THE BOX OF
DAYLIGHT

THE BOX OF DAYLIGHT

NORTHWEST COAST INDIAN ART

BILL HOLM

with contributions by Peter L. Corey,
Nancy Harris, Aldona Jonaitis,
Alan R. Sawyer,
and Robin K. Wright

Seattle Art Museum

University of Washington Press
Seattle & London

Copublished by
Seattle Art Museum
Seattle, Washington
and
University of Washington Press
Seattle, Washington

Exhibition dates: September 15, 1983 - January 8, 1984

This exhibition was organized with the aid of grants from
the National Endowment for the Arts, the Washington
Commission for the Humanities, PONCHO, and the Ethnic
Arts Council of the Seattle Art Museum.

Catalogue coordinator: Suzanne Kotz
Designer: Ed Marquand
Editor: Susan Pelzer
Photographer: Paul Macapia

Printed in Japan
Cover: Dancing headdress, Taku Tlingit,
       early 19th century (cat. no. 1).
Frontispiece: Dancing headdress frontlet, Northern
              Wakashan, mid-19th century (cat. no. 8).

Library of Congress Cataloging in Publication Data

Holm, Bill, 1925-
   The box of daylight.

   Catalog of an exhibition held at Seattle Art Museum,
Sept. 15, 1983-Jan. 8, 1984.
   Bibliography: p.
   1. Indians of North America—Northwest coast of North
America—Art—Exhibitions. I. Corey, Peter.
II. Seattle Art Museum. III. Title.
E78.N78H587 1983 709'.01'1097950740197777 83-50231
ISBN 0-932216-13-7 (S.A.M.)
ISBN 0-295-96088-4 (U.W.P.)

CONTENTS

FOREWORD

When Yehl, Raven, loosed light he brought sharpness and distinction to what was gray and hidden. The works of art shown in *The Box of Daylight: Northwest Coast Indian Art* are messengers of that ancient resolution. They carry the color and spirit of the place in which they were formed; they inspire us. We take great pride in both the exhibition and this catalogue. Rightfully, however, pride of creation belongs to the Salish, Kwakiutl, Westcoast, Northern Wakashan, Bella Coola, Haida, Tsimshian, and Tlingit, whose works of art are revealed here. It also belongs to their heirs.

In the summer and fall of 1983, three city institutions, the Burke Museum, the Pacific Science Center, and the Seattle Art Museum, are exhibiting Indian art of the Plains or of the Northwest Coast. Numerous excellent programs and activities accompany the exhibitions. In addition, the Fourth Annual Native American Art Studies Association Conference will mark the collection of these resources, though their gathering is, in fact, based on the efforts of one man—Bill Holm. Drawing on his almost endless energy and knowledge, Bill Holm has woven a garland in tribute to those who settled here before us. Our staff and coworkers have looked to him for unfailing guidance. The substance of our success is owed to him.

A project like *The Box of Daylight* requires numerous resources. Our first thanks go to the collectors, whose delight in works of art and whose generosity in lending them make the exhibition possible. Their counsel and patient support have shed warmth on the entire project.

To assist Bill Holm with the research and logistics of both the exhibition and the catalogue, Ellen Ferguson, project coordinator, and John Putnam, photographic coordinator, have undertaken well over a year's intense, dedicated effort. Our thanks also go to Peter Corey, Nancy Harris, Aldona Jonaitis, Alan Sawyer, and Robin Wright, whose research and articles are joined in the catalogue to the work of Bill Holm.

It is hard to enumerate those among the museum staff who have made special contributions to the exhibition or this publication. The subject has created a truly communal enthusiasm, and many individuals have contributed to a labor of love.

The museum and the Seattle community owe a great debt of thanks to the supporters of the exhibition: the National Endowment for the Arts, PONCHO, the Washington Commission for the Humanities, and the Ethnic Arts Council of the Seattle Art Museum. We hope they will share our pride in and admiration for this selection of the art of the people of the Northwest Coast.

Finally, I wish to thank the board of trustees of this museum who have, for fifty years, enabled our community to share in another box of daylight. In all our efforts we recognize their leadership and generosity.

Arnold Jolles
Director

ACKNOWLEDGMENTS

The initial impetus for the exhibition *The Box of Daylight: Northwest Coast Indian Art* came from the Ethnic Arts Council of the Seattle Art Museum which wished to participate in the celebration of the museum's fiftieth year with an exhibition within the expertise and interest of its members. Many of them, including then president John Putnam, have long been admirers and collectors of Northwest Coast Indian art and it seemed natural, given the fine material available, that it be the subject of the proposed exhibition. At the outset the officers of the Ethnic Arts Council, particularly John Putnam and his successor to the presidency, Ellen Ferguson, were joined by members of the museum staff, most notably Pam McClusky, Associate Curator of Ethnic Art, and Bonnie Pitman-Gelles, Chairman of the Education Division, in coordinating the Seattle Art Museum's schedule during a very busy year and in preparing a working outline and timetable for the proposed exhibition. From the first suggestion of an exhibition of Northwest Coast art from regional private collections, Arnold Jolles, Director of the Seattle Art Museum, was an enthusiastic supporter, and he continued to be even when the exhibition grew to nearly double its originally planned size. The staff of the registrar's office, particularly Dale Rollins, smoothly coordinated the loans from the two dozen lenders, whose generosity made the exhibition and catalogue possible. They are Mr. and Mrs. Alan Backstrom, Jim and Marilyn Bergstrom, Del Brink, Donn Charnley, Sylvia Duryee, John H. Hauberg, Dr. and Mrs. Allan Lobb, Mr. and Mrs. Philip McCracken, Eugene and Martha Nester, Del Nordquist, Philip S. Padelford, John and Grace Putnam, Mr. and Mrs. James Staley, David Storie, Jerrie and Anne Vander Houwen, Mary Winters, and eight others who prefer to remain anonymous. Jill Rullkoetter, Program Coordinator in the museum's Education Department, was responsible for planning and organizing the workshops, lectures, and other educational activities to accompany the exhibition. Mike McCafferty designed the exhibition.

As the exhibition grew, so did the catalogue. Every piece was to be illustrated, a task well calculated to test the stamina of the museum's genial photographer, Paul Macapia, who came through the ordeal with his usual superb photographs and with his good humor intact. Five Northwest Coast scholars, Peter Corey, Nancy Harris, Aldona Jonaitis, Alan Sawyer, and Robin Wright were invited to prepare essays on some aspect of their current research, and their provocative articles greatly increase the substance of the catalogue. Suzanne Kotz, Media and Publications Coordinator, editor Susan Pelzer, and proofreader Paula Thurman applied their talents and patience to the formidable task of shaping the myriad catalogue entries and five essays into a unified book, designed by Ed Marquand. Robin Wright, one of the authors, a doctoral candidate in art history and my assistant at the University of Washington, consulted with Suzanne and Susan when other responsibilities kept me away, made the editorial corrections to the texts on my word-processor disks, and entered the coding necessary to send the texts to the printer. My family put up with my long hours at the word processor and pondered with me the relative merits of dozens of names for the exhibition, ultimately agreeing unanimously on *The Box of Daylight*.

All the efforts of the council, the museum, the staff, authors, and lenders could not have produced an exhibition without the works of the native Northwest Coast artists, known and unknown, which together make up *The Box of Daylight*. It is to those artists that ultimate thanks must go.

Bill Holm
Curator

GITKSAN

NISHGA

TLINGIT

TSIMSHIAN

NORTHER

KAIGANI
HAIDA

HAIDA

NORTH

BELLA COOLA

WAKASHAN

COAST SALISH

Seattle

KWAKIUTL

COWICHAN

TWANA

NISQUALLY

WESTCOAST
(NOOTKA)

NITINAT

MAKAH

QUINAULT

INDIANS OF THE NORTHWEST COAST

A Taku Tlingit chief lying in state. Among his displayed clan emblems is the Raven Capturing the Sun Hat (cat. no. 1). Winter and Pond photograph, c. 1900, courtesy Thomas Burke Memorial Washington State Museum.

INTRODUCTION

There was darkness all over the world, a gloomy dark so that the myth people who fished and dug along the shores saw only a little of the mountains and islands around them. They talked and argued as they struggled to gather the fish and shellfish and roots that were their food. They argued about what they had heard was called "daylight," but no one had ever seen it. It was, someone said, kept in a box by a Nass River chief called Nas shuki yehl, Raven at Head of Nass. But there was no point in thinking about it because Nas shuki yehl guarded the daylight box in his house, and what good was it anyway?

At the same time there was in the dark world a person, or a bird, called Yehl, Raven. Wise and sly, greedy, generous, and meddling, he went here and there changing things to suit himself. It suited him to find out about "daylight," and he heard that Nas shuki yehl had a daughter who might provide a way to her father's treasure. This girl, Yehl discovered, went every day to a spring to dip water with her woven spruce root cup. It was easy for Yehl to become a hemlock needle and float right into that cup—again and again, until finally she just gave up and drank. And Yehl was born the grandson of Nas shuki yehl.

He grew very fast, and his grandfather thought, as grandfathers will, that this was the finest boy in the world. Never mind that they said his eyes looked funny, like a raven's. But he had a terrible temper, he rolled on the floor and screamed to get what he wanted to play with, the Moon Box. Nothing would do until he got that box, and when he did he rolled it around until it fell open and the moon escaped into the sky.

Grandfathers can forgive their grandsons anything; before long Yehl was playing on the floor again. And pretty soon he began to wail for the big box, the Box of Daylight. He screamed a long, long time before Nas shuki yehl finally gave in again, and when Yehl saw his chance he jumped up as a great raven, and with the box flew straight out the smoke-hole and into the night.

Yehl flew to where the myth people were fishing and threatened to break daylight on them, letting a few streaks out of the box to show he meant business. But when they scoffed at him and asked "Who do you think you are, Nas shuki yehl?" he threw the box of daylight open, flooding brightness over the world. The stunned myth people leaped into the sea or the forest and became the animals whose furs they wore: seals, sea otters, martens, and bears.

In western Washington State, centered on Seattle, but scattered over the area, are treasures that are kept, like Nas shuki yehl's box of daylight, in the homes of people who prize them for their great beauty, visual power, or ability to evoke the rich native heritage of the Northwest Coast. They were collected, one of them over two centuries ago and some within this year, from every meander on the coast. A great many of these treasures are superior examples and a few of them are recognized as being among the finest of their kind. To the credit of the owners, no hemlock-needle tricks nor temper tantrums were needed to gain access to their collections and to throw open this great Box of Daylight in the Seattle Art Museum.

In western Washington non-natives began collecting the art and artifacts of Northwest Coast Indian culture in the closing decades of the eighteenth century when Spanish and then British and American explorers and fur traders touched along the outer coast. The year 1792 brought the first collectors, Captain George Vancouver and his crews, into Seattle-area waters, and there has been a steady stream of them since. Most of this activity has been haphazard and indiscriminate over the years. Local settlers bought baskets and other objects of native make, but systematic collecting probably began in this corner of the country with James G. Swan and the Reverend Myron Eells in the last quarter of the nineteenth century. Both Eells and Swan began as private collectors, but their skills at the business of finding and buying Indian material and their knowledge led them into professional collecting. Both gathered material for the Washington State exhibit at the World Columbian Exposition in Chicago in 1893, and Swan assembled major collections from many parts of the coast for the great museums of the world.

Serious private collecting in the area in the early years of this century was limited. All the more outstanding because it was so very much larger and more comprehensive than most others of its time, the collection of Carolyn McGilvra Burke was

In the Raven House at Klukwan, a Chilkat
Tlingit chief surrounded by crest hats,
helmet, and mask wears the Raven blanket
(cat. no. 81). Winter and Pond photograph,
1909, courtesy Thomas Burke Memorial
Washington State Museum.

loaned to the Washington State Museum at the University of Washington (now the Thomas Burke Memorial Washington State Museum) for many years before being donated to that museum in the mid-1940s. Just about that time a few other Washingtonians, some of them artists or art patrons, began to regard as worthy of serious attention some of the things of Indian origin they saw around them. Most of these collections remained small, although many of the pieces in them were of the highest quality.

One collection, begun in the late 1940s by Sidney and Anne Gerber, became the largest in the region, and was generously given by Anne Gerber in 1968 to the Burke Museum where it significantly improved the coverage of the collections, especially in Kwakiutl material. Another Seattle art patron, John Hauberg, began his Northwest Coast collecting by buying several fine pieces for the Burke Museum and went on to assemble one of the finest private collections of Northwest Coast art in the world. The "daylight" in *The Box of Daylight* would be very much dimmer without John Hauberg.

The other collections represented in the exhibition range from single to many pieces; some of these collections have been years in the gathering, and have undergone shifts in their makeup intended to reduce the chaff and sharpen their focus on fine quality pieces. Several of the most spectacular collections are less than a decade old, and one particularly fine, small group was assembled within the last year. In living rooms and attics all around the region are, no doubt, other fine works from the hands of Northwest Coast artists. There are probably hundreds, if not thousands, of baskets in Washington homes. They are mostly family heirlooms, brought from British Columbia or Alaska by traveling forebears, or bought on the sidewalks of Seattle or Tacoma in the years when fine baskets were one of the main sources of cash for local native women.

Exhibitions of private collections have often had to bear a certain stigma. Reviewers sometimes feel bound to suggest that the owners' motivation to show their hoarded treasures is less philanthropic than economic—representation in a catalogue increases their market value—or that collectors who elect to be identified as "anonymous lenders"

do so to assuage their guilt at persisting in personal ownership of objects that ought to be in public collections. That there might be some justification for either criticism would be foolish to deny, but collectors are under no obligation to show their prized objects in public. They do so primarily because they appreciate those objects and believe that they should be seen. In a very real and practical sense the collections represented in this exhibition are analogous to the reserve collections of a great public museum. These collections have never been any more closed to examination and research by scholars than the storerooms of our public museums have been. Much of the quality of museum collections is owed to the discrimination of private collectors whose treasures have found their eventual homes in those museums.

There are enough pieces left in the collections represented in the exhibition to mount another show almost as fine as this one. My most difficult task as curator was not to locate the material, but to eliminate enough to bring the exhibit to a size suitable to the available space in gallery and catalogue. And I take full responsibility for the selection. Although I had the immeasurably helpful assistance of Ellen Ferguson and John Putnam in every aspect of the work—locating the material, assembling working photographs and documentation, offering sensible advice, buffering me and the Seattle Art Museum, and easing every headache—the final choice was mine.

A group of five essays accompany this catalogue. The theme is a simple one: scholars who are deeply and personally involved in the study of various aspects of Northwest Coast Indian art were asked to write essays of their own choosing. The coverage of the exhibition is so broad that we were sure that every article would relate to the objects in some way. These short essays represent new ideas and are real contributions to the literature of their subjects.

I hope that those who know this art, or come to know it, and are moved by it will find this Box of Daylight bright.

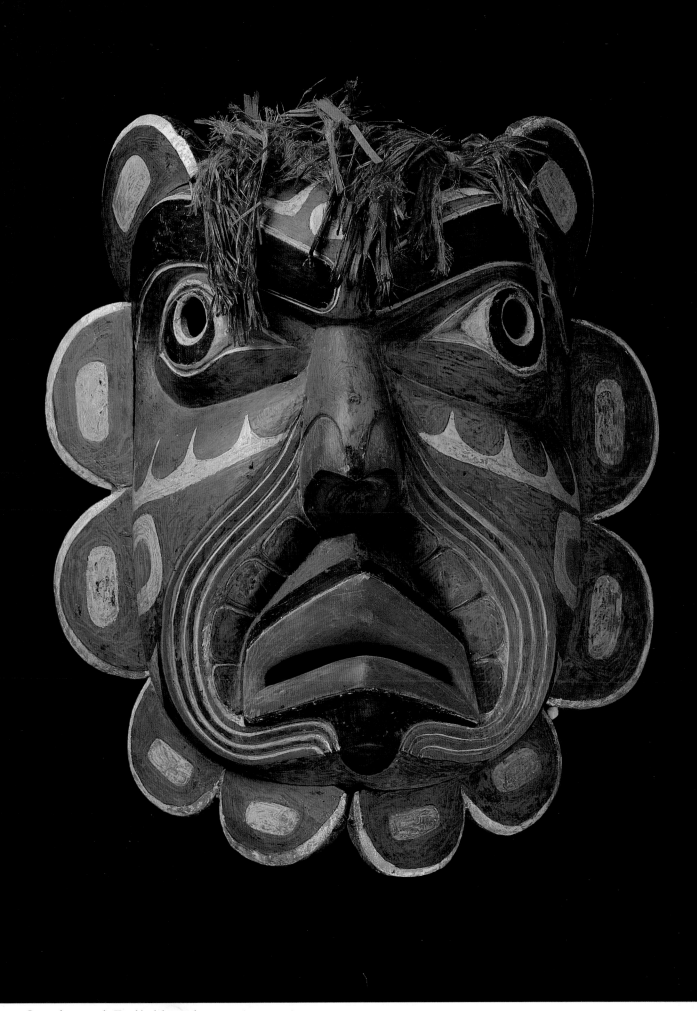

Goomokwey mask. Kwakiutl, late 19th century. (cat. no. 33)

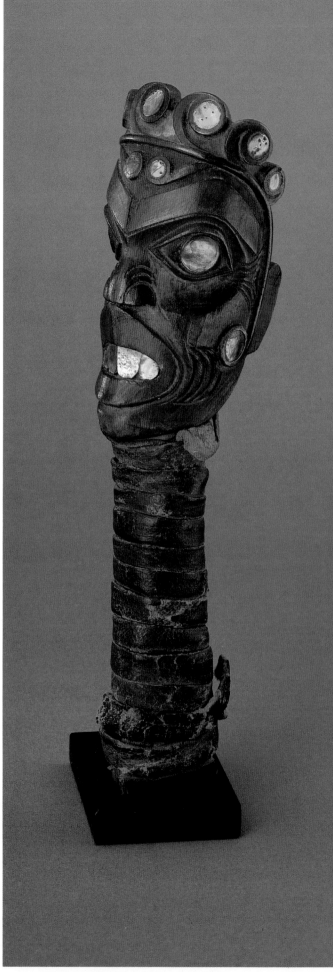

Spirit figure rattle. Quinault, 19th century. (cat. no. 23)

Dagger handle. Tlingit, early 19th century. (cat. no. 169)

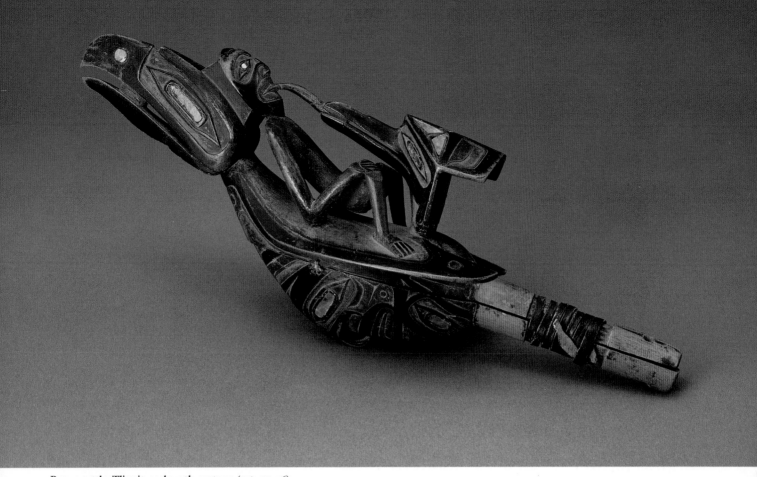

Raven rattle. Tlingit, early 19th century. (cat. no. 16)

Raven rattle. Haida (?), mid-19th century. (cat. no. 17)

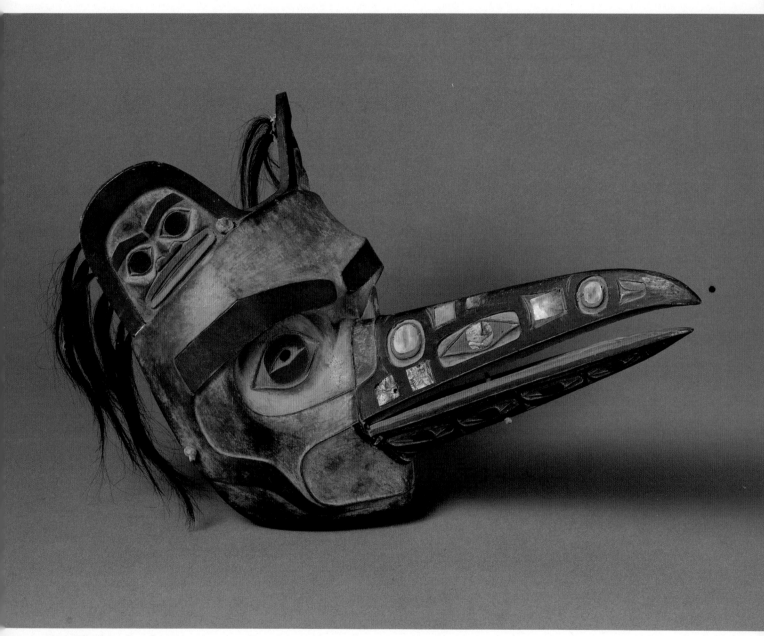

Mask. Tlingit, early 19th century. (cat. no. 47)

Dancing headdress frontlet. Tlingit, 19th century. (cat. no. 2)

Dancing headdress. Taku Tlingit, early 19th century. (cat. no. 1)

Chilkat blanket. Tlingit, 19th century. (cat no. 86)

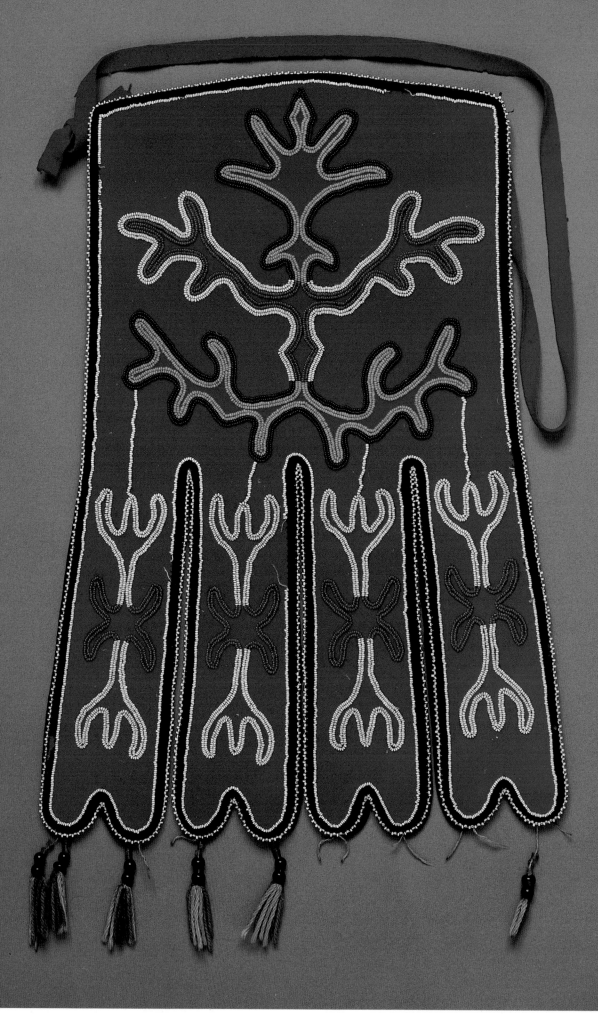

Octopus bag. Tlingit, late 19th century. (cat. no. 93)

Skhwaikhwey mask. Cowichan, Kuper Island, B.C., c. 1870. (cat. no. 28)

Bent-corner bowl. Tlingit, early 19th century. (cat. no. 116)

Horn bowl. Haida, 19th century. (cat. no. 123)

Chest. Bella Bella, 19th century. (cat. no. 109)

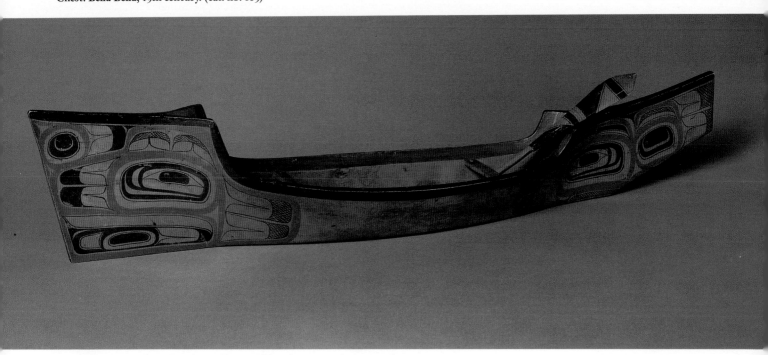

Model canoe. Northern Northwest Coast, mid-19th century. (cat. no. 156)

Tlingit baskets. Cat. nos. (l. to r.) 63, 66, 67, 65, 64 (r. foreground) 69, 68.

Basketry hat. Haida, late 19th century. (cat. no. 57)

Dancing headdress. Bella Coola, 19th century. (cat. no. 11)

DANCING HEADDRESS FRONTLETS

From the farthest northwestern reach of Tlingit country at Yakutat Bay, southward along the coast to the middle of Vancouver Island, dancing chiefs wore crowns as elegant as rich material and sculptor's skill could make. Traditions of the tribes assign various places of origin to the dancing headdress, but, whichever is correct, it must have been somewhere in the north. Some were collected very early in the historic period, one of the most beautiful by Malaspina in 1791 (Feder 1977: fig. 4). The features of the headdress are the same wherever it is worn: a cylindrical frame—often made of strips of whale baleen and covered with cloth—from the back of which hangs a long panel covered with rows of white ermine skins; an upstanding circlet of the long, springy whiskers of the Steller's sea lion; and a spectacular plaque carved of hardwood, painted and inlaid with abalone shell on the forehead. This plaque, or frontlet, is carved to represent a crest or a mythical character. The figure in the center is surrounded by a flange that is usually covered with inset plates of brilliantly iridescent abalone shell. Inlays of the same shell flash from the eyes, teeth, and joints. Sumptuous materials surround the intricate plaque. Often the crown is covered with a band of swan skin, luxuriant with white down, or ermines flank the frontlet. On Haida and Tlingit headdresses the plaque is often framed by rows of orange and black, spear-shaped tail feathers of the red-shafted flicker, with a band of iridescent green and black mallard head-skin across the forehead.

The dance must have traveled from tribe to tribe with the headdress as its use spread over the coast. The dancer appears with blanket and apron and often a raven rattle (Holm 1972:29 and Holm 1983). Knees slightly bent and legs spread, he jumps on both feet to the time of the song beat—short jumps, feet hardly off the floor, making the ermine rows covering his back jump in turn. The blanket was spread by the wearer's arms or elbows. The crown of sea lion whiskers holds a loose fluff of eagle down when the dancing begins. The whiskers rustle and clatter as the dancer bobs and tosses his head, shaking white whisps of down through the whisker barrier to swirl around his dancing figure. The white down means peace, or welcome, to the guests at a potlatch. Chiefs dance to greet canoes invited from far villages. Canoe-borne visitors dance in turn, and the swirling down from their headdresses drifts shoreward on the wind and over the host and his tribe on the beach. Among the Kwakiutl and their relatives, the dance is a preliminary to the appearance of a figure masked as a crest of the headdress dancer, who, possessed, runs from the house. In its rich composite of material, form, and movement, no Northwest Coast object expresses the ideas of rank and heredity, supernatural power, drama, and aesthetics so well as the dancing headdress.

1. DANCING HEADDRESS
Taku Tlingit, early 19th century
Maple, mirror, abalone shell, bird skin, sea
lion whiskers
H: 11 7/8 in. (30.2 cm.); W: 7 3/4 in. (19.7
cm.); D: 12 3/8 in. (31.2 cm.)
Collection of John H. Hauberg

Yehl crouched over the Box of Daylight, with the sun disk between his ears, is graphically portrayed in "Raven Capturing the Sun Hat," perhaps the finest illustration of this most famous myth of the Northwest Coast. Although it is essentially like other dancing headdresses, with its carved central figure, sea lion whiskers, swan skin, and ermine, it differs from most in the full sculptural treatment of the carving and in the structure of the hat. This masterpiece of classic northern coastal art is one of the hereditary treasures of the Taku Tlingit. Raven is shown in semihuman form, grasping the lid of the chest containing the daylight, which is represented by an inlaid mirror. The same material fills the center of the sun disk above Raven's head. According to tradition this mirror was acquired from the first white man encountered by the Taku and had the status of a treasured heirloom. Copper overlays the lips and eyebrows of the hero, and blue-green abalone shell is set in his mouth, nostrils, and eyes.

"Raven Capturing the Sun Hat" epitomizes the classic Tlingit sculptural style, with its rounded forms, large, round eyes in full orbs, blue-green, black, and vermilion painting, and embellishment of copper and abalone shell. It is a noble headdress.

2. DANCING HEADDRESS FRONTLET
Tlingit, 19th century
Maple, abalone shell
H: 7 1/2 in. (19 cm.); W: 5 1/2 in. (14 cm.)
Collection of Mr. and Mrs. Alan Backstrom

Most Tlingit frontlets have the form of this fine piece. The plaque is rectangular, with a slightly arched top. Abalone inlays cover the flange on three sides and surround the carved figures, a large, humanoid thunderbird and a smaller killer whale. The arrangement of a large, principal figure and a smaller, supplemental figure is typical of Tlingit frontlets and, to a lesser degree, of Haida headdresses, especially those of the Kaigani of Alaska.

Identification of the bird as a thunderbird is conjectural, but the theme of the thunderbird and whale is widespread on the coast. Here the bird, with human hands, surmounts the whale whose dorsal fin rises under the bird's humanoid chin. The whale's pectoral fins, turned downward, flank his head. Abalone-shell inlay encrusts the carving, which is painted typically in blue-green, vermilion, and black.

3. DANCING HEADDRESS
Tlingit, 19th century
Maple, abalone shell, sea lion whiskers, mallard skin, ermine skins, baleen, buckskin, and trade cloth
H: (frontlet) 7 5/8 in. (19.5 cm.); W: 6 1/2 in. (16.5 cm.); D: 1 3/4 in. (4.5 cm.)
Collection of Bill and Marty Holm

Some northern frontlets are carved with a figure in shallow relief, following the principles of the formline system of design most clearly seen on boxes and chests. This frontlet is thought to represent a swan, with a flattened, downturned beak merging with the twodimensionally rendered head of the bird. Abalone shell enriches the details of the head, body, and wings, but the enclosing flange is painted only with the familiar blue-green color. The rest of the painting is unusual in that the formlines that would ordinarily be black are brown, except for the lips. Vermilion feet and cheeks follow the usual color arrangement. Interestingly, the back of the frontlet, never seen while attached to the headdress, is painted with a highly abstract design of massive solid U forms in ochre red separated by narrow bands of unpainted wood.

The headdress is complete, with sea lion whisker crown, ermine trailer, and mallard skin brow-band. The frame of the cap is of baleen and copper wire.

4. DANCING HEADDRESS FRONTLET
Kaigani Haida, 19th century
Maple, abalone shell
H: 6 1/4 in. (15.9 cm.); W: 5 7/8 in. (15 cm.); D: 2 1/4 in. (5.3 cm.)
Collection of John H. Hauberg

Most dancing headdress frontlets are simply representations of crest figures, sometimes with associated supplemental creatures. A few, and this one is a good example, are more narrative in character, with the principal figure shown in action, illustrating a myth. The story represented here is of the Gonakadet, a great supernatural being from under the sea, who is described as a source of wealth and chiefly prerogatives. A young man who was unfairly ridiculed by his mother-in-law managed to trap the Gonakadet and by dressing in the monster's skin was able to catch all kinds of sea creatures—salmon, halibut, seals, and whales—which he left on the beach for his starving tribe. His mother-in law, discovering the bounty, claimed she had brought the food with her shamanic power. When the young man died after bringing two whales to the beach and his body was discovered in the

Gonakadet's skin, the pretending shaman, his mother-in-law, died of shame.

In the frontlet the hero is seen holding a whale, detailed in the formline system of design and inlaid with abalone shell. He emerges from the mouth of the Gonakadet skin, represented by the red face with abalone-inset teeth at the top of the frontlet and the claws below the man's ears. The Gonakadet is sometimes seen as a beautiful house front rising from the sea, or in the form of a huge wolflike creature with large ears, dorsal fins, and a curled tail. In this form it is called Wasgo by the Queen Charlotte Island Haida.

The frontlet was collected at Hydaburg, Alaska, and was identified by the Kaigani Haida owner as being the work of Albert Edward Edenshaw, a famous and powerful Haida chief who was also an artist and the maternal uncle and predecessor of the master artist Charles Edenshaw (cat. nos. 59, 60, 188-192).

5. DANCING HEADDRESS
Probably Kaigani Haida, 19th century
Maple, abalone shell, sea lion whiskers, flicker feathers, swan skin, ermine skins, buckskin, trade cloth
H: 7 1/3 in. (18.2 cm.); W: 6 in. (15.2 cm.); D: 2 in. (5 cm.)
Collection of John H. Hauberg

Most Haida headdress frontlets have the form of this one: a single figure of a crest animal filling the central area and an abalone inlaid flange bordering the sides and top. The figure's head is large, occupying the upper half of the space, and is often painted sparingly, the nostrils and lips red and the eyebrows and eyelid lines black. Abalone shell embellishes the eyes, teeth, and sometimes the nostrils. The body is compressed, often with the knees drawn up against the chest and the arms (or forelegs) raised with palms forward. This frontlet is a fine example of the type, except for the posture of the bear who clutches his knees with his forefeet. The style of carving suggests an Alaskan Haida, or Kaigani, origin.

Headdresses in fine condition and complete with down-covered cap, ermine trailer, and sea lion whisker crown are rare in most collections. Northern headdresses were typically ornamented with the tail feathers of the red-shafted flicker set upright around the top of the cylindrical frame, as in this example, or tied in overlapping layers flanking the frontlet.

7. DANCING HEADDRESS FRONTLET

Tsimshian, 19th century
Maple, abalone shell
H: 6 7/8 in. (17.5 cm.); W: 6 in. (15.3 cm.);
D: 2 1/8 in. (5.5 cm.)
Collection of Sylvia Duryee

The Tsimshian and their Nass and Skeena River relatives, the Nishga and the Gitksan, are credited with producing many of the finest frontlets of the Northwest Coast; they may even have been the originators of the concept itself. This is a fine example of a Gitksan frontlet from the upper Skeena village of Kitwancool. It was formerly the property of Chief Wee-Lezgu. The type is well represented here: a crest animal (this one a bear) with large, unpainted face, small red body, and delicately carved, rounded limbs flexed and inlaid on their forward surface with abalone shell. Small, supplemental figures are frequent adjuncts to the large, principal creatures in Gitksan sculpture and on frontlets they are often carved in a row around the rim or, as here, crouched in the ears of the main animal. The ear-men resemble little frontlets themselves, with compressed bodies and shell-inlaid rims.

The face of the humanoid grizzly illustrates the often benign expression of animals carved in the Tsimshian style, with their open eyes and taut orbs. Narrow lips drawn back against the smooth cheeks and thin eyebrows arched over wide sockets emphasize the otherwise unpainted but rich surface of the polished maple.

6. DANCING HEADDRESS FRONTLET

Probably Tsimshian, 19th century
Maple, abalone shell
H: 9 3/8 in. (23.9 cm.); W: 9 in. (22.8 cm.);
D: 3 in. (7.6 cm.)
Collection of John H. Hauberg

Accurate identification of the place of origin of Northwest Coast ceremonial objects is made especially difficult by their frequent transfer in marriage from one tribe to another. This spectacular frontlet, its circular corona set with large plaques of blue abalone shell, is a particularly good example. It was collected from a Kwakiutl of Fort Rupert, northern Vancouver Island, in whose family the headdress had been since about 1930. It first came to Fort Rupert as a gift (perhaps part of a dowry) to Chief Owadi from Chief Tlakwamot of the Bella Coola, in the late nineteenth century. It was subsequently transferred in marriage at least once more before coming to the family from which it was collected. The frontlet did not, however, originate with the Bella Coola. Stylistically it is Tsimshian, or perhaps Haisla, an adjacent people linguistically related to the Kwakiutl.

The spread of the frontlet's corona is emphasized by the extremely large and beautiful abalone-shell plaques laced to it through holes drilled in their margins. This method of attachment is unusual, although a few other frontlets are known in which the shell is laced in place (cat. no. 10). Most are set tightly into carved recesses and anchored with an adhesive, apparently made of pitch. This is the method used for the shell attachment in the eyes and mouth of this frontlet. The face is that of a humanoid bird, perhaps an eagle. The blue background was once over-painted with cream-colored enamel, and the vermilion lips and details with orange. Removal of the overpainting has revealed the original colors.

Many Tsimshian sculptural characteristics are represented in this frontlet: the smooth, open features suggestive of taut skin over underlying skeletal structure; large, rounded orb; sharply cut eyelid lines without defining ridge; pyramidal cheek structure; and arched, round-ended eyebrows. Tsimshian frontlets with round coronas are not unusual, but the width of the border makes this piece unique.

8. DANCING HEADDRESS FRONTLET
Northern Wakashan, mid-19th century
Maple, abalone shell
H: 7 1/2 in. (19 cm.); W: 6 1/2 in. (16.5 cm.); D: 3 1/2 in. (9 cm.)
Private collection

Although this elegant northern frontlet was collected in the Gwasila Kwakiutl village in Smith Inlet, it comes from the part of the coast occupied by tribes who speak the Northern Wakashan languages—the Hehltsukw or Bella Bella, the Haihais, and the Haisla. Distinctions of art style among these inlet dwellers are not yet understood so that work from the region has often been loosely called "Bella Bella" (see Sawyer's essay, p. 143). This frontlet is an example.

The humanoid bird is probably an eagle, a crest of the original owner. A small man, hands grasping his drawn-up knees, crouches against the bird's breast. Wings detailed in the formline tradition flank the man. In its general configuration the frontlet is very northern, but a number of details hint at origins other than Tlingit, Haida, or Tsimshian. The pointed arch of the top, the angular eyebrows, and the form of the eye socket and orb are more typical of the frontlets of the the Northern Wakashan area.

Blue bands painted diagonally upward across the eyes extend through the brows in double U form. The painting of the features is typical, as is that on the wing detail, with black primary formlines, red secondary U forms, and blue in the recessed, tertiary areas. An unusual and interesting feature is the alternation of large and small abalone inlays in the rim.

9. DANCING HEADDRESS FRONTLET
Bella Bella (?), 19th century
Maple, copper
H: 8 1/4 in. (21 cm.); W: 7 1/2 in. (19 cm.)
Collection of John H. Hauberg

Copper, rather than the usual abalone shell, highlights this spectacular and very unusual frontlet. It is another example of Northern Wakashan sculpture, although less in the true northern tradition than the previous piece. The wide, round eye socket, with flattened orb and sharply defined outline, is a feature of many pieces from this area. It can be seen in the small faces on the figure's body as well as on the large face. The creature's identity is not known. With man's hands, feet (now broken), and ears, the creature is basically human in form, but the long, beaklike nose, once hooked, shows that it is not an ordinary person.

The maker of this small masterpiece was a superior and imaginative crafts-man. The innovative use of copper, the piercing of the surrounding plaque, the detailing of the fingers right down to the fingernails set the frontlet apart. The painting is conservative but very effective, with vermilion body, lips and nostrils, black eyebrows, and dark blue painting on the face.

10. DANCING HEADDRESS FRONTLET

Bella Bella (?), late 19th century
Wood, abalone shell
H: 10 1/4 in. (26 cm.); W: 7 1/8 in. (18 cm.); D: 3 5/8 in. (9.3 cm.)
Collection of John and Grace Putnam

Another round frontlet illustrates some of the stylistic features of Northern Wakashan carvings and can be attributed to that area, even though it was collected from the Kingcome Inlet Kwakiutl and is documented as having been received in marriage from a chief at Gilford Island, another Kwakiutl village, in the early years of this century. The combination of bird and whale is similar to those in cat. nos. 2 and 11, but the stylistic differences are great. This one illustrates a typical arrangement of central coastal (that is Bella Bella, Bella Coola, and Kwakiutl) frontlets of a large, central face, often of a bird, with claws out-thrust below and a supplemental head above. A small red ball in the bird's beak is unusual. Its meaning is not known.

The paint colors are another clue to the place of origin. Black eyebrows and vermilion lips, nostrils, and claws are quite standard over much of the coast, but the blue painting over a large part of the surface, with background and relief slits in unpainted wood or vermilion, is typical of Northern Wakashan and Bella Coola pieces. This is another of the few examples in which the abalone rim plates are laced to the wood rather than glued.

11. DANCING HEADDRESS

Bella Coola, 19th century
Maple, abalone shell, copper, glass, baleen, swan skin, ermine skins, cedar bark, cloth
H: (frontlet) 9 1/4 in. (23.5 cm.); W: 6 1/4 in. (16 cm.); D: 5 1/2 in. (14 cm.)
Collection of Bill and Marty Holm

Bella Coola sculpture has a special power in its bold, swirling planes, in the juxtaposition of bulging, convex forms with flattened and hollow surfaces, and in the outward thrust of the carved characteristics. Frontlets typically feature a large central head and two supplementary faces, one or the other flanked with extended claws. The main figure is usually a bird with jutting, upward thrust beak, as seen here, but other creatures are depicted as well.

The hexagonal, flaring outline of the rim, with the upper figure breaking the outline, is often seen in Bella Coola frontlets. Coppers from the central coastal area have the same angularity, suggesting a possible relationship between the two forms (cat. no. 164), especially since northern coppers and frontlets show the same similarity in their flattened tops (cat. nos. 4 and 163). This frontlet has been modified several

times in its history, which would be very interesting if known, since it was collected from a Kingcome Inlet Kwakiutl woman, far from its Bella Coola birthplace. The abalone-shell inlay in the ears and cheeks of the thunderbird are much more recent and less skillfully done than the rest of the inlay, and the copper eyebrows are tacked over carved and painted originals. Shortly before it was collected the entire frontlet was renewed with an overall coat of dark maroon enamel. Fortunately it could be removed, revealing a typically Bella Coola painting of blue and vermilion on the unpainted maple ground. The eye sockets of the whale are a lively green.

Thin splints of amber baleen, split from the long plates taken from the mouths of whales, substitute for sea lion whiskers. Such a substitution is not uncommon in Bella Coola and Kwakiutl headdresses.

RATTLES

Throughout North America, ceremony is accompanied by rattles. The Northwest Coast is no exception. In fact, both in variety of types and complexity of design, rattles of the coast exceed all others on the continent. Their use and form change from one part of the area to another, but everywhere they belong to the ceremonial world. In spite of the great variety of rattles made and used on the Northwest Coast and the many different materials utilized in them, there are really only two concepts of structure involved: a thin-walled container holding small, hard particles and clusters of resonant objects loosely hung to strike together when shaken.

The sound of rattles is a conduit to the supernatural world. Everywhere on the coast shamans use rattles in curing the sick and in seeking assistance from spirit helpers. Although rattles are musical instruments and their sound often accompanies songs, their use always implies the presence of supernatural power, even in dances where the main motivation seems to be the dramatization of social rank.

RAVEN RATTLES

Long ago, on the northern coast, a rattle of very peculiar and very specific configuration came into being. No one knows today just what the complex of figures represented on this rattle means, or its original use. In the memory of its Indian users it has always been a chief's dancing rattle. We call it a "raven rattle," because the rattle itself is carved in the form of a bird, usually with a ravenlike head. Native accounts assure us that other birds were depicted on these rattles, and in fact there still exist a very few that can be recognized as puffins, eagles, and other non-ravens. There are, without exaggeration, hundreds of these rattles in existence, and of those less than a dozen are recognizably not ravens.

If the figure represented was merely a bird the rattle would not be the subject of so much conjecture and analysis. But, instead, it is a detailed composite of figures, some of which are always present in nearly the same form, some of which appear in one of two forms, and some which may or may not be included in the group. The rattle itself is a globular shell carved of hardwood, usually maple, and modified to bird form by the inclusion of a raven's head, wings, and tail. The head arches upward, giving the rattle a spirited S curve, and the wings sweep back along the sides. A close look at a raven rattle reveals that the head is pierced from top to bottom, which makes it seem to be a separate piece wedged onto the upthrust neck. Details of the bird's head are flattened into a shallow-relief design of formlines matching that which covers the body of the rattle. The raven always bites a small, red, usually rectangular block that may represent the daylight, or perhaps the

fire, which Yehl carried in his bill. It may also function to reinforce the fragile lower beak of the bird.

The belly of the rattle is elaborately decorated with a formline pattern, the central section of which depicts the face of another creature. It has often been identified as a hawk, because of the sharply hooked beak, or nose. There is some evidence that the figure may be a different supernatural being, perhaps not a bird at all. In any case, the design is analogous to the very abstract patterns on painted boxes (cat. nos. 99-111). The raven's tail stands upright as the formline-detailed head of a bird. Raven's tail feathers sweep back from the tail-bird's head. If this bird faces the handle of the rattle, his beak is hooked back to his mouth. If he faces forward over the raven's back, the beak is long and straight.

The most mysterious detail of the rattle is the reclining figure of a man, head resting on the raven's ears, knees drawn up and clasped by his hands. The man's tongue is always extended and bitten by the long-billed tail-bird or by a frog that crouches on his chest or is held in the tail-bird's beak. The extended tongue is a motif found often in Northwest Coast art and is a favorite subject for conjectural interpretation. It certainly must have meaning beyond what can be seen in this strange composition, but we do not know what it is. Most scholars believe that the raven rattle began its existence as a powerful instrument of the shaman. But in the memory of the native authorities who answered the queries of turn-of-the-century anthropologists, this rattle had always been used by dancing chiefs.

12. RAVEN RATTLE
Northern Northwest Coast, 19th century
Maple
L: 12 1/2 in. (31.7 cm.); H: 5 in. (12.7 cm.);
D: 5 in. (12.7 cm.)
Private collection

This rattle illustrates the very traditional arrangement of northern raven rattles, with the tail-bird reversed. All the features are present. As usual, the face of the man, the tail-bird, and the raven itself are rendered as formline patterns, reflecting the detailing of the raven's breast. Color follows the standard formline use, with black primary formlines, red secondary formlines, and blue-green tertiary area. The man's body is, as usual, red.

Wooden rattles were typically made in two pieces, each hollowed and then joined by tying with sinew through small drilled holes at the joining edges. Sometimes the divided handle was tightly pegged together as well. This raven rattle illustrates the construction technique.

13. RAVEN RATTLE
Northern Northwest Coast, 19th century
Maple
L: 13 in. (33 cm.); H: 5 in. (12.8 cm.); D: 5 in. (12.8 cm.)
Collection of Del Nordquist

Although it follows the same configuration as the previous rattle, this one is quite different in feeling. The body of the rattle is flatter, and the neck much more angular. Elbows firmly planted on the raven's back, the man arches his torso, from which a frog emerges and bites the tongue. A prominent nose, rather than a hooked beak, protrudes from the tail-bird's face. The two-dimensional detail conforms to the formline tradition.

Raven rattles are typically delicate and light. The thin hardwood shell is very resonant. A thimbleful of tiny rattles enclosed in the body—sometimes pebbles but more often, in historic times, lead shot—strikes against the thin enclosure to make the swishing sound imitated by all the northern tribes in their word for the rattle, *sasawkh*.

14. RAVEN RATTLE
Northern Wakashan (?), mid-19th century
Maple
L: 12 in. (30.5 cm.); H: 4 3/8 in. (11 cm.);
D: 4 3/8 in. (11 cm.)
Collection of Mr. and Mrs. Alan Backstrom

The sharply hooked beak of the rattle-bird suggests that this is an eagle, rather than the usual raven. On the other hand, the exaggerated upward thrust of the bird's head may have been deliberately countered by the curve for appearance's sake. The design of this rattle is very strong. The rake of the tail-bird's head, with its jutting nose, the reversing curl of the beak on the formline face on the rattle's breast, the long, angled tongue, and the bold hook of the head combine to make this rattle unique. Large ears force the man's head outward, opening up the space between him and the rattle. His masklike face is typical in its flatness.

The two halves of the rattle are ingeniously locked by an offset in the joint of the handle to keep them from slipping out of line. Sinew tied through drilled holes secures the two parts.

15. RAVEN RATTLE
Tlingit, 19th century
Maple
L: 13 1/2 in. (34.3 cm.); H: 3 1/2 in. (9 cm.); D: 4 in. (10.3 cm.)
Collection of Eugene and Martha Nester

The tail-bird of this slim Tlingit rattle faces the man and bites his tongue in the alternative rattle composition. The long-beaked bird has been called a kingfisher, although there is no solid information on which to base that identification. He resembles the raucous fisher, with his jutting crest feathers forming the raven's tail. The rattle is very slim and rounded, its wings sloping off at the sides.

The raven rattle is said to have been invented by carvers of the Nass River

people, the Nishga, and it has even been suggested that all raven rattles were made by them and traded to other tribes. However, rattles clearly in the styles of other tribes are common. Fragments of very early, precontact raven rattles in early Tlingit style have come from graves in the Tlingit country, proving that the Nishga were not alone in their manufacture, at least during the last two centuries.

16. RAVEN RATTLE
Tlingit, early 19th century
Maple, abalone shell
L: 13 1/8 in. (33.5 cm.); H: 3 3/4 in. (9.5 cm.); D: 4 7/8 in. (12.5 cm.)
Private collection

Although all raven rattles conform to a single arrangement of parts, with minor variations, they vary in excellence of design and craftsmanship. This old rattle stands at the top of the scale. Every detail of its design in sculpture and formline has been executed with the highest degree of skill. The two-dimensional design on the rattle's breast, although perfectly standard in every way, is, at the same time, a marvelous example of the artist's ingenuity. Every rule of the formline system has been followed, yet unique arrangements of detail are seen in the cheek designs at the corners of the long eyes and in the U complexes under the raven's neck. The abalone-shell inlays are perfectly fitted, both technically and aesthetically, in relationship to the long, black ovoids into which they are set.

Massive, somewhat angular formlines and long eyelids with little constriction are typical of early Tlingit work. They may be characteristic of the general northern art style from the early historic period. This fine rattle shows, in addition to early stylistic features, the patination of age.

17. RAVEN RATTLE
Haida (?), mid-19th century
Maple
L: 13 in. (33 cm.); H: 3 3/4 in. (9.5 cm.);
D: 4 1/8 in. (10.5 cm.)
Collection of John and Grace Putnam

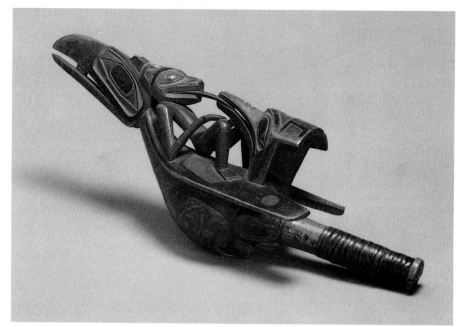

Very few old Northwest Coast pieces have any documentation at all, so the small bit of information accompanying this fine old rattle—that it was collected in the last century by a Hudson's Bay Company employee named Charles Beardmore—is tantalizing. Research in the Hudson's Bay Company archives may lead to a more informed guess about the origins of the rattle. It is a fine piece, another example of the highest standard of Northwest Coast carving. Although not so complex in detail as the previous rattle, the work is just as precise, and the artist's control of the formline conventions just as perfect.

Two unusual features highlight the rattle. The reclining figure has the head (or mask) of a bear, and a tiny frog crouches on the chin of the creature on the raven's breast, biting the tip of its downturned snout. Both of these variations are known on other rattles, but they are extremely rare; all known examples are of the highest quality.

Raven rattles are part of the regalia of a chief which includes the dancing headdress frontlet. When chiefs dance, shaking eagle down from their glittering headdresses, they use the raven rattle. The dance is stately but full of taut power. Arms spread to stretch the dancing blanket wide under the ermines cascading from his headdress, the dancer vibrates the rattle, held belly up. We can only guess what motivated the patience and fine craftsmanship expended on the perfection of detail in this whirring image only dimly seen in the firelit house.

18. RATTLE
Tlingit (?), 19th century
Wood
L: 9 3/8 in. (23.8 cm.); H: 4 in. (10.2 cm.);
D: 2 in. (5 cm.)
Collection of John H. Hauberg

This unusual rattle, carved in the form of a goose or swan, with its long neck arched over a round depression, is one of only two of its type known. Rattles representing birds of many kinds were made by the carvers of the Northwest Coast, but almost all of them utilize the body of the bird as the globe of the rattle. Here the bird sits on a lozenge of wood that has been split, hollowed, and reassembled with its contained rattles. It is an elegant figure, naturalistic in pro- portion, with spread wings and tail elaborated with formline ovoids and U forms representing the joints and feathers. Black and red paint remain on the formlines, with traces of blue in the tertiary areas and red on the bird's body and neck. Nostrils, lips, and eyes are red on a black head.

There is no record of how this rattle was used. It may have been a shaman's rattle, but more probably was one used in dancing. Whatever its purpose, it is a remarkably elegant example of Northwest Coast sculpture.

19. CLAPPER

Tlingit (?), mid-19th century
Wood, spruce root
L: 9 3/8 in. (23.8 cm.); H: 2 3/4 in. (7
cm.); D: 2 1/2 in. (6.4 cm.)
Collection of John H. Hauberg

Although not strictly a rattle in that
there are no enclosed pebbles or shot,
the clapper is used much like the rattle in
dancing. It is held in the outstretched
hand by the knob at the end of the handle and shaken rapidly. The clapper is in
two parts, joined only at the end of the
thin, flattened handle; the upper part
springs up and down, snapping together
with its lower mate at each shake. The
hollow hardwood clicks like a castanet.

The figure on the upper shell functions as a weight to separate the halves
in action. It represents a white-headed,
adult bald eagle. The eagle is rendered in
a naturalistic manner, resting on the
clapper with its wings slightly spread.
Its head and tail match the natural color
of the living eagle, as do the black formlines of its wings and body. The figure

on which it sits is too abstract to identify
with certainty, but is a fine example of
northern relief-carved painting, with red
primary formlines, black secondary, and
pale blue tertiary areas. Clappers are
very fragile, and few have survived
intact. This one was repaired at the thin
section of the handle, the place where
they typically break.

20. CLAPPER

Tlingit, mid-19th century
Wood
L: 10 5/8 in. (27 cm.); H: 2 3/4 in. (7
cm.); D: 1 3/4 in. (4.4 cm.)
Collection of John and Grace Putnam

The raven head of this clapper recalls
that of the familiar rattle, even to the red
block in the bird's beak. The resemblance ends there. The clapper has the
characteristic flattened, flexible handle
and divided shells. Raven is shown with
the sun on his back, a reference to his
adventure with Nas shuki yehl and the
liberation of the daylight. The sun is
rendered as a half-round stylized face

surrounded by a vermilion corona. The
bird's wings are detailed with black
formlines carved in relief.

Among the Kwakiutl tribes of northern Vancouver Island clappers are used
only in the Mitla dance, in which the
performer wears the dancing headdress
with frontlet and shakes the clapper
much as the usual headdress dancer uses
the raven rattle. Just how northern clappers like this one were used is uncertain,
but perhaps they were a similar part of
dancing regalia.

21. CLAPPER

Tlingit, early 19th century
Wood
L: 8 7/8 in. (22.5 cm.); H: 2 in. (5 cm.);
D: 2 in. (5 cm.)
Collection of John H. Hauberg

The oldest of the clappers in this group
probably dates from the early years of
the last century. A fine carving with simple, elegant detail, it may represent the
kind of baby bird, with an oversized
mouth and a stubby tail, often seen in
the tobacco pipes of the Tlingit. Perhaps
this is young raven with his insatiable
mouth. Almost all the color has worn
away from the hardwood surface; it has
adhered most tenaciously on the end-
grain surfaces where the paint medium
finds its best grip. Outer details exposed
to handling have acquired a deep polish
typical of old pieces. The bird once had
slightly spread wings that have long ago
split off, the broken edges now softly
rounded. The extent of the wings can be
guessed from the fragmentary formline
detail that remains. Unfortunately, the
upper slat of the extremely thin handle
has broken through, and it has been
secured with a wrapping of cord.

The exaggerated mouth and rounded
belly graphically express the boundless
extent of the bird's hunger. It is a
humorous image as well as a powerful
one.

22. MOUNTAIN SHEEP HORN RATTLE
Cowichan, early 19th century
Mountain-sheep horn, yew wood
H: 14 in. (35.5 cm.); W: 6 1/2 in. (16.5 cm.); D: 2 in. (5 cm.)
Collection of John H. Hauberg

Rattles made of horn softened by heat and folded over to form a triangular chamber were confined to a limited area of the Northwest Coast in northern Washington State and southern British Columbia. The folded horn rattle reached its a state of great elaboration among the Salish tribes of Georgia Strait, where it was a very important ritual instrument used in purifying participants in the critical rites of passage (Suttles 1982: 59). The heavy, coiled horn of the mountain sheep was cut open, boiled, thinned, and folded back on itself. When softened by boiling it could be easily shaped and carved, and Salish carvers made the most of its properties in making the rattles. A highly developed system of design convention was used to form designs representing faces, birds, mammals, fish, and combinations in sharply cut relief carving. Elements such as crescents, U forms, T or wedge shaped cuts, as well as stacks and combinations of them, formed feathers, eyes, and body details.

On this fine rattle are carved, on one side, two hook-beaked birds, perhaps thunderbirds, whose silhouettes outline a human face, and whose feathers intertwine in the overlap of their bodies. On the other side is a pair of circling creatures in the same stylized detail. The handle, of yew wood, is lashed to the horn chamber. At the end there is a carved head—the features indicated by crescent cuts—apparently wearing a bird headdress with inlaid button eyes. Missing is a massive, hanging fringe of white, mountain-goat wool yarn suspended from the slanted edges of the horn. More yarn was tightly wound on the handle. These rattles are highly prized by their Salish owners, although none of them have been made for generations (Feder 1983: 46-55).

23. SPIRIT FIGURE RATTLE
Quinault, 19th century
Wood, deer hooves, buckskin, cloth, horsehair
H: 20 1/2 in. (52 cm.); W: 4 1/8 in. (10.5 cm.)
Collection of Mr. and Mrs. Alan Backstrom

This little figure is much more than a rattle. In fact its function as a rattle is secondary to its real purpose, the giving of assistance to a shaman at work. A number of similar carvings are known and something of their use and significance recorded. It is a representation of a spirit helper of the shaman, said to look just like that spirit experienced by the owner in a trance. The facial painting of yellow forehead, red from brow to cheek, and pink chin are just as the spirit appeared. The clustered deer hooves, which clatter with any movement of the figure, symbolize his rattling bones.

Quinault power figures are among the most striking examples of Salish sculpture. Their angular bodies, pierced to separate arms and legs, present a bold pattern of positive-negative interaction. Salish stylization of the face— an oval outline with sharply undercut brow, and straight nose and incised eyes and mouth—is perfectly represented in this power figure.

24. GROUSE RATTLE
Nitinat, Clo-oose Village, 19th century
Wood, cotton twine
L: 12 in. (30.5 cm.); H: 5 in. (12.8 cm.); D: 5 in. (12.8 cm.)
Collection of John and Grace Putnam

One of the most distinctive of the bird-shaped rattles used on the Northwest Coast is the smoothly streamlined, globular rattle generally described as representing a grouse. Usually very sparsely decorated, and then only on the head and neck, grouse rattles depend on their swelling form and the interesting juxtapostion of the flattened breast and globular body for their aesthetic strength. They very effectively evoke the impression of a fat bird, small head stretched grouselike to survey his territory. Some grouse rattles have inset, bead eyes and sporty, angular topknots. This one is plain, and resembles in profile the alert prow of a Westcoast (Nootkan) canoe.

Most of these rattles retain the facets of the carving knife. Their fine network emphasizes the undulating surface of the bird's body.

25. GLOBULAR RATTLE
Tsimshian, 19th century
Wood, buckskin
H: 13 in. (33 cm.); W: 5 in. (12.8 cm.); D: 5 in. (12.8 cm.)
Collection of John and Grace Putnam

Beautifully polished and deeply patinated, the smooth globular form of a Tsimshian shaman's rattle stands in striking contrast to the elaborate pierced-work of the chief's raven rattle. Some round shamans' rattles from the Tsimshian are elaborately carved in relief, but many are, as this one, left plain except for simple fluting along the joined edges of the shells. The rattle is not simply oval, but subtly angled, with slightly flattened top and side edges. There is a very slight and smooth transi-tion from the swelling surface of the center to the barely concave confluence with the rim groove. A trace of red paint remains in the grooves.

Globular rattles are associated with shamanic practice throughout the coast. Tlingit shamans also use other forms, including the spectacular oyster-catcher rattle, but round forms prevail. Many are carved with human faces, sometimes with the expression and bony aspect of corpses. Perhaps the similarity of the round rattle to the human skull explains its association with supernatural power.

26. GLOBULAR RATTLE
Kwakiutl, 20th century
Wood, red cedar bark, twine
H: 12 1/2 in. (31.7 cm.); W: 9 in. (22.8 cm.); D: 4 1/2 in. (11.5 cm.)
Collection of John H. Hauberg

Just as is customary among the northern tribes, the Kwakiutl associate round rattles with shamans' practice. They have, however, an elaborate ceremonial complex, Tseyka, or the Winter Ceremonial, in which all active participants are referred to as "shamans" (*pipakhula*) and in which round rattles are used. This is such a rattle, and the rim of shredded, red-dyed cedar bark, the emblem of Tseyka, ties it to that ceremony. Rattles are shaken by the ritualists who call the motivating spirits and who consecrate the shredded cedar bark that the participants wear. All dancers are accompanied by attendants, who shake round rattles to calm them and to signal the singers. The rattles used by the attendants of the Hamatsa, the Cannibal Dancer, are often specifically in the form of skulls.

This rattle is the work of the well-known Kwakiutl chief and artist, Mungo Martin. The white background painting is characteristic of twentieth century Kwakiutl style, and the sweeping, narrow lines and sharply constricted eyelids, among other details, are recognizable features of Mungo Martin's work.

27. WHISTLE
Northern Northwest Coast, 19th century
Wood, rawhide
H: 5 in. (12.8 cm.); W: 2 7/8 in. (7.2 cm.); D: 2 1/2 in. (6.4 cm.)
Collection of John and Grace Putnam

Whistles are a part of the larger aspect of Northwest Coast ceremonial tradition that includes rattles. More than noise-makers, they usually function to make audible the unseen powers that are present on ritual occasions. Like rattles, they are wooden shells, usually made by splitting the globular or cylindrical block, hollowing both parts, and joining them by means of lashing. Unlike rattles, whistle parts must be joined in an airtight match, or the result will be a weak or nonexistent tone. The joint is often sealed with pitch, and Kwakiutl ritualists pour water in their whistles just before use to swell the joints tight.

Whistles are unlike rattles in another way: they were usually unseen. Intended to represent the voices of spirits, or the sound of unseen power, they were sounded in secret. Yet many were carved elaborately as if for display. This little whistle may have been made for use with a bellows, which would allow it to be blown in the concealment of a dancer's or attendant's blanket. As in the case of many carved whistles, the open sound hole is formed out of the figure's mouth.

MASKS

Masks, along with totem poles, symbolize the Northwest Coast in the popular view. For much of the coast this idea is a valid one. But the great depth of tradition and the heritage of styles behind Northwest Coast sculpture is often unrecognized, and masks and totem poles have been stereotyped as crude carvings of grotesque faces.

The tribes of the Northwest Coast share a great many cultural features, but the coast is a long one, with varying climate and topography and resulting differences in the resources that support life and culture. The masking tradition extends over a long stretch of that coast, roughly from northern Washington State to the northern limit of the culture area, reaching even beyond it to the western Alaskan arctic, but it too is not uniform. Masks vary in physical form, size, complexity, and purpose from one part of the coast to another. They are much more important to some coastal cultures than to others, and the motivations for mask wearing are as diverse as the masks themselves. Yet it can be said fairly that, for all parts of the coast, masks are the means by which the supernatural world is made visible. They may represent powerful spirit helpers whose potency infuses a shaman, or dramatic manifestations of fabled creatures of family history. Handsome or frightening, fanciful or naturalistic, masks enrich the Northwest Coast.

28. SKHWAIKHWEY MASK
Cowichan, Kuper Island, B.C., c. 1870
Wood, feathers, cloth, beads
H: (without appendages) 19 5/8 in. (50 cm.); W: 12 in. (30.5 cm.); D: 8 in. (20.2 cm.)
Collection of John H. Hauberg

On the Northwest Coast, important times of change—puberty, marriage, death—are marked by ritual. The changing one and his relatives are precariously balanced in their relationships to the supernatural world and the realm of ordinary life. Ritualists, skilled and equipped to cleanse and purify those closely involved in life changes, are prominent in Coast Salish ceremony. Their tools include the mountain sheep horn rattle (cat. no. 22) and the dress and mask of the Skhwaikhwey. Individuals own the Skhwaikhwey mask, the right to use it for cleansing, and the right to pass it on to descendants. Its form comes from a story that recounts how an ancestor first was given the Skhwaikhwey's dress and the instructions for its use.

When the power of the Skhwaikhwey is needed, the host arranges for two, or a multiple of two, dancers to perform at a potlatch in which the cleansing is to take place. They appear from an enclosure, one by one, jumping from foot to foot, the deer-hoof rattles on their ankles clattering. Wooden hoops strung with large, pierced scallop shells form their rattles, and they crash like metal shards. Row on row of feathers shingle the dancers' bodies and flutter with the jumps. Crowning all are the great masks, angled on the dancers' foreheads so that each dancer looks out through the mouth, over a broad tongue-projection. Peg eyes jut from round sockets and creature heads form the horns and noses. Stiff ruffs of feathers frame the masks and bobbing plumes crown them.

The dancers run with short steps up to the object of their cleansing, brushing him with hemlock boughs and shell rattles. Then they resume the jumping dance. Host family members tuck the corners of blankets, as payment, in the hands of the dancing Skhwaikhweys, who drag them until they are retrieved by a relative. One after another they return to their cubicle, their cleansing finished. Strong dancers, proud of their skill and stamina, prolong the dance.

Identified with the raven by the bird-head nose and upstanding horns, this fine Skhwaikhwey mask was made sometime around 1870 by Chief Jim Charley of Nanaimo. The raven's wings sweep around the rim of the mask face, his tail feathers stripe the forehead and his claws curl under the horns. Other masks are detailed with different creatures: sawbill duck, serpent, and ghost among them (Suttles 1982: 60-62). The feather ruff is covered with a velvet band beautifully beaded in abstract floral patterns.

29. MASK
Westcoast, Nitinat, late 19th century
Red cedar, cedar bark
H: 12 in. (30.5 cm.); W: 8 1/2 in. (21.7 cm.); D: 8 in. (20.3 cm.)
Collection of Dr. and Mrs. Allan Lobb

The masking customs of the Westcoast (Nootkan) tribes are more like those of their northern relatives, the Kwakiutl, than those of their southern Vancouver Island Salish neighbors. Many more masks, of a variety of types, were worn by Westcoast dancers. Some represent human forms, mythical ancestors or spirits associated with the Winter Ceremonial, while others are likenesses of birds or animals. Southern Westcoast sculptural style is well illustrated in this humanoid mask. Deep from front to back, with the sides forming planes angled away from the median line, the mask achieves strong, sculptural form with minimal carving. The large, open eye rimmed with long eyelids, tapered to points, on the slightly modeled cheek plane is a typical feature of this style of carving. The area above the eye is wide and gently slanted up to the narrow arched eyebrow. Flaring nostrils and a wide, straight mouth above a short chin complete the form.

30. MASK
Westcoast, Nitinat, late 19th century
Red cedar, cedar bark
H: 11 3/8 in. (29 cm.); W: 8 1/2 in. (21.5 cm.); D: 6 7/8 in. (17.5 cm.)
Collection of John H. Hauberg

Westcoast masks are often made in pairs to be danced together (cat. nos. 29 and 30). Almost identical in sculptural form, the two masks differ mainly in their painted design. We have little understanding of the painting tradition of the Westcoast artists. Masks such as these are often painted with asymmetrical designs, consisting of angled stripes, running straight across the carved forms. Sometimes the stripes have rounded ends that resemble, and may be related to, the U forms in northern formline painting. Young Westcoast artists today are studying these nineteenth century masks in order to gain an understanding of their forefathers' art. The results of these efforts are powerful new images growing directly out of traditional Westcoast forms.

31. MASK
Westcoast, 19th century
Wood, cedar bark, twine
H: 12 3/8 in. (31.5 cm.); W: 7 1/4 in. (18.4 cm.)
Collection of John H. Hauberg

Although the age of this striking mask is unknown, it is probably much earlier than the previous two. Collected near Tofino on the central Vancouver Island coast, it shows the ravages of time and a strong carving style unlike that of known late nineteenth and early twentieth century masks. The jaw is carved of a separate piece and loosely attached to the mask with a twine tie. The moving jaw and opening mouth supply lifelike expression, even to such a fanciful face. The angled, prismatic principal form is related to later southern Westcoast masks, but the deeper recess defining the eye sockets increases the sculptural effect. Once there were eyes in those hollow sockets; wooden orbs pivoted at their ends to roll and blink—stiff wood made alive.

The black face with red border paint explains the sculpture's forcefulness, which is sometimes diminished by elaborate surface design. The tassel of red cedar bark is a recent addition; whether the mask originally had attached bark is not known.

32. MASK
Kwakiutl, 19th century
Wood
H: 10 in. (25.3 cm.); W: 9 in. (22.7 cm.)
Collection of Mr. and Mrs. Alan
Backstrom

Kwakiutl carvers are best known for their fanciful stylization, bold carving with exaggerated planes, and elaborate surface decoration. This old mask, with its naturalistic proportions, smoothly merging contours, and restrained paint might easily be misread as a northern carving, but in fact it is Kwakiutl. Many Kwakiutl masks and carved figures of the nineteenth century have features like this one: small, naturally proportioned eyes and lips, and rounded cheek planes. The lips, nostrils, and ears are painted red, and the eyes, eyebrows, moustache, and beard black. The painted moustache terminates in dashing spirals that are only faintly visible against the dark patination of age. Most Northwest Coast male masks have painted, carved, or fur whiskers. Contrary to popular notion, moustaches and beards were common on the coast at the time of the first arrival of white explorers, who frequently commented on them in their journals.

There are many Kwakiutl human face masks lacking obvious characteristics that distinguish them as specific beings. Some of these were used in a dance called Gitakhanees, which represented Tlingits of the north. Others were used to depict ancestors or supernatural humanoid beings. The use of this one is not known.

33. GOOMOKWEY MASK
Kwakiutl, late 19th century
Wood, cedar bark
H: 19 1/4 in. (49 cm.); W: 17 in. (43.2 cm.); D: 5 7/8 in. (15 cm.)
Collection of John H. Hauberg

Kwakiutl mythology and dance drama are peopled by a bewildering multitude of beings, many of which are not identifiable today. Some, however, do have known distinguishing features and, even more important, recent Indian use in traditional, ceremonial settings makes their proper identification possible. This mask has both characteristics. The creature represented here is the Goomokwey, the chief of the undersea world and a source of wealth and prestige for those lucky enough to gain his benevolence. The Goomokwey mask is usually large, in humanoid form, with scalelike painting details and a corona, often composed of a series of U forms with central spots, perhaps representing the suckers of octopus tentacles. Sometimes sea anemones in the form of raised disks on the cheeks or eyebrows, or other marine attributes such as spines or a starfish, are attached to the mask.

The Goomokwey appears in the Tlasula series of dances which dramatize family crests. A new dancer wearing the frontlet headdress loses his self-control when teased by an attendant and dashes out of the house. The attendants follow and return with his headdress and blanket, announcing that the dancer has disappeared. They try to continue his dance, in a deliberate, awkward burlesque, a comic interlude in the long ceremonial series. Later on, during a pause in the dances, an eerie, wailing call echoes from the shore, the voice of a cedar reed-horn. Reluctantly, after many false starts and excuses, the attendants investigate the dismal cry, and bring a masked figure into the spreading firelight of the house. This time it is the Goomokwey, who has come in the place of the missing dancer. The singers begin the song of the mask, striking time with their batons on a carved plank. Goomokwey moves slowly, as if under the water, turning his head to reflect the firelight, or to be silhouetted against it. Eagle down swirls around him, blown by attendants. As the song ends, they shout *wuh wuh wuh* and, shaking their rattles, surround the dancer and retreat behind the screen at the back of the house. Other headdress dances and other masks follow until all the Tlasula privileges have been shown.

34. NOOHLMAHL MASK
Kwakiutl, mid-19th century
Wood, horsehair, copper, opercula
H: 10 3/8 in. (26.5 cm.); W: 8 1/8 in.
(20.6 cm.); D: 5 7/8 in. (15 cm.)
Collection of John H. Hauberg

A very strange being occupies an important place in the Winter Ceremonial of the Kwakiutl. Irrational, bad-tempered, physically dirty, the Noohlmahl (Foolish, or Reckless, Dancer) acts as the enforcer of rules in the dance house. Mistakes or infractions send him into a mindless frenzy. His big nose is his most salient feature, and any reference to it, or abuse of it, is intolerable to him.

This is one of two types of Noohlmahl (pronounced noothl-mawthl) masks (Holm 1975). The other, more characteristic form has a very large, protruding nose, drooping eyes, and grinning mouth. It is possible it represents an actual malformation, the Treacher-Collins syndrome. The mask seen here has another source: decorative carvings of lions common on European sailing ships from the sixteenth to the nineteenth centuries. Lion-type Noohlmahl masks have a uniform set of features: a swirling, twisted mane with rounded projections on the sides; a long, rounded nose with septum extended over the upper lip; a swelling, striated muzzle; a glowering mouth; round, drooping eyes; and slanting eyebrows with vertical drops in the center forehead flanking several wrinkles or knobs. Lions in ships' carvings share all these features!

Documented examples are rare and old. The earliest dated example was collected in 1842. This one could well be that old.

35. THUNDERBIRD MASK
Kwakiutl, late 19th century
Red cedar, cedar bark
H: 11 in. (28 cm.); W: 10 1/2 in. (26.6 cm.);
D: 14 1/2 in. (37 cm.)
Collection of Jim and Marilyn Bergstrom

Thunder as a bird is a continent-wide conception in North America, but nowhere as graphically portrayed as on the Northwest Coast, where he is found in monumental sculpture, masks, paintings, and every manifestation of art. And of all coastal artists, those of the Kwakiutl have embraced the thunderbird as a favored subject. Kwakiutl mythology abounds in references to this powerful tribe of birds. Thunderbird, or his brother Kolus, perches on memorial poles as a lineage crest, masked Tlasula dancers mimic his hunching stride, and his spreading feathers and arched beak glitter on button blankets. The Kwakiutl perceive the thunderbird as a giant eaglelike bird, horns or ears curling over the head, which often carries a whale or clutches the horns of the Sisiutl (cat. no. 132).

This Thunderbird mask is very simply and directly carved, with none of the deep modeling of features often seen in Kwakiutl sculpture. Instead, the planes of the eye, cheek, and beak merge in a smoothly flowing surface on which the details are painted. Only the crescentlike nostril is carved. The green-painted eye socket, yellow beak, black eye detail and brow, and red lip and nostril are characteristic of Kwakiutl painting. A bold, white stripe painted over the eye socket green is a very striking but unusual accent, and probably a later addition.

Profuse hanging of shredded cedar bark partly dyed red and a rope of bark rimming the mask indicate its use in the Winter Ceremonial, called Tseyka by the Kwakiutl. Thunderbirds appear in several parts of this ritual complex, in which dancers dramatize the power acquired by ancestors in adventurous contact with supernatural beings. The mandible is hinged with leather straps and controlled by a cord run over a cross bar. Dancers, every day seeing eagles soaring, fishing, preening, strolling the beach, combine the natural bird's movements with a sense of the mythical bird's fabled power.

36. RAVEN HAMATSA MASK
Kwakiutl, c. 1910, by Mungo Martin
Wood, cedar bark, leather, woolen blanket
L: 37 3/8 in. (95 cm.); H: 14 3/8 in. (36.5
cm.); D: 10 in. (25.5 cm.)
Collection of Mr. and Mrs. Philip
McCracken

Hamatsa, the Cannibal dance, stands highest in rank in the Tseyka, the Winter Ceremonial. Originating in an ancestor's adventure with Bakhbakwalanooksiwey, the man-eating spirit, and counted as one of the most important privileges to be brought by a bride to her husband in marriage, the Hamatsa dance has loomed large in our perception of Kwakiutl ceremonial drama. Each succeeding heir to the dance reenacts his forebear's transformation into a manifestation of Bakhbakwalanooksiwey and his taming through dance, song, and ritual. The drama begins with the disappearance of the new initiate, who is taken by the motivating spirit. Later, when the people begin to dance, he is lured back from the spirit's house and appears wild and hungry to eat men, and dressed in ornaments of hemlock branches. His wildness is gradually softened and red-dyed cedar bark replaces the hemlock regalia in his dance; but suddenly the Cannibal power overcomes him and he runs, shouting his wild cry, behind the painted screen. A great beak snaps and clatters, and from behind the

screen steps a bird, shaggy with cedar bark. He dances upright at first, then in crouching jumps. Finally he sits on the floor, swinging the great beak slowly down and down. Then the dancer half rises and clatters the beak. He shouts the Hamatsa cry and steps, dancing, to the far corner of the house. Another bird enters the firelight, and the two dance. As many as four birds, the companions of Bakhbakwalanooksiwey, appear at one time. When they disappear, one by one, the Hamatsa returns and finally is quiet in his dance.

The great masks of the man-eating birds are unsurpassed in dramatic power, with their long beaks, staring eyes, and swinging folds of shredded cedar bark. Their characteristics are surprisingly uniform: primarily black, with white eye sockets and red lips, nostrils, and details; and masses of cedar bark strands, braids, and twists dyed partly red. Mungo Martin, the maker of this mask, judging from the very distinctive style of the carving and painting, was a renowned carver from Fort Rupert, near the north end of Vancouver Island. He was probably only in his twenties, though already an experienced and respected carver, when he made this raven. The slight extension of the beak past the lip is an unusual and innovative feature, but the most interesting and

unique detail is the small, red hands clasping the joint of the jaw. No other Hamatsa mask, of over 200 known, has these hands. Otherwise, the construction and decoration are perfectly characteristic of the traditional form.

Hamatsa masks are heavy and awkward to wear, and the dance is very strenuous. A strong harness of cord and strips of woolen blanket is needed to tie the mask on and hold it at the proper angle. The blanket strips on this mask are from the white Hudson's Bay Company blankets that were used as potlatch currency during the late nineteenth and early twentieth centuries.

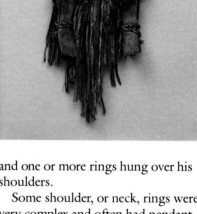

37. HOKHOKW HAMATSA MASK
Kwakiutl, c. 1940, by Mungo Martin
Wood, cedar bark, leather, woolen blanket
H: 14 1/2 in. (36.8 cm.); L: 37 in. (94 cm.)
Collection of John H. Hauberg

Mungo Martin continued to make masks and other carvings until a few years before his death in 1962. Quite a few of those masks were the wild birds of the Hamatsa dance. Around 1940 he made a pair of them, one a raven and the other this Hokhokw mask, for Tlakwagila, Tom Johnson, the highest ranking Kwakiutl chief. The Hokhokw is a long beaked man-eater with a prominent nostril. Generally the beak is very long and thin, but Mungo Martin chose to carve this one shorter and more massive. Both the raven and the Hokhokw masks show design characteristic of Martin's style, particularly in the form of the eye, with its inner and outer circles joined at the front and very constricted eyelid, and in the long, white eye socket running out onto the beak (Holm 1983).

A very unusual feature in the Hokhokw mask is the cluster of feather designs rising over each eyebrow and edged with cedar bark rope. "Head feathers" in the form of curled horns stand over the eyebrows of some Hokhokw and Crooked Beak masks by Willie Seaweed, a contemporary of Mungo Martin (Holm 1983), and a few other masks show similar elaboration, but the arrangement here is unique.

38. HAMATSA'S CEDAR BARK RING
Kwakiutl, early 20th century
Yellow cedar, cedar bark, human hair
H: 68 in. (172.7 cm.); W: 12 in. (30.5 cm.);
D: 6 in. (15.2 cm.)
Collection of John H. Hauberg

As he becomes progressively more tame in his dances, the Hamatsa exchanges cedar bark ornaments for more and more elaborate arrangements. The exact form of these ornaments depends on the tradition on which the particular Hamatsa's dance is based. In the old days, the character of the braided bark and the various knots and fringes were significant. The dancer wore a cylindrical ring of elaborately worked and red-dyed bark around his head, braids or twists of bark around wrists and ankles, and one or more rings hung over his shoulders.

Some shoulder, or neck, rings were very complex and often had pendant parts of carved and painted wood with designs related to the Hamatsa's tradition. This example represents a man, himself wearing the ornaments of a Hamatsa. In use it probably hung over the dancer's shoulders, the head and arms on his chest and the legs down over his back. There are only two or three other extant examples of these man-shaped neck rings. They probably symbolize the corpses upon which the Cannibal Spirit feeds. An appropriate skin color, the yellow cedar was left largely unpainted except for details of the face, hands and feet, and ovoid joint marks at the knees and elbows.

39. CEDAR BARK NECK RING
Tsimshian, 19th century
Cedar bark, bird skin, ribbon
Neck ring: Diam: 13 3/8 in. (34 cm.);
D: 2 1/8 in. (5.5 cm.)
Pendants: H: 19 3/4 in. (50 cm.);
W: 2 3/4 in. (7 cm.)
Collection of John and Grace Putnam

From one end to the other of the Northwest Coast, shamans and participants in certain ritual activities with shamanic overtones have worn rings of shredded cedar bark as emblems of their calling. The origin of this custom is a mystery. Perhaps the cedar bark harness worn by Puget Sound and Georgia Strait Salish Spirit Dancers in their first year, which is actually held by attendants to control and restrain the dancer, exemplifies what might have been the functional prototype of the elaborate bark rings of the Kwakiutl and the northern tribes. This Tsimshian neck ring illustrates the complexity of materials and technique seen in the Winter Ceremonial regalia. A circular core, probably of a bark bundle, is covered with a multiple-strand wrapping of cedar bark cord except for a section at the top over which flat strips of bark are plaited. Two broad pendants made of neatly spun, two-ply cedar bark cords sewn side by side into flat strips are lashed to the sides. The cords are alternately plyed in opposite directions to form a herringbone pattern in the finished pendants. At the hanging ends the individual cords hang freely as a fringe.

Bird skin, perhaps of an eagle, with the feathers removed and only the thick,

white down remaining, is sewn in strips at two places on each pendant. All trace of the down is gone, perhaps destroyed by moths. Bird down-skin was often used on ceremonial regalia on the Northwest Coast. It is a particularly rich material. Three bands of dark red sateen ribbon are sewn around the ring, probably as a repair of a worn spot. Thick rings such as this one, with elaborate, broad pendants, are characteristic of Tsimshian regalia.

40. MASK
Bella Coola, 19th century
Alder
H: 13 5/8 in. (34.6 cm.); W: 9 5/8 in. (24.5 cm.)
Collection of John H. Hauberg

The Bella Coola are Salish speakers living deep in the inlets and along the Bella Coola River. Their coastal neighbors are Northern Wakashan tribes: the Awikenokhw, the Bella Bella, and the Kitimat. In many ways, Bella Coola culture and art resemble that of the neighboring tribes, but there are many

distinctive differences, reflecting perhaps their Salish heritage. A complex cosmology constructed on a multi-layered universe populated with myriad supernatural beings presented Bella Coola artists with inspiration and endless subject matter. A well-documented mask in the American Museum of Natural History, collected by George Hunt in 1897, is nearly identical to this one. Identified as Ahlkhula'tunoom, the figure holds a speaker's staff striped like his face and announces the arrival of the Thunder.

Bella Coola sculpture is strong in its interplay of bold planes and bulging forms; a stylized naturalism characterizes it. The structure of cheek and mouth reflects human anatomy, but is bolder in thrust and curve. Heavy brows angled over the temples and a conical orb are identifying features. Dark green, red, and white enamel stripes are probably repainting of an earlier pattern of less contrast. Red cedar bark whisps remain across the forehead.

41. MASK
Bella Coola, late 19th century
Alder, cloth, cedar bark, hair
H: 13 1/2 in. (34.3 cm.); W: 11 1/4 in.
(28.6 cm.)
Collection of John H. Hauberg

The significance of this powerful Bella Coola mask is unknown. It too has been repainted in enamel, roughly following the original colors. The areas now painted in white were probably originally natural wood, and the dark green might have been the characteristic ultramarine blue of turn-of-the-century Bella Coola art.

The stylistic features that make Bella Coola sculpture so distinctive are here in emphatic form. Bold, interlocking projections of cheek, nose, and mouth, flaring nostrils, tapered lips, strong, conical orb—all proclaim its origin. The turban-like band encircling the head suggests a massive, twisted cedar bark ring. Bella Coola art's dramatic power is evident.

42. MASK
Bella Coola, late 19th century
Alder, cedar
Diam: 42 3/4 in. (108.5 cm.)
Collection of John H. Hauberg

Bella Coola masked performances were dramatizations of the actions of the inhabitants of the supernatural universe. This mask, with its huge corona, may represent the sun or, perhaps more likely, the moon. In a Bella Coola ceremony, the illusion of the moon traveling across the heavens has been described as the movement of a great image, perhaps like this one, drifting across the back of the house.

An early photograph shows another mask, now in the collection of the Museum of Anthropology of the University of British Columbia (A8367), in the center of the moon disk. The present central mask was substituted for it long ago. In form and paint it is typically Bella Coola, and was no doubt made as a replacement for the original, which was collected before 1910.

Bella Coola flat painting stands just at the edge of the northern formline tradition. Some examples follow the northern precepts exactly; this one uses them freely and impressionistically. The lateral birds appear to be ravens, and the upper creature must be a killer whale, judging by his long dorsal fin. An unknown creature composed of floating, formline features spreads across the bottom of the corona. Black, vermilion, and blue are the usual colors; the white accents on this example are less common.

43. MASK
Bella Coola and Kwakiutl, 19th century
Alder, cedar
H: 19 1/4 in. (48.3 cm.); W: 17 in. (43.2 cm.)
Collection of John H. Hauberg

This strong mask of the Goomokwey illustrates a frequent and puzzling problem in Northwest Coast art studies. A mask obviously from the hand of a master Bella Coola sculptor is painted in Kwakiutl style and surmounted by an eagle figure clearly Kwakiutl in both form and decoration. Should it be called Bella Coola or Kwakiutl or both, as I have done? There is no doubt of the carving's origin, although it was collected in 1968 from the descendants of George Hunt at the Kwakiutl village of Fort Rupert, where it had been for many years. After coming from Bella Coola, it must have been renewed to fit the tastes of the new owner by overpainting it in flamboyant Kwakiutl style and by the addition of the eagle and surrounding projections, perhaps representing the starfish.

44. MASK
Northern Wakashan (Kitlope ?), 19th century
Alder
H: 11 3/8 in. (29 cm.); W: 8 in. (20.3 cm.)
Collection of Mr. and Mrs. Alan Backstrom

There is an area on the Northwest Coast that is stylistically mysterious. We might call it the "Northern Wakashan triangle," using the anthropologists' name for the linguistically related tribes who occupied it in historic times. It is a big area, extending from Rivers Inlet in the south to Kitimat in the north, and from the Bella Coola country in the east out to the sea. Probably this stylistic area would not be such a mystery if the Northern Wakashan tribes had not abandoned many of their old villages so long ago and established their homes in a few widely separated villages at just about the time in the nineteenth century that traditional sculpture ceased for most of them. Add to that the almost complete lack of firsthand collection information and the difficulty becomes apparent.

Alan Sawyer attempts to shed some light on the variety of styles represented in masks from this area (see Sawyer's essay, p. 143). As he points out, gaps in our information make it very difficult to reach firm conclusions, but his identification of this mask as from Kitlope? (the ? is Alan's) seems logical and acceptable—unless and until more information comes to light.

There are perhaps a dozen known masks in this distinctive style. Paul Kane, the Canadian painter, sketched one in the early 1840s, which may be the earliest solid date obtainable. It is unpainted except for the eyebrows, beard, and moustache. All the others have painted detail like this one. A fine and very imaginative formline design in black is symmetrically painted on a green background. Rendered in narrow, elegant formlines, the pattern follows the classic rules of the northern system with the single exception that there are no inner ovoids, a very unusual circumstance given the traditional handling of all the other elements. Streaking across the cheeks and over the eye sockets and orbs is a broad orange stripe matching the color of the lips and nostrils.

45. MASK
Northern Wakashan (?), mid-19th century
Alder
H: 9 1/8 in. (23.2 cm.); W: 7 1/2 in. (19 cm.); D: 5 in. (12.7 cm.)
Collection of John H. Hauberg

Naturalistic masks from the northern part of the Northern Wakashan triangle, from the Coast Tsimshian, and from the Queen Charlotte Island Haida are very difficult to tell apart. Naturalistic representation always blurs tribal distinctions, especially when styles are already similar. Alan Sawyer identifies this mask as from the Haisla village of Kitimat, the northernmost of the Northern Wakashan groups (see Sawyer's essay, p. 143).

Very little is known of the use of masks by the Haisla. Their neighbors, the Tsimshian, used very similar masks in the dramatization of hereditary spirit figures called Nakhnokh. Haida face masks were used in somewhat the same way to dramatize different spirits. Some of them are in the form of easily identified creatures, while others, like this one, are human faces without distinguishing features recognizable to us.

The face paint probably resembles that used directly on the face of a dancer. It is in the form of a broad band of color across the eyes, with extending formlinelike elements on the cheeks. A moustache and beard of hair were once glued in place.

46. MASK
Tlingit, Sitka, pre-1869
Alder
H: 8 3/4 in. (22.2 cm.); W: 8 in. (20.3 cm.); D: 4 1/2 in. (11.4 cm.)
Collection of John H. Hauberg

Even without very solid documentation that this mask was collected at Sitka in 1869, it can easily be identified as mid-nineteenth century Tlingit. It very closely resembles others collected in Alaska during the Russian administration and the early years of the American presence. All the stylistic features point to that identification: large, rounded forms; broad, flat lips raised at the outer corners; heavy, arched brows; large, open eyes with little or no constriction of the lids; and the upper cheek plane continuous from the orb to the mouth. The painting too is typical, with its blue-green, asymmetrical design of broad U forms covering much of the mask.

This is probably a shaman's mask, representing a spirit with which the shaman had association and whose power he assumed in donning the mask. There were a number of masks in the shaman's kit, along with rattles, amulets, and other objects that were repositories of the supernatural powers used in his work. Many Tlingit spirit masks have no eye holes, leading to the unfounded supposition that they were not made to be used. This one does have small holes roughly cut in line with the wearer's eyes. Their irregularity, in contrast to the carefully executed carving, suggests that they were added at a later time.

47. MASK
Tlingit, early 19th century
Alder, abalone shell, human hair, leather
H: 10 1/2 in. (26.5 cm.); W: 7 7/8 in. (20 cm.); L: 9 1/2 in. (23.5 cm.)
Private collection

Raven, changer of the world, was a man as well as a bird. This beautiful mask, a masterpiece of Northwest Coast sculpture, combines both forms. In its accurate portrayal of natural form and proportion, Raven's beak, growing from a humanoid face, is almost an ornithologist's rendering. The beak is elaborated with massive, black formlines in a complex of ovoid and U forms. Abalone-shell inlay and blue-green paint in the tertiary areas enrich the design. The lower mandible is decorated with a pair of formline faces closely spaced along each side. Vermilion lines the beak.

Raven's human face is skull-like, with deeply sunken eyes on round orbs. The eye is peculiar, the inner ovoid slit with an incised, miniature eye painted vermilion. Heavy eyebrows stand sharply forward from the forehead, which slopes back on a taut, concave plane, reinforcing the impression of a corpse. Thin, expertly carved ridges border the eye sockets and continue the line of the upper lip over the cheeks and around the chin. A subtly raised plane curves down

from the eyebrow to join the chin line. The carving is masterful. Under this thin surface of detail presses the skull, the cheekbone curving under the corner of the eye socket and emphasized by its patination. Only traces of the original blue paint remain, except deep in the sunken socket where it was protected from wear.

The animal ears of Raven stand upright, carved with human faces and fringed with human hair. These locks of hair are sewn to skin strips that are tied with sinew to the ears; in the usual method the hair is inserted and peg-wedged in holes drilled directly in the wood.

There is no documentation with this mask, and its real use is unknown. It may be a shaman's mask, but more probably is a mask used in dramatizations of mythology. In conception and execution it is among the finest of Northwest Coast ceremonial objects.

HEADDRESSES

The lines between masks, headdresses, and hats are hard to deter-
mine. The Hamatsa mask (cat. nos.
36, 37), for example, could be considered a headdress since it is worn
on the forehead rather than over the
face; but since the dancer's face is
covered with the shroud of red-dyed
cedar bark, it may be properly considered a mask. All hats are headdresses, but the woven hats of the
Northwest Coast deserve a category
of their own. Many carved wooden
headdresses, on the other hand, are
replicas of woven hats so the distinction is blurred. My definition for a
headdress is a carved, masklike
object worn like a hat.

The function of the headdress varies with its type and with its area on
the coast. Northern, that is, Tlingit,
Haida, and Tsimshian, headdresses
are usually crest objects. They display the clan affiliation of the wearer
and often achieve the status of crests
themselves. A very specialized northern headdress is the functional war
helmet. Further south along the
coast, headdresses may display crests
or may be representations of supernatural beings associated with the
dramatic Winter Ceremonials.

48. RAVEN HEADDRESS
Tlingit, early 19th century
Wood, abalone shell, human hair
H: 8 1/2 in. (21.5 cm.); W: 7 in. (17.8 cm.);
D: 12 in. (30.5 cm.)
Collection of John H. Hauberg

A slave, the story goes, saw a hat, or
headdress, floating on the river. It was
shaped like a raven's head with abalone
eyes and had high, hair-fringed ears like
the killer whale's dorsal fin. His chief,
Anatlahash, chief of the Ganaxtedi Taku,
ordered it brought out of the river. It
was named Raven Floating on the Nass
Hat, and came to be one of the great
treasures of the Ganaxtedi. The Ganaxtedi claim Raven as a crest because he
once declared himself to be one of them,
and so the Raven Floating on the Nass
Hat had special significance for them.

This marvelous old carving, a rich
example of Tlingit crest art, has the ability to communicate to us something of
the life and values of its ancient owners.
It stands for chiefly prerogative, lineage
pride, and the rivalry between clans. It
reminds us of the depth of history on
the Northwest Coast, and of a rich oral
literature detailing the origins of families and the adventures of Raven and the
creatures of myth. It is a stirring object
of art.

Whoever made the Raven Floating on
the Nass Hat, he was a master of classic
Tlingit sculpture. Here he has combined
the fully three-dimensional representation of Raven's head with a formline
frame, mirroring the structure of the
heads on boxes and chests (cat. nos.
99-110). In order to soften the transition
between formline and stylized representation, a T shaped relief recess, painted
vermilion, was carved in the formline
border to define the end of the eyebrow.
The compact little men in the ears are
very similar to the men carved in the fin
of the Killer Whale hat of the Nanyaayi
clan of the Stikine Tlingit, a clan crest
object of similar significance, now in the
Thomas Burke Memorial Washington
State Museum.

50. CREST HEADDRESS
Tlingit, early 19th century
Wood, abalone shell
H: 10 5/8 in. (27 cm.); W: 15 in. (38 cm.);
D: 7 1/2 in. (19 cm.)
Collection of John H. Hauberg

Not all wooden hats were warriors' helmets. Many, carved as emblems of noble lineages, were worn in ceremonial times to display the family privileges. This is such a crest hat. The figure is a bird, perhaps, judging by the form and the painting on the long, tapered neck, the red-throated loon.

On the loon's breast is carved the face of a creature with a beaklike nose curled back to a human mouth. This figure is often shown on the breasts of birds, for example on raven rattles (cat. nos. 12-17), and usually called a thunderbird in the old descriptions. However, its real meaning is not clear. Wings sweeping back from the breast-face are designed as massive formline patterns painted vermilion, which vibrates in contrast to the rich ultramarine blue of the bird's body and the black of the neck and head. This blue paint, like the vermilion, is a trade pigment, and may even be powdered from commercial laundry bluing that was widely used for paint by tribal artists in the nineteenth century. The eyes of both loon and breast-bird are of abalone shell.

49. HELMET
Tlingit, Angoon, late 18th century
Wood, human hair, brass buttons
H: 11 3/8 in. (29 cm.); W: 11 in. (28 cm.);
D: 8 1/8 in. (20.5 cm.)
Collection of John H. Hauberg

When Europeans first met the Tlingits they were surprised and impressed by the elaborate armor of the leading warriors. The most striking detail of Tlingit armor was the helmet, carved of hardwood in the form of a fierce, scowling human face, a dangerous creature, or a crest animal. The helmet was shaped to fit close down to the level of the warrior's eyes, and his face was covered with a visor of bentwood that he held in place by biting a loop of twisted spruce root fastened to the inside.

This old and fine helmet is made in the form of an eagle, recognizable by its hooked, yellow beak and white head. The legs and feet are raised in relief from the conical helmet surface and carved with scales, while the wings and tail are detailed with formlines to represent joints and feathers. This massive, angular style is characteristic of formline designs of the early historic period.

Tlingit helmets are typically set with locks of human hair, sometimes described as being from the scalps of enemies. A closely packed crest of hair locks sweeps back over the eagle's head, and tufts embellish the wings and tail. Brass buttons give the eyes a metallic flash.

Family traditions of the Tlingit owners identify the eagle helmet as the one worn by their ancestor, Kitch-Tyee, at the battle of Sitka in 1802 when the Tlingits destroyed the Russian fort and drove them, however temporarily, from their land. After helmets became obsolete as defensive armor, they were retained as chiefly crests worn on ceremonial occasions. This helmet is an example of that transformation.

51. CREST HEADDRESS
Tsimshian (?), 19th century
Wood, abalone shell, copper
L: 16 in. (40.6 cm.); H: 6 1/2 in. (16.5 cm.);
D: 8 in. (20.3 cm.)
Collection of Sylvia Duryee

The eagle helmet (cat. no. 49) was carved as a conical hat with appendages that gave it its animal character. In contrast, the loon headdress (cat. no. 50) and this one, representing a bear, are sculptured as animals with head-shaped hollows in the bellies that allow them to be worn as crest hats.

The painting utilizes the same deep blue, vermilion, and black as the loon hat, but wear has darkened the colors. Large, copper canine teeth fill the front of the mouth and could lead to an identification as a beaver, since they resemble that animal's incisors. However, there is no sign of the beaver's tail, one of his primary identifying features. Abalone-shell inlays sparkle as teeth and eyes. The animal's fur is indicated by vermilion dashing over a dark grey-brown paint. The ears appear to have been replaced.

52. HEADDRESS
Bella Coola, 19th century
Wood, cedar bark, copper
H: 4 1/8 in. (10.5 cm.); L: 11 3/8 in. (29.5 cm.)
Collection of John H. Hauberg

The powerful thrust of Bella Coola sculpture distinguishes this small headdress, probably made for the Kusiut ceremony, the Bella Coola equivalent of the Kwakiutl Tseyka. It's likely the bird is a raven, even though the beak is curved. Bella Coola artists usually give the eagle a much more pronounced downward hook. The raven's head juts from the forehead of its wearer, and masses of cedar bark stream over his head and down his back. The jaw is articulated, the jaw hinge typically Bella Coola with pins joining the lower beak through holes drilled in the cheeks. Flaring nostrils and a hooked beak give the bird a voracious look, and the copper eyes peering under heavy brows add to that effect. Blue painting in great, interlocking lobes of color follows the usual Bella Coola scheme. Wooden vanes fastened the length of the forehead represent head feathers and add to the effect of the thrusting force.

53. CREST HEADDRESS
Kwakiutl, late 19th century
Red cedar
H: 15 1/2 in. (39.4 cm.); L: 22 7/8 in. (57.2 cm.); D: 12 3/8 in. (31.5 cm.)
Collection of John H. Hauberg

There are relatively fewer crest hats among the Kwakiutl than among the northern tribes, and most of those in collections are of a much later date. This heron hat is a particularly elegant one. It was made by the Kingcome Inlet carver Herbert Johnson, Gayoosdisulas, for his father and was later returned to Johnson in a memorial potlatch. The heron hat was in ceremonial use until sometime in the 1960s.

Several pieces of wood were joined to make the hat. Wings, tail, and neck were nailed to the very thinly carved body. The sweeping head feathers were also made of a separate piece of wood fitted to the bird's head. Made of red cedar, the headdress is very light, and all its parts are carved to delicate proportions. The typical Kwakiutl color scheme was used in the painting, with white background and details of black, red, and green. The body and neck of the heron are painted in grey, the natural color of the real bird. The curved neck, downward pointed daggerlike beak, and drooping tail are all features that enhance the naturalism of the image.

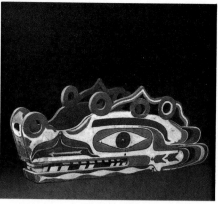

54. HAMATSA HEADDRESS
Kwakiutl, early 20th century
Yellow cedar, cedar bark, cloth
L: 24 1/2 in. (62.2 cm.); W: 14 1/2 in.
(36.8 cm.)
Collection of John H. Hauberg

When the wildness of the Cannibal
Spirit has finally been pressed from the
Hamatsa by the songs and dances of
Tseyka, he dances quietly, dressed in a
blanket and apron and often wearing a
headdress decorated according to his
inherited tradition. This impressive,
composite headdress was worn in the
Hamatsa's final, tame dance. It is carved
to represent a thunderbird; the head,
wings, and tail were made separately
and joined to a heavy ring of shredded
cedar bark wrapped with red cloth.
Cedar bark rope and tassels decorate the
carving and establish it as a Tseyka headdress. The natural color of the yellow
cedar forms the background, and the
features are painted black, red, and
green.

When worn, the bird's head projects
from the Hamatsa's forehead, the wings
flank his face and sweep back over his
ears, and the tail hangs over his neck. He
wears a blanket, either the skin of a black
bear decorated with cedar bark braids
and pendants and perhaps wooden
skulls, or a button blanket. Certain
Hamatsas have the right, through relationship to the Tlingit, to wear the
Chilkat blanket. Around his neck hangs
a large, elaborate cedar bark ring, and
similar, smaller rings circle his wrists
and ankles. His dance is quiet and
sedate, indicating that he is no longer
the personification of the Cannibal
Spirit. A female relative, his
Heyligyakhstey, dances near him,
accompanied by his many attendants
shaking their rattles.

55. DANCE HEADDRESS
Westcoast, Ahouset, early 20th century
Red cedar, brass tacks
L: 25 in. (63.5 cm.); H: 9 1/2 in. (24.3
cm.); D: 8 1/2 in. (21.5 cm.)
Collection of John H. Hauberg

Flat-sided, constructed forehead masks
are unique to the tribes inhabiting the
west coast of Vancouver Island and the
adjacent western shore of Washington's
Olympic Peninsula. They are not simply
lesser substitutes for sculptured masks,
but make up a special class of ceremonial
objects that traditionally take this form.
All the people who use flat-sided masks
also make fully sculptural ones. None
were collected before the middle of the
nineteenth century. Most of the known
examples represent the supernatural
wolves, the principal creatures of the
Westcoast Winter Ceremonial. Some
however are made to represent the light-
ning serpent, the belt and harpoon of
the thunderbird. There are also thunderbird masks made in the same technique
of very thin wooden boards joined
together and a framework of light slats
and rods intended to hold the shape and
fit the dancers' heads. This lightness
allows the use of very large masks.

Characteristic of these masks is the
elaborate fretwork along the top and
rear edges, and complex painting in circles, U forms, and curvilinear, formlinelike shapes. This one is painted with red,
black, blue, and grey on a white ground,
with accents of brass tacks.

56. DANCE HEADDRESS
Westcoast, Hesquiat, late 19th century
Red cedar, cedar bark
L: 22 3/8 in. (57 cm.); H: 9 1/4 in.
(23.5 cm.)
Collection of John H. Hauberg

This very interesting Westcoast headdress combines the flat-sided construction with a fully carved mask. All the
features of a typical constructed wolf
mask are seen in the body of the headdress, including the scrolls and piercing
along the edges. The flat sides merge
with a sculptured face that is closely
related to the style of the two humanoid
face masks pictured earlier, particularly
their deeply prismatic form and large
eyes on the cheek planes. In this mask
the eyes are separate pieces pivoted at
their ends, allowing them to roll and
change expression. A flat jaw is hinged
with leather straps.

The exact meaning and use of this
forehead mask is unknown, but similar
masks depicting the merging of mythical beings with humans are quite common on many parts of the coast, and
there are other examples from the Westcoast tribes.

HATS

Hats finely woven in conical form are a cultural feature shared by tribes all along the Northwest Coast, although the specific shapes, techniques, materials, and decoration differ from one area to another. They have often been likened to Chinese hats and from time to time it has been suggested that they were actually derived from them. James G. Swan went so far as to state, in a note accompanying hats he collected at Neah Bay for the Smithsonian Institution, that the form had been introduced to the Northwest Coast by Chinese seamen with John Meares in 1788. Of course, the conical woven hat is a natural development from a highly developed basketry technology and the needs of people on the rainy coast; its very early existence is proven by similar hats recovered from precontact archaeological sites.

Finely woven hats are marvelous aesthetic accomplishments in themselves, but they become artistically important through surface decoration applied by painting or woven in at the time of making. Basically functional, hats were also important in the ceremonial life of Northwest Coast peoples, and certain ones achieved the status of crests, every bit as esteemed as their carved-wood counterparts. Others were utilized to display lineage emblems without themselves being considered crest objects.

57. BASKETRY HAT
Haida, late 19th century
Spruce root, ermine pelt, leather
H: 8 3/4 in. (22.3 cm.); Diam: 12 1/2 in. (31.7 cm.)
Collection of Donn Charnley

This small hat, perhaps made for a noble child, illustrates the style of the crest hat, with woven basketry cylinders topping the crown and the painted design of an animal encircling the brim. The hat is tightly woven with finely split spruce root in the technique of twining. Two very narrow strands from the outer surface of the root are passed, one inside and one outside, around each vertical (warp) strand. Between each warp they are crossed so that the two weft strands constantly twist around one another. The resulting fabric is tight and firm. The surface appearance is varied by the number of warps crossed between twists, and combinations of twining around single or multiple warps. The concentric diamond pattern on the rim of this little hat is an example of such "skip-stitch" twining.

The animal painted on the hat in black, red, and pale blue-green is a wolf, conceptually split so that one side of the animal occupies each side of the hat. The style of painting is very distinctive, with its narrow and rounded formlines, asymmetrical eyelid lines, and some peculiar combinations of elements. Because of this it is easily recognized as the work of an artist who has been tentatively identified as Tom Price, a Haida artist who worked at the close of the nineteenth and the beginning of the twentieth centuries (Gessler 1971, Holm 1981: 193-97). The basketry cylinders at the top of the hat are prestigious emblems, often called "potlatch rings." Their true meaning is the subject of debate, the usual story being that they represent the number of potlatches given by the owner of the hat. This is too simple an explanation, but at least we can be certain that their presence indicates chiefly status.

58. BASKETRY HAT
Haida, late 19th century
Spruce root
**H: 5 1/2 in. (14 cm.); Diam: 16 1/2 in.
(42 cm.)**
Collection of Sylvia Duryee

Another hat painted by the Haida artist
Tom Price illustrates his distinctive
style. The design is a whale, recognizable as a baleen whale rather than the
more commonly seen orca, or killer
whale, by its short, curved dorsal fin and
the fringe of baleen represented by parallel, red lines attached to the toothlike
U forms in the mouth. Internal organs
are rendered almost exactly like those of
the wolf. The whale's long pectoral fins
trail back from his jaw, the flukes of his
tail curve forward on each side of the
hat, and dashes of black paint billow
upward from his blowhole, a conventional way of rendering the mist of his
spout. The five-pointed red star on the
flat top of the hat is apparently a Tom
Price signature; it appears on all his recognizable hats except the little wolf hat
with the potlatch rings (cat. no. 58), and
on none painted by other artists.

Skip-stitch twining on the brim forms
diagonal lines. Both of these Price hats
are made with plain twining on the
crown, which produces a texture of vertical ridges. The hat is in exceptionally

fine condition. Spruce root basketry
often gets very brittle with age, and such
hats are frequently broken.

59. BASKETRY HAT
Haida, late 19th century
Spruce root
**H: 5 1/2 in. (14 cm.); Diam: 17 in. (43.2
cm.)**
Collection of John H. Hauberg

Probably the most recognized name in
the area of Northwest Coast art is
Charles Edenshaw, and with good reason. This Haida master produced a great
body of work during his long career,
and many of those pieces are among the
finest ever made. He was an innovative
artist and developed an elegant style that
makes his art easily distinguishable from
his contemporaries. He painted many
hats, most of them woven by his wife,
Isabella, who was a renowned basket-
maker. This fine hat, with its painting of
a killer whale, was probably made by
her.

Edenshaw was faithful to the established rules of form in northern Northwest Coast art, but he often successfully
bent those rules to produce striking
variations, such as the thin red line outlining the whale's body. Smoothly
rounded forms are another characteristic
of his work, as are the smooth flow and
openness of the designs. On his hats, the
master artist painted a unique emblem
that, like Tom Price's mark, appears only
on Edenshaw's hats. It is a four-pointed
star with each point divided into red and
black segments, and it can be considered
a signature (Holm 1981: 181-88). The
killer whale hat is in perfect condition
and may never have been used.
Although he produced many traditional
pieces for use within Haida culture,
much of Charles Edenshaw's work was
made for sale to non-Indians, as this hat
may have been.

60. BASKETRY HAT
Haida, late 19th century
Spruce root
H: 7 1/8 in. (18 cm.); Diam: 15 3/4 in.
(40 cm.)
Private collection

The painting on this hat shares many characteristics with the previous one, and has also been attributed to Charles Edenshaw. The painting—representing a beaver with identifying features of large incisors and a broad, cross-hatched tail—extends from rim to crown. In order to fill the space with an even distribution of formline elements, the head of the beaver has been enlarged and modified to fit against the rim of the crown, while the legs, feet, and pelvis are extended close to the brim. This is very different from the somewhat naturalistic body proportions and recognizable silhouettes of other hat paintings in the group.

A higher and larger crown also distinguishes this hat from the others. Skip-stitch twining forms closely spaced concentric diamonds on the rim, while the upper half is woven in three strand twining that results in a smooth, regular texture rather than the vertical ribbing seen on the Tom Price hats. The star on the top is four-pointed and solid red, rather than the more typical Edenshaw red and black star. A number of other hats use this form of top painting and most of them resemble this one in composition and detail. They may have been painted earlier in Edenshaw's career, or may be the work of another artist whose style was similar to his.

61. BASKETRY HAT
Westcoast, late 19th century
Cedar bark
H: 6 in. (15.3 cm.); Diam: 13 in. (33 cm.)
Collection of John and Grace Putnam

Several different kinds of hats were woven on the Northwest Coast. Most common on the southern coast was a dome-shaped hat twined of red cedar bark. In addition to its shape, a number of other distinctive features serve to differentiate the typical Westcoast hat from those of the northern coast. They were usually made double, with a somewhat coarsely woven liner joining the outer hat at the rim. The typical material was cedar bark, rather than spruce root, although one style of domed hat was woven of split root. The usual starting technique was to plait four broad strips of cedar bark in a square at the top, then to split them and commence the twining. This hat clearly shows the square-plaited start.

The majority of dome-shaped hats were plain and depend for their handsome appearance on an elegant shape and the fine texture of expertly twined cedar bark. Some, however, were painted. This one has a bold design of black stripes and abstract forms that defies interpretation. On what is apparently the front of the hat the figure of a man stands out in black detail on a white ground. The painting is simple and bold, characteristic of the art of the Westcoast people.

62. BASKETRY HAT
Westcoast, Makah, late 19th century
Cedar bark, grass
H: 6 in. (15.3 cm.); Diam: 13 in. (33 cm.)
Collection of John and Grace Putnam

Another double, dome-shaped hat differs from the other in both technique of manufacture and decoration. The outer hat is made by a technique called "wrapped twining," in which an outer weft of split grass, some of it dyed, is wrapped around the cedar bark warp and standing weft. The technique results in a diagonal texture rather than the vertical ribbing characteristic of plain twining. Patterns are made by introducing grass dyed various colors. Often, as in this example, the designs are geometric, although animal and bird forms are also used. The hat is much faded, but red and yellow, and, perhaps, green can still be distinguished.

Wrapped-twined hats differ from the famous whalers' hats of the early historic period in technique and materials. In recent years, however, basket-makers have been weaving replicas of the older hats, with their bulb tops and whaling scenes, in the wrapped-twined technique. They can always be recognized by the distinctive diagonal texture.

BASKETS

Some of the world's finest baskets were made on the Northwest Coast of a great variety of materials and construction techniques. Their practical importance to the cultures of the coast was responsible for the enormous numbers produced and for the perfection of technical skill on the part of the makers. Basketry was a woman's art everywhere in the area. Women gathered and prepared the materials, developed the forms and designs, made and used the baskets. When a new barter and cash market opened up with the Euro-American settlement of the Northwest Coast, native women entered it enthusiastically with their baskets, and for a period of at least half a century—from the 1870s through the 1920s—one of the chief sources of money for Northwest Coast families was the sale of baskets to non-Indians. Thousands were made for sale during those years and came into Northwest homes where many remain to this day. Some very large collections, made up of superb examples from tribes of every part of the coast, were assembled; but most collections were small, the baskets thought of not as art objects but as curios, often used to hold sewing materials, trinkets, or even wastepaper.

Baskets as art deserve to be exhibited separately and within much more space than this exhibition can provide. They represent a large and very important aspect of Northwest Coast Indian art and the major design contribution to it of female artists of the area, a contribution that only recently has begun to receive its deserved recognition.

63. BASKET
Tlingit, late 19th century
Spruce root, grass, maidenhair fern stem
H: 11 in. (28 cm.); Diam: 12 3/4 in. (32.5 cm.)
Collection of Dr. and Mrs. Allan Lobb

When Tlingit women began making baskets to sell to white newcomers, they continued to use traditional shapes and designs (see Corey's essay, p. 137). The most popular basket form, usually referred to as a berry basket, flares slightly and is a bit wider than it is high. Tlingit baskets were twined with very finely split spruce root, the outer, smooth surface of which was used for the weft, or twining element, while the inner, less fine grained parts were used for the foundation strands, or warp. Several twining techniques were employed by Tlingit basket-makers, though plain two-strand twining was the principal technique. In the best baskets, the strands are amazingly even and tightly and regularly twined to form a thin, light, waterproof fabric. New spruce root is flexible and strong, and many baskets were creased and folded flat when not in use, to be dampened and opened up when the time of use arrived.

Tlingit basket decoration utilized three techniques: textures derived from the twining methods; dyeing the spruce root wefts; and false embroidery with split and dyed grass straw and maidenhair fern stems. Traditional basketry designs often consisted of a pair of broad horizontal bands of repeated geometric patterns separated by a narrower, contrasting band. The designs were produced by weaving colored stripes with dyed root and wrapping the stitches as they were made with the false embroidery material to form the geometric elements on the dyed background color. The background stripes can be seen on the inside of the basket where they are not camouflaged by the false embroidery. This basket illustrates the technique.

Dark red-brown is the natural color of the glossy stems of the maidenhair fern, split and wrapped over the spruce root weft. Light patterns are grass stems, which originally were dyed in several colors, but which have faded to a nearly uniform gold. The pattern in the upper and lower bands combines designs called "cross" and "double war club," while the central band is a variant on the "butterfly" pattern (Emmons 1903:263-277, Paul 1944:49-68).

64. BASKET
Tlingit, early 20th century
Spruce root, grass, maidenhair fern stem
H: 7 1/2 in. (19 cm.); Diam: 8 1/2 in.
(21.5 cm.)
Collection of John and Grace Putnam

This basket is a very fine example of an early twentieth century piece designed and made for sale. The bands of design have become narrower and more open, and the areas lacking embroidery are patterned all over with diamond figures made by twining over two warps to produce raised lines. This skip-stitch twining was not a new technique but was traditionally used to pattern the rims of earlier utilitarian baskets.

Another old method of producing a pattern is illustrated here in the narrow checkered lines bordering the upper and lower bands. It was produced by twining with one dyed and one plain weft. In the succeeding row the colors alternate with the first row to form the checker pattern. A reinforcing ridge near the turn of the bottom is the result of twining with three strands of split root.

The upper and lower bands use the "tattoo" pattern in fern stems and the "shaman's hat" pattern in dyed grass. The intermediate band, made up of interlocking triangles called "half the head of a salmon berry," resembles a larger pattern called "the mouth-track of the woodworm."

65. BASKET
Tlingit, late 19th century
Spruce root, grass, maidenhair fern stem,
cotton cloth
H: 10 in. (25.5 cm.); Diam: 4 3/4 in.
(12 cm.)
Collection of John and Grace Putnam

This beautifully woven and richly decorated Tlingit basket is an unusual type. Baskets of cylindrical form are the norm for early Tlingit examples, but they are usually wider than they are tall. An elaborate embroidered design, which is a favorite on old baskets and is called "the tail of the raven," makes up the traditional pair of broad bands. The center band, a variant of the "tying" design, is repeated, half at the rim and half at the base. Except for the fern stems, the colors have faded so that only subtle differences are discernible. Although the upper and lower matching designs sometimes align, it is not at all unusual, even on the finest baskets, to find them jogged to the right or left as they are here. Our aesthetic sense ordinarily demands alignment or regular alternation of patterns like these, but the Tlingit artists apparently were not bound by such restrictions.

66. BASKET
Tlingit, late 19th century
Spruce root, grass, maidenhair fern stem
H: 5 1/2 in. (13 cm.); Diam: 4 3/8 in.
(11 cm.)
Collection of Dr. and Mrs. Allan Lobb

A number of exotic shapes began to appear in Tlingit basketry of the late nineteenth century as the artists began to cater to the market. Some were startlingly farfetched, such as basketry tea sets complete with sugar bowl and creamer, miniature shoes, and Euro-American hats. Others were more basketlike, such as this shapely example, described as a "ginger jar" type. Some were actually woven over the jars, and many bottles of various sorts were tightly and expertly covered with basketry.

This one is an excellent example and in fine condition. It displays several interesting features: a closely fitted, embroidered lid, solid bands of false embroidery, and rows of cross-warp, open twining. In twining a basket, vertical walls require the least effort since the number of warps remains uniform. Flaring baskets require the regular addition of warps to gradually increase the diameter. A basket with swelling sides must have warps added or deleted to control the complex form.

The upper and lower bands of false embroidery show alternating designs based on the "half the head of a salmon berry" motif, while the central band combines the two.

67. BASKET
Tlingit, early 20th century
Spruce root, grass
H: 4 in. (10.2 cm.); Diam: 8 in. (20.3 cm.)
Collection of Dr. and Mrs. Allan Lobb

A traditional basket type used to store a woman's sewing tools or small objects of value became one of the most popular baskets for sale in later days. It was a rather small, cylindrical basket with a lid, often completely covered with false embroidery, and distinguished by a hollow, flat knob on the lid which enclosed tiny pebbles or shot. Today these are called "rattle top" baskets and are prized by collectors. This one, very simple in its decoration compared with many, is elegant and perfectly formed.

The weaving of a rattle top basket is an exercise in complete control of the medium. To make the lid the weaver begins in the center of the knob, adding warps as she weaves to expand the circular top. When she reaches the limit of the knob, she decreases warps as she weaves the constricted neck. Then she joins the neck to the lid proper, which has been woven to the diameter of the neck, by twining over the knob and lid warps together. The finished lid shows a perfect juncture of the two parts. On this basket the knob, lid, and wall of the basket itself are decorated with repeated bands of an S shaped figure, perhaps a variant on the "blanket border" design.

68. BASKET
Tlingit, 19th century
Spruce root, grass, maidenhair fern stem
H: 9 in. (23 cm.); Diam: 3 1/2 in. (9 cm.)
Collection of Mr. and Mrs. Alan Backstrom

Among the rarest and most visually striking of the products of Tlingit basket-makers' art is the double, or telescoping basket, said to have been used to hold shamans' equipment or eagle down. Some of the very finest Tlingit baskets take this form. The inner basket, slightly tapered toward the top so that its telescoping cover can be easily fit tightly in place, is almost always completely covered with fine embroidery. Usually the outer basket is of plain root, elaborated with skip-stitch weaving, but this fine example continues the false-embroidery decoration on the cover. The inner design alternates "waves" with "tying," while the outer, cover basket is decorated with bands of designs that are similar to those that Emmons identified as "rainbow" (Emmons 1903:267).

This large double basket, in perfect condition, is one of the finest of its type, both in the perfection of the work and in the aesthetic quality of the design. A particularly elegant touch is the use of stitches of unembroidered spruce root to form the lines of division between the design bands on the cover and to subdivide the diagonal stripes of the pattern.

69. BASKET
Tlingit, 19th century
Spruce root, grass, maidenhair fern stem
H: 4 in. (10 cm.); Diam: 2 in. (5 cm.)
Collection of John and Grace Putnam

The coating of lead oxide on its inner surface is clear evidence of the fact that this fine double basket, less than half the height of the shaman's basket, was used as a shot pouch. When muzzle-loading guns came into use on the Northwest Coast many of the accessories needed for them were made by native craftsmen. Powder horns and measures, percussion cap horns, and bullet pouches were among the objects made of the materials available on the coast and they were often decorated in traditional motifs. Tlingit basket-makers wove pouches for the paper cartridges used with muzzle-loading muskets as well as these miniature double baskets for gunpowder or lead shot.

The inner basket is entirely covered with false embroidery in a design called "tattoo." The cover is without grass embroidery and is decorated with simple bands of dyed spruce root weft that have faded so as to be nearly unnoticeable.

70. BASKET
Haida, 19th century
Spruce root
H: 15 in. (38 cm.); Diam: 12 3/8 in.
(32 cm.)
Collection of Dr. and Mrs. Allan Lobb

Haida basket-makers of the nineteenth century limited their production to very simple, cylindrical containers of a great range of sizes. Many Haida baskets were decorated with simple bands achieved by twining alternate sections with undyed spruce root wefts and with wefts dyed black or a dark purplish brown. Usually, as in this basket, these stripes are plain; but by using weft pairs of two colors, undyed and dyed, patterns of vertical or diagonal stripes, or checkerlike arrangements were achieved.

The upper part of the typical Haida basket was elaborated with textural patterns made by manipulating the twining stitches of the weft. The rim was finished with one of several possible complex twining stitches that used multiple strands of root and that turned the ends of the warp strands back into the weave. In this classic basket the decorative band at the top is formed of alternating two- and three-strand twining to form a series of parallel ridges.

The choice of the cylindrical basket form was aesthetic and practical and was not related to the degree of skill of Haida basket-makers. Haida weavers were renowned for their hats, which were among the most sophisticated basket forms.

71. BASKET
Westcoast, late 19th century
Cedar bark, grass
H: 10 in. (25.5 cm.); W: 16 1/2 in. (42 cm.);
D: 2 in. (5 cm.)
Collection of Dr. and Mrs. Allan Lobb

The technique of twining was known all over the Northwest Coast and was sometimes combined with other basketry methods. This utilitarian wallet-shaped basket from the Northwest Coast of Washington, or southwestern Vancouver Island, is made in a combination of checkered plaiting and wrapped and plain twining. The bottom, characteristic of baskets from this area, is plaited of flat strips of the inner bark of the red cedar. At the turn of the bottom, the cedar bark strips were split into a fine warp and about two inches of the sides were woven with grass in a technique called wrapped-twining. In this method of basketmaking one stiffer twining strand remains on the inner side of the warps while a flexible strand is wrapped over the outside of each warp strand and around the inside of the standing, or inner, weft. Designs, quite faded in this example, are formed by changing the wrapping strand to one of another color.

The upper part of the wallet is woven in plain twining, basically the same technique as that used by Tlingit basket artists, which uses grass weft on cedar bark warp. A representational whale surrounded by a rectangular design is painted on the basketry surface in black with accents of white. Painting on hats was common all over the coast, and many plainly woven Haida baskets were painted, but otherwise it is a combination uncommon on Northwest Coast baskets.

72. BASKET
Makah, early 20th century
Cedar bark, grass
H: 3 1/2 in. (9 cm.); Diam: 7 5/8 in.
(19.5 cm.)
Collection of Dr. and Mrs. Allan Lobb

The wrapped-twining technique has been used to produce untold numbers of decorated baskets for the market since the late years of the nineteenth century. Apparently based on an ancient method of constructing utilitarian baskets, it appears to have been perfected in the area of Neah Bay, Washington, sometime in the last century. The technique has spread widely in the Northwest and is the favorite basketry method along the outer Washington and southern Vancouver Island coasts.

The quality of wrapped-twined basketry varies from extremely rough to some of the technically finest baskets in the world. This cylindrical, lidded trinket basket is an example of the highest quality. Although there are baskets from the region with a higher stitch count, none surpass it in regularity of technique or perfection of form and detail. Geometric designs in black and green alternate with representational whales, birds, and canoes. Perky birds stand in rows on floating logs. Some of them, about to fly, spread their wings. They look for all the world like the seagulls that even today ride tide-driven driftwood along the Northwest Coast.

73. BASKET
Makah, early 20th century
Cedar bark, grass
H: 3 1/2 in. (9 cm.); W: 4 1/2 in. (11.5 cm.); D: 4 in. (10 cm.)
Collection of Dr. and Mrs. Allan Lobb

Makah basket-makers excelled at controlling the form of their products. Most examples made for the basketry market were cylindrical, like the preceding one (cat. no. 72), but some were flaring and others square or rectangular. Lids were common, and some, like this one, had integral knobs. But fanciful forms tempted the makers to demonstrate their skills, and a favorite display of virtuosity was to cover an object of whatever shape with tightly twined cedar bark and grass elaborated with colorful designs. Bottles and jars were the most common, but mussel and moon snail shells, whales' eardrums, Japanese glass fishing floats, and even deer antlers were encased in basketry.

Flying birds alternate with abstract, rectangular motifs in this finely woven, rectangular basket. Representational designs are common, and traditional, on Westcoast basketry, including that of the Makah. The elaborately embellished whalers' hats seen and collected from the Westcoast people by the earliest European visitors to the coast depicted whales, canoes, and thunderbirds. They were made with somewhat different materials and techniques, but were clearly the precursors of the trinket baskets of the later nineteenth and twentieth century baskets.

74. BASKET
Westcoast
Cedar bark, grass
H: 2 1/2 in. (6.5 cm.); Diam: 3 in. (7.5 cm.)
Collection of Mr. and Mrs. Alan Backstrom

Westcoast wrapped-twined basketry comes in all sizes. Some baskets are very much smaller than this tiny example. Long whales circle the basket and lid. They seem to symbolize Westcoast culture, which gave such importance to the whale of myth and of the everyday world. Whaling was the most prestigious activity: whalers were always of the noble class, whales were the prey of the thunderbird. They furnished food, blubber, oil, and meat. Tools and weapons were made from their bones. And they often appeared in the art of the Westcoast tribes. Here they are quite naturalistic in their proportions compared to the geometric renditions on the ancient whalers' hats.

Wrapped-twined basketry shows a characteristic diagonal texture on the outer surface. The direction of slant is determined by the direction of twining. On the inner surface the standing weft, spiraling around the wall of the basket, produces a horizontally ribbed pattern. Unlike Tlingit basketry, where the false-embroidered designs appear only on the outside, patterns appear inside and out in wrapped-twined work, although the forms are clear and regular only on the outside.

75. BASKET
Twana, late 19th century
Cattail leaves, grass, cedar bark
H: 14 1/4 in. (36 cm.); Diam: 14 1/2 in. (37 cm.)
Collection of John and Grace Putnam

Among the most distinctive of Northwest Coast baskets are those from the Twana of the Hood Canal region in western Washington. The Twana, or Skokomish, basket-makers specialized in moderately soft, twined baskets that have slightly rounded sides, and are decorated with a variation of the overlay technique. Typically these baskets show a broad, complex zigzag design (called "salmon gills") in reddish and dark brown on a tan ground, or four vertical stacks of concentric rectangles (called "boxes") spaced evenly around the surface of the basket. Almost all of them feature a narrow band below the rim which has evenly spaced figures of animals woven in a simple, diagrammatic form. Those figures with two slanted legs are thought to represent mergansers, those with four legs and upturned tails are dogs, and those with downward slanting tails are wolves, or, according to more recent interpretation, horses (Thompson et al. 1980: 12-19).

In the Twana version of the overlay technique the designs, which are made of dyed cedar bark weft, appear only on the outside of the basket; there they contrast with the grass, which forms the other element of the weft. The warp, which is entirely enclosed, is of cattail leaves. The box designs on this fine basket are very complex and expertly done. Alternating bands of dark and reddish brown overlay add a rich variation to the concentric rectangles of the design.

76. BASKET
Quinault, early 20th century
Spruce root, bear grass
H: 8 1/2 in. (21.5 cm.); Diam: 9 1/2 in.
(24 cm.)
Collection of Dr. and Mrs. Allan Lobb

Several different basketry techniques were practiced by Quinault weavers. Their home on the west side of the Olympic Peninsula put them in contact with wrapped-twined basket-makers to their north and with makers of plain-twined and coiled baskets to their south and east. All these techniques were utilized by the Quinault, but they are best known for elegantly formed twined spruce root baskets decorated in the overlay technique with bear grass. It is possible to produce almost any kind of design with overlay, and the technique has many advantages over others, such as false embroidery, if the design is limited to two colors and if these colors change at every stitch, as they frequently do in Twana and Quinault basketry.

Quinault baskets resemble their Twana counterparts in a number of ways. They are similar in shape and often share design elements, such as the "salmon gill" pattern and the animal border. They are stiffer than the Twana baskets with their cattail warp, and the color arrangement of pale bear grass on darker spruce root has a very different appearance from the nearly black cedar bark patterns on the tan grass backgrounds of Twana basketry. Quinault weavers tend to orient their designs vertically, a tendency exemplified in this basket. Although the interlocking vertical meanders create a very complex pattern, the total effect is direct and elegant, perhaps because of the controlled repetition and the simple color arrangement.

77. BASKET
Nisqually, late 19th century
Cedar root, bear grass, cedar bark, horse-tail root
H: 5 1/2 in. (14 cm.); Diam: 7 in. (18 cm.)
Collection of Dr. and Mrs. Allan Lobb

The tribes of Puget Sound excelled in the making of hard baskets of cedar root sewn so firmly as to be watertight. The roots were split into long splints and a narrow strip from the smooth, outer surface of the root was used to sew a bundle of the coarser strips from the inner part into a continuous coil. Nearly all coiled cedar root baskets were decorated to some degree, usually by a process called imbrication in which strips of decorative material were folded and tucked under the stitches of cedar root as they were made. This small and extremely fine basket, entirely covered with imbrication, shows none of the cedar root sewing on its outer surface. The light colored areas are imbricated with the leaves of bear grass, the dark red areas are the bark of the cedar root, and the black areas are probably the root of the horsetail rush.

This beautiful, little lidded basket was collected in the 1890s by James Wickersham on the upper Nisqually River. It is the work of a master basket-maker named Si-a-gut.

78. BASKET
Puget Sound Salish, mid-19th century
Cedar root, bear grass, cherry bark, horse-tail root
H: 8 1/2 in. (21.5 cm.); W: 13 in. (33 cm.)
Collection of Dr. and Mrs. Allan Lobb

This elongated basket is very similar to coiled baskets collected in the 1840s by the United States Exploring Expedition under Lieutenant Charles Wilkes in the Cowlitz area of southern Puget Sound. It is completely covered with imbrication in complex designs. Coiled cedar root baskets are strong, and many have survived hard and long use. This one shows the marks of wear and age, but the natural colors of the design materials have resisted fading and have only darkened with the patina of time.

Coiled cedar root baskets were made all over the western half of Washington and southwestern British Columbia. They vary in size and shape, and in some of the materials used. Some baskets made in the area of the Fraser River use flat cedar splints for the core of the coils, but most of these durable, practical baskets are built of coils made of a bundle of split cedar root.

80. BASKET

Puget Sound Salish, 19th century
Cedar root, bear grass, horsetail root (?),
buckskin
H: 12 in. (30.5 cm.); Diam: 13 5/8 in.
(34.5 cm.)
Collection of Mr. and Mrs. Alan
Backstrom

Hard use shows in the worn imbrication, notched rim, and blackened interior of this fine, large cedar root basket. The dark patination of the inside may be largely the result of berry staining, since baskets such as this one were used in the gathering of the food plants of the region.

The interlocking zigzag pattern is a favorite one in the Puget Sound region. A line of small dog figures, very similar to those on the twined baskets of the Twana, is spaced around the rim. Animal designs like this one, an almost invariable feature of Twana baskets, are also found in the work of other Puget Sound people, and it is not surprising since there was a great deal of trade and intermarriage among those tribes, and ideas of all sorts were shared throughout the region.

79. BASKET

Nisqually, late 19th century
Cedar root, bear grass, cedar bark, horsetail root, buckskin
H: 11 1/2 in. (28 cm.); Diam: 14 1/8 in.
(36 cm.)
Collection of John and Grace Putnam

Most Puget Sound cedar root baskets were of this shape—slightly elliptical in plan, with sides rounded down to a smaller bottom. They were used for many purposes, among them gathering and storing berries and roots for food, general storage, and cooking. A well-made coiled basket was watertight, and red hot stones dropped in water contained in the basket quickly brought it to a boil. This basket, another masterful piece by Si-a-gut, is fitted with buckskin loops by means of which a tumpline, or burden strap, could be attached.

The unusually complex design is imbricated in the natural pale bear grass, yellow-dyed bear grass, reddish cedar bark, and black horsetail root. The inner triangles at top and bottom are only partially covered with bear grass imbrication, leaving the rich, light brown cedar root stitches exposed.

Basketry is tedious work, requiring long hours of gathering and preparing materials before the actual construction begins. Even though expert basketmakers worked very quickly, their compensation per hour of work was very small. When baskets were no longer required in day-to-day life, and better paying work could be found, basketry declined. Recently, pride of heritage, along with better prices resulting from an increased respect for baskets on the part of collectors, has encouraged a renewal of basketmaking on the Northwest Coast.

CHILKAT BLANKETS

When the Spanish ship *Santiago* approached the north end of the Queen Charlotte Islands in 1774, the Haida chiefs who met her were wearing beautifully patterned robes twined of mountain-goat wool. The Spanish seamen collected some of them, but none of these are known to have survived. From the graphic descriptions recorded by two priests accompanying the expedition we have a picture of what they must have been like: fringed, rectangular capes, very tightly woven with elaborate designs in black, white, and yellow which the Spanish thought were embroidered. This description does not match what we know as the "Chilkat blanket," but an earlier textile that we might call the northern geometric twined blanket. They are extremely rare today. There are less than a dozen in the world and only a single complete example (Vaughan and Holm 1982:110-11) and a few fragments are in the United States.

By the early nineteenth century a new form of blanket had evolved that incorporated techniques of the geometric tradition and the conventionalized figurative painter's art. It was called the Chilkat blanket after the Tlingit tribe that produced most of them, although there is good evidence that women of other tribes made them as well. They were, and are, the robes of nobility, highly esteemed the length of the northern coast. Extremely complex twining techniques were used to produce exacting copies of painted designs; the resulting textile had a new and sumptuous quality derived from the subtle relief of the patterns, rich color, and a magnificent, heavy fringe.

81. CHILKAT BLANKET
Tlingit, late 19th century
Mountain-goat wool, yellow cedar bark
H: 45 7/8 in. (116.5 cm.); W: 68 3/8 in. (173.5 cm.)
Collection of Mr. and Mrs. Alan Backstrom

Most Chilkat blankets are designed as highly abstract representations of crest animals, so patterned and conventionalized in the formline design system that they are not recognizable to those lacking special knowledge. This one is an exception; it is one of a number of blankets made near the end of the nineteenth century in which the represented animal is shown configuratively on a white background. It displays four ravens, their bodies and heads spread to show both sides at once. Two salmon appear flanking the large raven in the center. The coho salmon is a crest of the Raven phratry and is probably the one represented here. Chilkat blankets from this time, especially if they are configurative in design like this one, often have floating elements unlike the continuous formline patterns of more standard blankets. Although the U complexes spaced around the edge between the raven figures are primarily decorative space fillers, they would often be assigned meaning by the blanket owners.

This blanket was photographed at the turn of the century at the time when it was worn by a Chilkat chief in the Raven House at Klukwan. Although there are several other known blankets of this pattern, subtle irregularities and color variations make it possible to establish the individual identity of the blanket. (See photograph, p. 2.)

82. CHILKAT BLANKET
Tlingit, late 19th century
Mountain-goat wool, yellow cedar bark
H: (without fringe) 45 7/8 in. (116.5 cm.);
W: 68 3/8 in. (173.5 cm.)
Collection of Dr. and Mrs. Allan Lobb

Because of the fact that Chilkat blankets were woven from painted pattern boards, a necessity because of the complex relationships of the design elements, many shared the same design or varied only slightly. Most blankets also fall within a few compositional arrangements. The most common of these has traditionally been called the "diving whale" pattern. The decorated field within the black and yellow border is divided into three fields: a large central panel and two symmetrical lateral panels. The central panel, which hangs over the shoulders and down the back of the wearer, is completely filled with a representation of the crest animal, which in this case is an elaborately conventionalized whale. The design is in broad, black formlines on a white background, elaborated with detail in yellow, blue, and white. The whale's head is at the bottom, indicated by the two large eyes and a snout represented by a pair of ovoids in the center bottom. The large, stylized face in the center of the blanket

has been identified as the body of the whale. Any supplementary meaning it might have is uncertain since it depends largely on interpretations given by different native informants. Flanking the face are designs representing the pectoral fins or, perhaps, the two halves of the dorsal fin. The tail, spread wide to show the flukes, covers the width of the panel's upper part.

Interpretation of the designs on the side panels is much more difficult. Knowledgeable Indians at the turn of the century often failed to agree on their meanings. This one has been called a raven sitting, as well as the profile of the whale. The design is the same as that in figure 568b in George T. Emmons' *The Chilkat Blanket*. Emmons, studying Chilkat blanket designs early in this century, was given the native names of many of the design elements. They are descriptive terms, necessary for weavers' communication, but have little to do with the larger symbolism of the blanket.

83. CHILKAT BLANKET
Tlingit, late 19th century
Mountain-goat wool, yellow cedar bark
H: 53 1/4 in. (135 cm.); W: 70 in.
(178 cm.)
Collection of John and Grace Putnam

The "diving whale" blankets are the most common, and the casual viewer might perceive them to be all alike. In fact, there are a number of compositional variations among them, and very seldom are there two alike in every detail. Although the central panel figure on this blanket is similar to the previous one in basic arrangements, there are many differences. The panel is narrower so the tail flukes are joined in the upper center of the design, and all details are relatively simpler. The pectoral fins on either side of the central face, or "body," are of formline U complexes, rather than the ovoid-U combination of the other blanket that has the secondary symbolism of a bird's head. The lateral panels are very different, and include among their details profile-stylized faces.

This blanket shows almost no sign of wear, and one might be tempted to assign it a twentieth century date and assume that it was made for sale, as many were, rather than for native use. However, it is documented as having been collected from Chief Johnson of the Auk Tlingit in 1890. Many old blankets lack the appearance of age because of the native custom of keeping them stored in chests rather than displaying them when not in use. In fact, the only traditional time for spreading blankets out for public view was at the memorial for a deceased noble.

  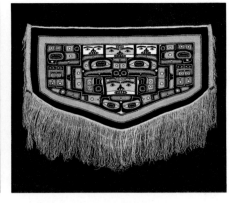

84. CHILKAT BLANKET
Tlingit, late 19th century
Mountain-goat wool, yellow cedar bark,
commercial wool yarn
H: 49 1/4 in. (125 cm.); W: 65 3/4 in.
(167 cm.)
Collection of Bill and Marty Holm

There are at least twenty Chilkat
blankets in private collections in the
Seattle area, well over half of which
share the design of the diving whale. No
two of them are alike in all details, and,
in fact, most differ from one another in
many ways. The similarity of this
blanket to the previous two (cat. nos.
82, 83) is obvious, and yet examination
reveals many differences. Fewer and
simpler design elements give this blanket
a bolder and more open feeling.

Blankets vary widely in the fineness of
yarn and quality of weave. Generally
speaking, the blankets of the early and
mid-nineteenth century are finer than
later examples; but there are exceptions.
The quality of a blanket can be quickly
judged by noting the degree of similarity between the woven forms, especially the ovoids, in a blanket and in a
fine northern formline painting. The
finest blankets very closely approximate
the painted formline characteristics:
relief "slits" properly define the edges of
ovoids; inner ovoids display the traditional quality of nonconcentricity;
curves are smooth; and corners are
square and sharp. This blanket illustrates those qualities.

85. CHILKAT BLANKET
Tlingit, mid-19th century
Mountain-goat wool, yellow cedar bark
H: 55 in. (140 cm.); W: 67 in. (170 cm.)
Collection of John H. Hauberg

Another very fine blanket illustrating
the skill of the weaver in copying the
subtleties of painting is documented as
having been the property of Son-i-hat, a
famous Kaigani Haida chief. It too has
been identified as the image of a whale
diving, although it is very different from
the designs of the preceding blankets
(Emmons 1907:fig. 563b). The whale's
head is easily seen at the center bottom.
The wide head above it represents the
body; large eyes represent the shoulder
joints and attached fins flank the human
face. At the top the tail flukes differ from
the usual arrangement in not being
inverted. Large, angular U forms thrusting laterally into the side panels can be
interpreted as the sides of the dorsal fin.
Side panels, as usual, are freely interpreted as a sitting raven.

The technique of producing a Chilkat
blanket involves bordering every color
change, during the weaving process,
with multiple rows of three-strand
braiding (Samuel 1982). These rows
outline the details with black and white
lines and refine the shapes. They also
impart a rich, textural relief that is one of
the features of Chilkat tapestry weaving
that sets it apart.

86. CHILKAT BLANKET
Tlingit, 19th century
Mountain-goat wool, yellow cedar bark
H: 53 1/4 in. (135.3 cm.); W: 65 in.
(165 cm.)
Collection of Philip S. Padelford

The configuration of this blanket design
is very different from these four diving-
whale patterns. There are no clear divisions between panels, and the head of
the crest animal is at the top rather than
at the bottom of the blanket. The figure
is a sea grizzly, a monster combining features of the grizzly and the killer whale.
Two large eyes near the top center are
the eyes of the bear, which surmount his
wide mouth with black teeth and his
nostrils. The human face at the upper
center is his forehead and the two flanking faces are his ears. The creature's
body is shown as a large human face in
the center, and his paws with their massive, arched claws stand upright beside
it. Large, rectangular U complexes
extend into the undefined side panels,
representing here the elbow fins of the
sea grizzly. His hindquarters occupy the
lower center of the design in the form of
an inverted formline face, representing
the pelvis or tail joints, and laterally
extending fin designs. The designs at the
side seem most logically to represent the
profile of the animal, although one interpretation, describing the entire design as
a grizzly with cubs, identifies the sides
as the young bears (Emmons 1907:fig.
546a,b).

87. CHILKAT BLANKET
Tlingit, 19th century
Mountain-goat wool, yellow cedar bark
H: 51 1/2 in. (131 cm.); W: 66 7/8 in.
(170 cm.)
Collection of John H. Hauberg

The difficulties in interpreting Chilkat
blanket designs and in assessing the
accuracy of interpretations are well-illus-
trated by this blanket. There seems no
logical explanation of the design other
than that it is a bird sitting upright,
wings spread. The configuration is so
nearly like well-documented bird
designs that it is hard to see it as any
other creature. At the top is the head,
formed of two profiles with the tip of
the beak turned down at the center
between the ovoid nostrils. The ubiq-
uitous body-face is flanked by inverted
double-eye wing bones from which
hang rows of U shaped feathers. Below
the body are two ovoid joints with their
appended tail feathers and the bird's feet
and claws spread out to the sides. But a
nearly identical blanket was interpreted
by a native at the turn of the century to
be a bear under the water (Emmons
1907:fig. 560b). There are many examples of such contradictions in blanket
design interpretation. Blankets that
clearly represent a specific creature in
the view of most informants are sometimes thought by others to depict
entirely different beings. These informants base their interpretations on heirloom blankets that have always been
accepted as certain crest figures within
their families. One can accept one interpretation or the other, but there is no
way to say with certainty that one is
right and one wrong.

Although this is not an extremely old
blanket, the design appears to be similar
to one painted in the 1820s by Alex-
ander Postels, an artist with the Litke
expedition (Holm 1982:fig. 11), and is
the earliest accurate illustration of a classic Chilkat blanket. This blanket is
somewhat unusual in the angularity of
the corners of the ovoids.

88. CHILKAT BLANKET
PATTERN BOARD
Tlingit, 19th century
Red cedar
H: 20 7/8 in. (53 cm.); W: 37 3/8 in.
(95 cm.)
Collection of Bill and Marty Holm

Pattern boards typically include a little
more than half of the blanket design, not
including the black and yellow border.
Since the designs were invariably bilaterally symmetrical, only the beginning
of the repeat was needed. Only the black
color of the design was shown. Placement of the yellow and blue was so
nearly fixed that skilled weavers knew
just where those colors were to be. The
weaver placed the pattern board to one
side of her weaving frame, though
always within reach, and she measured
the size and placement of each element
from the board. The weaving technique
allowed her to work within a narrow
section to avoid constant shifting of her
position.

Most old pattern boards were made of
broad, handmade boards. Although this
one is a well-painted board with a traditional design, it is made of milled lum-
ber. The design is an unusual one, seen

on only a few blankets. Emmons' (1907:
plate 572a) shows a very similar pattern,
which differs mainly in having an ovoid
formline surrounding the central face,
with a break in the upper outline indicating that it represents the blowhole of
the diving whale. This pattern lacks clear
definition of the lateral panels because
the pectoral fins and the tail flukes
extend far into them.

Pattern boards are relatively more
rare than blankets in collections. The
weavers have always been reluctant to
part with them, and they were traditionally passed down from one generation to the next. And any number of
blankets might be produced from a
single board, so that there were never
a large number. New boards were also
copied from old blankets, and some
variations in them surely resulted from
this process.

BUTTON BLANKETS
AND BEADWORK

With the introduction of woolen cloth by European and Euro-American traders in the last years of the eighteenth century, ceremonial dress of the Northwest Coast tribes began a change that culminated in the development of the button blanket. It probably reached its classic form around 1850, although no solid documentation is available for that time. From northern Vancouver Island to the northern end of the Northwest Coast at Yakutat, there is a remarkable uniformity to the arrangement of button-blanket parts and decoration. They were typically made of navy blue Hudson's Bay Company blankets bordered on three sides with broad, red bands of woolen trade flannel. A crest animal was usually worked out in flannel appliqué, often outlined in iridescent mother-of-pearl buttons. Buttons also edge the red borders.

At about that same time the techniques of bead appliqué were being developed or introduced through trade contacts with the interior Athapaskan people, who represented the northwestern fringe of a continent-wide bead sewing tradition. Northern American beadwork developed from aboriginal porcupine-quill and moose-hair embroidery, after the introduction by traders of small glass beads. Northwest Coast beadwork began rather late in the historic period, and most of it owes much more to Athapaskan influence than it does to the traditional art concepts of the coast.

89. BUTTON BLANKET
Kaigani Haida, late 19th century
Woolen cloth, pearl buttons
H: 54 in. (137 cm.); W: 69 in. (175 cm.)
Collection of John H. Hauberg

A killer whale is represented in this typical northern style button blanket. It came from Klinkwan village on Prince of Wales Island, Alaska, and was said to have been designed by John Yaehltatsee around 1890. The whale is shown spread out so that both sides of the body are visible. Broad pectoral fins, elaborated with formline U complexes, stand out at the sides. The whale's dorsal fin is divided and bent outward from the central backbone, and appears as two symmetrical curved forms pierced with round holes. This hole frequently appears in the fins of killer whales depicted in northern Northwest Coast art and is said to be a characteristic of certain supernatural whales. Tail flukes take the usual form below, while the divided head, with blowhole between the halves, displays the large eyes and toothed mouth characteristic of killer whale designs.

Northern button blankets usually have simple borders such as this one. A single row of buttons along the juncture of the red and blue is common. Until very recently, button blankets were never bordered along the lower edge; a lower border cuts across a dancer's legs and interferes with the appearance of flowing movement. Modern blanket makers are becoming aware of this, and the innovation is not as popular as it once was.

90. BUTTON BLANKET
Tlingit, late 19th century
Woolen cloth, pearl buttons
H: 53 1/4 in. (135 cm.); W: 69 in. (175 cm.)
Collection of John H. Hauberg

Three salmon jump across the blue field of a Tlingit blanket. When the blanket is worn the wild asymmetry is not so apparent, as the salmon in the corners swim diagonally down toward the front. Multiple-button borders and outlines are very spectacular in the firelight. The iridescent buttons glisten like living salmon.

Many old button blankets use, like this one, the white, undyed selvedges of red trade cloth as a decorative detail. Woolen cloth was a very important trade item in the nineteenth century all over North America, and much of it was piece-dyed in such a way that the selvedges were "saved," or left undyed. The irregular, zigzag edges of the white bands are the result of the dying technique and are characteristic of this kind of trade cloth. On the Northwest Coast a very tightly woven, fine variety of this cloth, with a feltlike nap—as is seen here—was popular as an appliqué material.

91. BUTTON BLANKET
Kwakiutl, early 20th century
Woolen cloth, cotton cloth, pearl buttons
H: 60 1/2 in. (153.5 cm.); W: 73 1/2 in. (186.7 cm.)
Collection of John H. Hauberg

The difference between typical northern blankets and Kwakiutl blankets is graphically illustrated by this one. The three-sided red border and central design, both outlined with buttons on a dark background, are shared by blankets throughout their geographical range. Some northern blankets also have the upper border broken by a gap in the red cloth, often filled with a contrasting panel of another material. But only a very few have button designs on the border itself, and never with the flamboyance of the typical Kwakiutl blanket. Border designs are usually geometric, although images of coppers are also common. Kwakiutl blankets are sometimes elaborated with large plaques of abalone shell sewn to the borders, especially along the upper edges, which fall like a pair of spectacular lapels as the blanket is worn.

The tree is a fairly common crest design on Kwakiutl blankets. Colors other than blue are also seen for the background; green is the most common alternative. There are also Kwakiutl blankets with light blue, orange, or maroon backgrounds, but dark blue or green, with red borders, are the standard colors.

92. APPLIQUÉ TUNIC
Tlingit, early 20th century
Woolen cloth, pearl buttons, beads
H: 44 in. (112 cm.); W: 44 in. (112 cm.)
Collection of John H. Hauberg

Tlingit dancers have traditionally imitated the Gonana, as they call their Athapaskan neighbors, in festival dances in which they wear clothing and ornaments acquired from them or derived from Athapaskan styles. Late in the nineteenth century this dress began to feature spectacular cloth tunics with contrasting panels on the lower borders, cuffs, and yokes. These panels, typically red on blue, or the reverse, were lavishly embroidered with abstract floral motifs in small glass beads. The Tlingit beadworkers developed their own variation on the style, of which the decoration on this tunic is a fine example. Elaborate curvilinear designs outlined in multiple rows of beads that have symmetrical changes of color and open, cloth centers are characteristic of the style.

This shirt combines a Tlingit crest design of a raven, in red cloth and button appliqué, with the abstract foliate beadwork. It was collected in Angoon, a village on the west side of Admiralty Island, Alaska.

93. OCTOPUS BAG
Tlingit, late 19th century
Woolen cloth, wool tape, glass beads, yarn
H: 21 1/4 in. (54 cm.); W: 13 in. (33 cm.)
Collection of John H. Hauberg

A decorative bag of unique form is found among Indian groups all across the northern half of North America. It is usually called an "octopus bag" because of the eight tabs, in four pairs, which are pendant from it. Tlingit bags can be distinguished from octopus bags of other inland tribes by the character of the beaded designs. Multiple outlining of open-centered, abstract foliate shapes in a symmetrical composition characterizes Tlingit bags. Nineteenth century bead colors are somewhat softer than the colors of modern beads, and they produce a very rich effect on the red background of the trade cloth.

94. OCTOPUS BAG
Tlingit, late 19th century
Woolen cloth, wool tape, glass beads, yarn
H: 17 1/2 in. (44.5 cm.); W: 13 in. (33 cm.)
Collection of Dr. and Mrs. Allan Lobb

This octopus bag features a double-headed bird beaded in typical Tlingit style in the center of the bag. Seemingly casual color changes occur in the outlines of the abstract foliate patterns, but examination shows that they are nearly all arranged to form symmetrical pairs. Beadwork on Athapaskan bags tends to be somewhat more flowerlike in contrast to the free curvilinear forms of Tlingit beadwork.

Although these bags were derived from functional pouches, they have become decorative accents for ceremonial costume. They are worn slung over the shoulder on a tape or braided yarn carrying strap. Sometimes they are worn in pairs, one hanging on each side of the dancer.

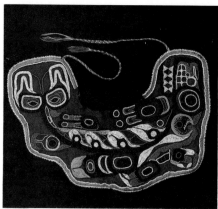

95. OCTOPUS BAG

Tlingit, 20th century
Woolen cloth, wool tape, glass beads, yarn
H: 20 1/2 in. (52 cm.); W: 15 3/4 in.
(40 cm.)
Collection of John and Grace Putnam

The navy blue background contrasts with brilliant bead colors in this Tlingit bag collected in Sitka. Even this relatively recent bag retains all the typical details of decoration and construction of traditional octopus bags from across the continent. The beadwork of many northern North American tribes features a border of a narrow binding of cloth, which usually contrasts with the color of the decorated area. The border is edged on its inner side with a single line of appliquéd white beads and on its outer edge with white beads applied in a serrate pattern of beads on edge alternating with beads sewn flat. This widespread border fashion is shared by all Tlingit octopus bags.

96. DANCE BIB

Tlingit, late 19th century
Woolen cloth, ribbon, glass beads, yarn
H: 8 1/2 in. (21.6 cm.); W: 12 1/2 in.
(31.7 cm.)
Collection of Mr. and Mrs. Alan Backstrom

Tlingit dancers wear decorative bibs beaded in the local style on trade cloth. Sometimes they follow the abstract foliate tradition of design, but many are beaded in patterns derived from the formline painting of crests. This bib features a design of a killer whale. Although each design element has a counterpart in the formal painting system, the multiple colors and somewhat less precise forms change the design so that it becomes quite a different kind of art.

All the whale's parts are recognizable according to the Tlingit system of design. Tail flukes rise to the left, and the head with toothed mouth to the right. A round, human head, outlined in yellow, fills the blowhole. The head's body, in blue beads, flows out as the spout of the whale, its clawed hands and feet pushing against the border of the bib.

97. BEADED ERMINE TUNIC

Tlingit, late 19th century
Ermine, buckskin, woolen cloth, glass beads
H: 42 in. (106.7 cm.); W: 45 in. (114.3 cm.)
Collection of John H. Hauberg

The most elegant of the Tlingit beaded dance shirts are those made of the pelts of ermine sewn to a cloth or buckskin foundation. This fine example has a strongly Athapaskan flavor in the style of the floral beadwork and the thick fringe around the yoke, at the cuffs, and around the lower edge. Over one hundred ermine were used to make this shirt. The white skins have always been prized as a chief's emblem on the Northwest Coast, just as they are considered a mark of royalty in Europe. Their most frequent use is as the trailer of the dancing headdress, but they also appear hung from the top of the cylinders on crest hats, decorating shamans' rattles and hats, and on many other objects, including chiefs' tunics such as this one.

BOXES AND CHESTS

If any single object can characterize the culture of the Northwest Coast it must be the remarkable container called the bent-corner box. This is especially true on the central and northern coast, beyond the limits of hard, coiled cedar root basketry. The wooden boxes of the coast served as storage receptacles for food, clothing, ceremonial regalia, and tools. They were the utensils for cooking and serving food. Specialized forms of boxes served as cradles, quivers, and canteens. And, finally, they were the coffins of the dead.

Technically, bent-corner boxes were a remarkable achievement. Their existence depended upon a tool-use technology applied to native woods especially suitable for splitting into thin, flat slabs, and the development of techniques for carving specialized grooves that allowed the planks to be bent after being made pliable by heat. Box planks were made from straight-grained red and yellow cedar, spruce, yew, and perhaps other woods split with wooden or antler wedges, adzed to a regular thickness, and shaved with knives to a flat surface. The bending grooves, or kerfs, were carefully spaced so that the resulting sides of the box were even and the box symmetrical. The final, joining corner was fitted with great skill and fastened with pegs or lacing through drilled holes. A fitted bottom was similarly fastened, and a lid was matched to the upper edges. In the end, the box was watertight, oil-tight, and vermin-proof, suitable for the storage of preserved food, or the regalia of a chief.

The scale of box perfection ranges from rough, quickly fashioned containers to masterpieces of art, painted and carved with crest creatures, inlaid with glistening abalone shell and row on row of sea snail opercula. Most collectors of Northwest Coast art have at least one bent-corner box; without one the culture is not truly represented. There are probably a hundred of them in private collections in the Northwest.

It was in just such a box that Nas shuki yelhl kept his hoard of Daylight.

98. BOX
Tlingit (?), 18th century
Wood, spruce root
H: 12 in. (30.5 cm.); W: 10 1/4 in.
(26 cm.); D: 8 1/2 in. (21.5 cm.)
Private collection

The estimate of an eighteenth century origin for this enigmatic box is not based on its condition, but on the character of the carving. Wooden objects exposed to the weather and fungus-rich environment of the Northwest Coast can take on this appearance in a very few years. But the style of rendering the human figure and the subject matter are similar to carvings acquired by the earliest European collectors on the coast and to pieces collected in the mid-nineteenth century which even then had the appearance of great age.

It is a very unusual little box. Probably it was the property of a shaman, and perhaps it was used as a container for the equipment of his trade. The crouching man, legs and arms spread in a very typical Northwest Coast configuration, is seldom seen on the face of a box. But even more surprising are the two severed heads which he holds by their hair. Once human hair hung out over the tiny faces and was secured in place by pegs, a few of which still remain in place. Traces of what appears to be red paint remain on his body.

Most early boxes were sewn together with spruce root drawn through drilled holes connected with grooves so that the root was protected from wear. An accidental split repaired with this same technique is visible near the bottom of the box. Later boxes were typically fastened with hardwood pegs driven through diagonally drilled holes, although some boxes were sewn until the end of the nineteenth century.

99. BOX
Tlingit, 19th century, collected at Klukwan
Red cedar
H: 28 in. (71 cm.); W: 21 1/4 in. (54 cm.);
D: 20 1/2 in. (52 cm.)
Collection of Jim and Marilyn Bergstrom

The most common decorated box in the northern coastal area is somewhat higher than it is wide, with a nearly square plan, and with a bilaterally symmetrical formline design painted on two opposite faces. The designs represent animals or supernatural beings, but they are so highly conventionalized that it is usually impossible to identify them with any certainty. In fact, there is some evidence to suggest that the two decorated faces, at least on some boxes, represent the front and hindquarters, respectively, of the creature. Almost all boxes of this kind share a basic compositional arrangement that varies in a few predictable ways (Holm 1974:23-24). The upper third—even half in some boxes—is taken up by a design representing the animal's head, rendered in one of two standard formline constructions. Almost always the primary formlines are black, with secondary detail in red. The center of the box is filled with a more or less rectangular design field for the body. On either side of this field are narrower panels that contain the forelimbs of the crea-

ture. The two lower corners are elaborated with ovoid joints that probably represent the hips. The compositions of each side may be very similar, but they are never exactly alike; and, of the many hundreds of boxes in existence, there are no two with exactly the same design.

The proportions of the body parts, the choice of formline detail, and the character of the formlines themselves vary from artist to artist, and these variations make it possible to cluster box paintings into individual styles. This box was painted by a master of massive formline style. The parts are beautifully proportioned and expertly rendered. All design details and relationships follow the classic northern system (Holm 1965). Boxes with two opposite, symmetrically painted sides always have the intervening faces painted with designs that are quite different. Usually these are very simple circles or ovoid forms, but some boxes have very imaginative designs such as this one. A single black line divides the side vertically, and filling the upper part of one half is a hook-beaked bird, simply and elegantly painted in black. This bird's significance is not known.

100. BOX

Tlingit, 19th century, collected at
Angoon
Red cedar
H: 23 in. (58.5 cm.); W: 19 in. (48 cm.);
D: 18 1/2 in. (47 cm.)
Collection of Eugene and Martha Nester
and Mr. and Mrs. James Staley

Another masterfully painted box exhibits many of the stylistic features of the preceding one, but the formlines are less angular. It is an early, classic box with a typical composition on the front, which has clawed feet occupying the lateral forelimb panels. The back, however, shows an unusual variation on the standard format, with the base ovoids joined back to back in the lower center and angled upwards. It is a very fine painting with imaginative variations. The side panels have simple circle designs, a fairly typical choice.

The top inch or so of this box is missing, as revealed by the incomplete ovoid designs at the upper edge. This missing inch is very common in boxes of this kind, and, at first, seems very mysterious. Since these boxes always have lids that fit very closely, to get at the contents a mouse gnaws a half-round hole through the rim just under the lid. In order to refit the lid to its proper tightness, the box owner trims the sides down. This box is minus its original lid—just as many of the boxes in collections are.

101. BOX

Northern coast, 19th century, collected in
Hydaburg
Red cedar, opercula
H: 22 in. (56 cm.); W: 15 in. (38 cm.);
D: 14 in. (35.5 cm.)
Collection of John and Grace Putnam

Although the arrangements of the symmetrical designs on this box are very similar to those on the previous two, the style is radically different. The formlines are narrower and the spacing of the formlines and their associated thin, tertiary lines is much wider, giving the whole painting an open, airy effect. The heads on both sides of this box take up half the area. Black primary formlines on the two sides follow almost identical patterns, but the red secondary details are quite different in most of the areas. The side panels show a typical arrangement of outlined ovoids, drawn around the bark templates that the northern artists used to achieve the remarkable symmetry of their art. Thin vertical lines, reminiscent of the vertical red corners on simpler Tlingit storage boxes, parallel the box corners.

The lid of this box illustrates the usual form. Slightly flaring and overhanging the sides, it forms a massive capital atop the tracery of the painted design. It is not as solid as it looks, but is hollowed from the bottom. Front and back faces are inlaid with opercula of the red turban shell, a marine snail.

102. BOX

Northern Coast, 19th century
Red cedar, opercula
H: 26 in. (66 cm.); W: 18 in. (47 cm.);
D: 15 in. (38 cm.)
Collection of John and Grace Putnam

One side of this fine northern box has a painting that follows the usual organization in all its parts. The other side (illustrated) has a mouth structure so unusual that it's seen on less than one percent of square boxes. Instead of the usual red cheek designs filling in the lower corners of the creature's head, the mouth extends to the edges of the painting, and a downturned snout occupies its center. No doubt there is a special significance to this variation, but any attempt to interpret it would be conjectural. The painting is characterized by formlines of moderate weight, with large, wide ovoids and more detail than usual in the red, secondary designs.

Large, red circles with appended U forms decorate the sides. The lid is a modern replacement, but is correct in its form and decoration of inlaid snail opercula. These glossy shells are the trap doors with which the snails close their shells for protection. They were widely used throughout the coast for inlay in box lids, the rims of dishes, and as teeth in masks and helmets.

103. BOX
Bella Bella, 19th century
Cedar
H: 20 in. (50.7 cm.); W: 14 1/2 in.
(36.7 cm.); D: 13 in. (33 cm.)
Collection of Mr. and Mrs. Alan
Backstrom

A number of stylistic features separate this small box from the others. The formlines are very thin and the inner ovoids are small and very nonconcentric. There are areas of red hatching, or diagonal parallel lines, all slanting from upper right to lower left. These are all characteristics of painting that is known to have been done at the village of Bella Bella in the nineteenth century and seem to represent a Bella Bella style. Boxes painted in this style generally follow all the compositional rules of northern box painting: large head; central rectangular body; lateral forelimbs; and ovoid hip joints in the lower corners. The illustrated side of this box is an example of the most common alternative composition; the head design incorporates nostrils and long, double eyes with pointed eyelids. Those seen on the previous boxes lack nostrils and have eyes, represented by profile formline heads, without eyelid points.

The opposite side of this box shows the more common head form. Interestingly, all boxes that have these two forms of head design on their opposite sides have the pegged or sewn corner of the box on the side without nostrils or eyelid lines. This most remarkable consistency suggests that the eyelid-nostril style of face was considered to be the front of the box. That idea is reinforced by the fact that many bent-corner bowls that have recognizable animal heads on one end and hindquarters on the other always have the joined corner adjacent to the back end.

Simple designs, consisting of formline ovoids with attached U forms, are painted on the box sides. They are typical of the almost fragmentary designs found there. Although the side designs rarely fill more than a small part of the area, they are always placed with sensitivity and give the impression that the artist was fully aware of the total space and the effect of the painted design on that space.

104. BOX
Bella Bella, 19th century
Cedar, opercula
H: 19 1/8 in. (48.5 cm.); W: 16 1/2 in. (42
cm.); D: 14 1/2 in. (37 cm.)
Collection of Jim and Marilyn Bergstrom

Another small box with Bella Bella painting characteristics uses the same two head designs as the preceding one (cat. no. 103). These two boxes are clearly related, but judging by significant differences in the proportions and relationships of design elements, they are probably not by the same artist. The artist used a very unusual arrangement in the lower corners, eliminating the rectangular forelimb panels at the sides and filling those spaces with U forms that, rising from the lower ovoid joints, suggest fins or flukes of a sea mammal. The whole lower part of the design is very compressed, giving the head more than half of the space.

The moderately thick lid is inlaid with opercula. In use, most box lids were secured with an ingenious lashing of cord of cedar bark or spruce root. The lashing reinforces the structure of the box as well as fastens the lid. Loops run over the corners of the lid and are joined with a tie that is easily released to open the box. The lashing material gets brittle with age and seldom survives.

105. BOX

Bella Bella, 19th century
Cedar
**H: 24 1/2 in. (62.3 cm.); W: 19 1/4 in.
(49 cm.); D: 17 in. (43.3 cm.)**
Collection of John H. Hauberg

An unusual variant on the northern symmetrically painted box is almost unique
to the Bella Bella. The artists eliminated
the lower ovoid joints and extended the
head and body areas vertically to fill the
resulting space. When combined with
the characteristically thin Bella Bella
formlines, the result is a light and open
design. All the space divisions of standard northern boxes are present, except
for the lower details. The head fills more
than half of the side of the box, the body
occupies a rectangular panel in the lower
center, and the forelimbs fill the lateral
panels. In this example, the U forms
resemble fins or, perhaps, feathers.

Most Bella Bella boxes use the two
head-forms. The side with pointed eyelid lines and nostrils always has a tongue
design in the mouth and a combination
of U forms and ovoids over the head.
The opposite side, lacking nostrils and
eyelid points, always has a pair of red U
forms in the mouth and simple formline
U designs over the head. These relationships are typical for similar boxes from
all the northern tribes. It is difficult to
imagine how these rather complex rules
of composition became so firmly established for so long and over such a stretch
of coast.

106. BOX

Northern Coast, 19th century
Red cedar, opercula
**H: 23 1/4 in. (59 cm.); W:15 3/8 in. (39
cm.); D: 15 3/8 in. (39 cm.)**
Collection of Bill and Marty Holm

Another composition seen in the paintings on northern boxes covers all four
sides with elaborate formline patterns.
At first glance, the designs seem to be of
a completely different arrangement than
those on boxes with two opposite
painted sides, but actually they are
closely related. The basic design of head,
body, forelimb panels, and lower joints
is retained, but expanded laterally to
cover two adjacent sides of the box with
the midline of the symmetrical design
on the corner. The ovoid joint designs
are moved outward to flank the body,
and an outer extension of the head
design may enclose the forelimbs or,
more typically, a design that can be interpreted as a profile of the body.

The opposite sides of this box are
painted with a very different, more elaborate composition, but still retain the
basic head, body, and limb arrangement.
This box, with its beautiful painting,

was reassembled from a pile of broken
parts. The imposing lid, with its ninety
opercula, was discovered in another collection and reunited with the matching
box.

69

107. BOX

Tlingit, early 19th century
Cedar
H: 16 7/8 in. (43 cm.); W: 12 5/8 in. (32 cm.); D: 12 in. (30 cm.)
Collection of Jerrie and Anne Vander Houwen

So many unusual features mark this old box that one might not notice that the composition of the design is typical for corner-oriented boxes. A large head, filling most of the upper halves of adjacent sides, tops a small body flanked by clawed feet. Ovoid hip joints fill the lower corners in the standard way. A stylized human face fits between the eyes on the forehead of the represented creature. The whole design has been elaborated with shallow carving that brings the formlines and inner ovoids into delicate relief.

The most startling feature of the design is the color of the primary formlines, which are dark red rather than black; while the secondary formlines are also red, although brighter. This combination is extremely rare. The inner ovoids, claws, and eyebrows of the stylized face are black. Interesting and unexpected asymmetry appears in the painting on the forehead face and, less obviously, in the switch from black cross-hatching to dashing in the U forms surmounting the base ovoids. Other variations appear to the careful examiner.

The opposite side of the box is even more surprising. An inverted human face dangles from the jaws of a fearsome monster, whose wide, sharp-toothed mouth extends from edge to edge of the box. Tricks of asymmetry hide in the complexities of the pattern; some of this asymmetry is the result of the proportions of the box itself—it is somewhat longer in one dimension than in the other—and some of this is just the artist's play.

108. CHEST FRONT

Northern Coast
Yellow cedar
H: 18 in. (45.7 cm.); W: 30 in. (76 cm.)
Collection of John and Grace Putnam

The ultimate achievement of the northern box maker was the great chest. On state occasions, chiefs sat upon them; and they were used to store clan emblems, the chief's ceremonial regalia, and, on a chief's death, his remains. They were constructed exactly as the boxes and differed principally in their proportions, which were much longer than deep. Chests varied in size, from tiny receptacles for a shaman's charms to great lockers as long as a man. They were frequently carved as well as painted. Many of them were double, with an inner chest attached to the bottom and an outer, telescoping chest attached to the lid.

The finest chests, like this fragment, were masterpieces of design and craftsmanship. The designs follow the rules for box painting. Opened out, a corner-oriented box would show much the same arrangement as this chest front. Here is an example of the highest quality illustrating the double-eye face structure with nostrils and pointed eyelids. The body formlines, which also become the forelegs, contain a facelike design that is mirrored in profile in the panels flanking the great head. Curved claws fill the space between the body and the lower ovoid joints. Ovoid and U combinations elaborate the space over the head.

There are many examples of relief carving combined with painting in northern Northwest Coast art, and the combination frequently offers clues to the artists' methods, to their ways of conceiving the art, and perhaps to the development of the tradition itself. Except for the six large eyes or joints, which were carved to a recessed bulging form before painting, the design was first painted on the flat, unrelieved surface of the wood. Then the background and tertiary areas were carved. This sequence is most apparent in the occasional unpainted area that, accidentally overlooked by the artist, was left uncarved. In this chest front this omission was made in all of the cheeks of the faces forming the eyes and lower joints except one. The old carved box (cat. no. 107) shows similar oversights that corroborate the painting-carving sequence.

109. CHEST
Bella Bella, 19th century, collected in Ketchikan
Yellow cedar, red cedar
H: 21 1/4 in. (54 cm.); L: 35 3/4 in. (91 cm.); D: 20 1/2 in. (52 cm.)
Collection of John and Grace Putnam

Although this chest was collected from the family of the Tlingit chief Kian, it is stylistically identical to chests and boxes made at Bella Bella and probably was originally traded from there. The Bella Bellas were apparently responsible for boxes and chests that were eventually collected from all parts of the coast. The bright blue of the tertiary areas contrasting with vermilion secondary and black primary formlines produces a vibrant effect.

The two different head types common to boxes and chests are represented on the opposite sides of this chest. Otherwise the compositions are essentially alike, but vary in the details of body, profile body, and forelimbs, which take the form of human hands on one side (illustrated) and clawed feet on the other. The chest ends are painted much like symmetrical boxes, except that the heads of the creatures are designed as stylized faces. These ends, characteristic of chests of this kind, are uncarved.

110. CHEST PANELS
Tlingit (?), late 18th century
Red cedar
H: 9 in. (23 cm.); W: 40 1/4 in. (102 cm.)
Collection of Eugene and Marth Nester

Massive formlines, minimal background, simple detail, and ovoid reliefs in eyes and joints are all characteristics of ancient Tlingit painting and carving that are present on this old chest. It is a small one, but the character of the design imparts a monumental quality to it. Both face types are represented in simple, bold style. The long eyes of the face with pointed eyelids and nostrils lack the elaborate double eye form of more recent chests in the exhibition, and the nostrils are shorter and raised in high relief, but otherwise the facial structure is the same. The arrangement of body parts is highly simplified though comparable to the others. This is not just a function of the much smaller size of this chest, but also a characteristic of the art of the protohistoric period.

Colors conform to the classic arrangement, with black on the broad, primary formlines, red on the secondary elements, and blue-green in the recessed, tertiary areas. When the chest was carved, possibly 200 years ago, this system of design and color placement was fully developed. Its fundamentals remained unchanged for more than a century, until the breakdown of traditional culture. The design system has been revived in the last twenty years.

111. BOX
Tlingit, 19th century
Red cedar
H: 14 3/8 in. (36.5 cm.); W: 13 3/8 in. (34 cm.); D: 12 in. (30.5 cm.)
Collection of Jim and Marilyn Bergstrom

The imaginative and skillful design on this small, square box, is completely unlike any of the other boxes in the exhibition. It is in fact a different kind of a container, one which could properly be called a food box or a bent-corner bowl. It has been modified by trimming the undulating form of the top edge flat and fitting a lid. Bowls like this often have asymmetrical painting, different on each side, and every design oriented in the same direction rather than mirroring adjacent sides. The designs seem to represent a series of animal heads, although the artist and his patron might very well have identified them differently.

The red pattern at the bottom is an example of ultraprimary painting. The artist first divided the designed area with simple stripes or areas of color and then painted traditional formline patterns. The painting is particularly elegant, with its many unusual and imaginative details. A number of these deep bowls have been altered to boxes. They can be identified by the fact that the designs on two sides arch upward and are incomplete, while the adjacent designs are flat or concave at the upper edge and have been trimmed slightly if at all.

BOWLS

Wood and mountain-sheep horn were the materials of food bowls on the Northwest Coast. Some of the early inhabitants of the coast had bowls of birch bark, which suggests that they had ties of some kind with the interior regions where bark bowls and containers have been a cultural feature from prehistoric times to the present. Even wood and horn bowls of the historic period show vestiges of birch-bark bowl characteristics, which reinforces the idea that many of the coast dwellers may have migrated from the interior long ago.

A universal characteristic of Northwest Coast bowl form is the undulating rim that is high at the ends and dips at the sides. The derivation of this shape is unclear, but there is a good possibility that it is the result of the natural change that occurs when the sides of a hollow vessel are spread apart—such as when a horn bowl or a canoe, for instance, is widened by steam-bending. Whatever the origin or function of the undulating rim, it is so characteristic that its presence identifies a bowl, no matter what other features the container might have.

Bowls come in all sizes, from tiny individual containers for candlefish or seal oil into which food was dipped to great feast dishes as long as twenty feet. They take the form of bent-corner boxes, of rectangular trenchers carved from solid blocks of wood, of hollowed, sculptured animals, or globular forms. They are often elaborately decorated by painting, carving, or inlay of shell. Some became valued family heirlooms transferred as privileges in noble marriages or prestigious relics passed down by high-ranking ancestors. Like the bent-corner boxes to which they are related, bowls are significant delineators of Northwest Coast culture.

112. BENT-CORNER BOWL
Northern Coast, 19th century
Yellow cedar, red cedar, opercula
H: 6 in. (15 cm.); L: 14 in. (35.5 cm.);
D: 12 in. (30.5 cm.)
Collection of Eugene and Martha Nester

Using pegging, lacing, lashing, and fitting with various sorts of tenons and scarfs, Northwest Coast craftsmen developed wood-joining technology to a high degree. Yet they avoided the tedious fitting of joints in boxes and bowls whenever possible by bending the corners. To do this they relied on a complex technique of thinning the plank that formed the sides with grooves of unique design and of steaming the thinned wood until it became flexible enough to bend. It is tempting to imagine that the idea of bending the sides of boxes is another concept linking the coastal craftsmen with the interior people and their birch-bark technology.

The bent-corner bowl illustrates this technique. A long plank of fine-grained wood, in this case probably yellow, or Alaska, cedar was prepared by splitting and then carving with adze and knife to the shape required to form the slightly bulging, high-ended form when bent. It was then joined to a bottom of red cedar. Typical bowls have rims hollowed to form a flange all around the edge, and this flange was often elaborated with inlay, usually of opercula. The sides often had painted decaration. This bowl has a classic painted design in delicate formlines representing animals whose identities are obscure. The heads are on the shorter, arched ends and are painted in profile with open mouths. The bodies are stretched along the lowered sides. Each has a large, elaborated ovoid as its central feature, with claws and fins appended to it. Traditional black primary and red secondary formlines follow the canons of northern painting. Although the primary compositions are similar for the two designs, the details differ in many ways—a circumstance to be expected in northern boxes and bowls.

113. BENT-CORNER BOWL
Bella Bella, 19th century
Yellow cedar, red cedar, brass tacks
H: 6 in. (15.3 cm.); L: 16 1/2 in. (42 cm.);
D: 14 1/2 in. (37 cm.)
Collection of Jim and Marilyn Bergstrom

All the features of the previous bowl are repeated in this one, but with significant variations. Both the form and the decoration point to Bella Bella origin. The exaggerated arch of the rim is uncommon among more northerly bowls, and the style of painting—narrow formlines, extreme non-concentricity of small inner ovoids and single-hatching of red secondary U forms—is Bella Bella. Animals as obscure as those on the northern bowl (cat. no. 112) are arranged in the same manner, with the heads on the bowl's ends and the bodies on the sides. And again the compositional arrangements are the same from one side to the other, with many slight differences in detail. Brass tacks are used here in the place of the sea snail opercula, with which the rims of bowls were traditionally inlaid. Tacks were very popular in some parts of North America (particularly among the Plains tribes) for decoration on weapons, ceremonial implements, belts, and so forth. They are less common on Northwest Coast objects, and, when used, they frequently take the place of opercula inlay.

115. BENT-CORNER BOWL
Northern Coast, mid-19th century
Yellow cedar, red cedar, opercula
H: 5 3/4 in. (14.7 cm.); L: 10 3/4 in. (27.3
cm.); D: 9 3/4 in. (24.7 cm.)
Collection of Sylvia Duryee

If this bent-corner bowl was ever painted, it too has lost all trace of color; yet the design follows the forms and relationships of painting. The arrangement is the same as the previous bowl (cat. no. 114): symmetrical head and tail on opposite ends and the body of the animal filling the sides. It must be a mythical monster, perhaps the sea grizzly. The two large teeth in the mouth of the creature suggest a beaver, but the face is divided into two profiles and the teeth can then be viewed as the canine teeth of a bear. This identification is reinforced by the whalelike tail on the opposite end and flippers and claws on the sides. A stylized face above the creature's nose can be read in several ways, but similar faces have been used to represent the blowholes of whales and sea monsters. Closely studded with opercula, the bowl's rim is deeply undercut. The swelling sides, undulating, inward-flaring rim, and oily sheen all give bent-corner bowls an organic vitality.

114. BENT-CORNER BOWL
Tlingit (?), mid-19th century
Hardwood, red cedar, brass tacks
H: 7 in. (17.7 cm.); L: 10 in. (25.4 cm.);
D: 8 1/2 in. (21.5 cm.)
Private collection

Bent-corner bowls differ from boxes in that the sides are carved into more or less convex form. This old northern bowl shows this convexity well. It is amplified by the sheen of the surface patination, partly the result of the infusion of oil that typifies Northwest Coast bowls. The bending process reverts the bulging sides to flat surfaces at the corners. Most bowls, including this one, were probably painted at one time, but the oily wood forms a poor bond with native salmon-egg tempera, and generally the bowls have come down to us richly patinated but without paint.

The design follows the same principles as those governing the painting on boxes and chests, but without color the positive-negative relationships of forms are much harder to see. In this particular piece the formlines are especially hard to recognize because they are so massive. Narrow, recessed relief slits define the edges of the wide formlines. Beveled and hollowed tertiary areas appear to float on a plain background, which is in fact the grid of primary formlines that defines the body parts of an animal. The creature is a bird, with head represented on one end; shoulder joints, wing feathers, and hips on the sides; and feet, joints of the tail, and tail feathers on the other end. The head and tail ends are bilaterally symmetrical, while the sides are asymmetrical, mirror images. Invariably, the corner on which the ends of the bent plank meet and are joined is on the tail end. Bowls like this suggest that the artist always chose the end with a bent corner on each side for the head. If this concept can be transferred to boxes, it means that the painted side without a joined corner must be seen as the front of the box, and, perhaps, represents the front end of the represented animal (see cat. no. 103).

116. BENT-CORNER BOWL

Tlingit, early 19th century
Hardwood, red cedar, opercula
H: 5 3/4 in. (14.5 cm.); L: 13 3/4 in. (35
cm.); W: 11 in. (28 cm.)
Collection of John H. Hauberg

Boldly sculptured faces in an archaic
Tlingit style thrust outward from the
ends of this fine old bowl. They are masterfully carved and have the wide eyes,
rounded nostrils, and broad lips characteristic of Tlingit sculpture. Very
unusual formline detail covers the sides,
which are quite different from one
another. The symmetrical designs
appear to include whales' dorsal and
pectoral fins, and it is possible that the
bowl represents a highly imaginative
rendering of the double killer whale
crest hat of the Stikine Tlingit. This hat,
with killer whale heads front and back,
each with flippers and dorsal fins flanking a central column of potlatch rings,
was represented on a memorial totem
pole at Wrangell and on Chief Shakes'
ceremonial pipe. If the bowl does indeed
represent this crest, then the faces are
humanoid whales. Each has a wide
mouth studded with teeth, one set
carved and the other of opercula. In this
interpretation, the large ovoids at the
upper corners of the sides represent the
blowholes of the two whales.

This bowl is a fine early example, with
unusually powerful sculpture in the
faces. The thick red cedar bottom, bulging sides, and opercula-studded rim
flange conform to classic bent-bowl
characteristics.

117. SQUARE BOWL

Northern Northwest Coast, 19th century
Alder
H: 7 3/8 in. (18.8 cm.); L: 8 1/2 in. (21.6
cm.); W: 7 1/2 in. (19 cm.)
Collection of Dr. and Mrs. Allan Lobb

This bowl, carved of a block of alder, is a
superb example of the object that seems
to point most graphically to some kind
of connection between the historic coast
dwellers and the people of the interior. It
is nearly square in plan, and its two
arched ends are painted and carved with
bilaterally symmetrical formline faces.
These designs are classic examples of
true northern coastal art, but they share
the surface of the bowl with decorations
that at first seem mysterious but, on
reflection, understandable. At each end
of the low sides there is always a series
of vertical, parallel grooves limited at
their lower ends by a thin groove slanting down to the corner. This design
arrangement is universally followed in
square bowls from the northern coast
and although it is aesthetically satisfying, it seems somehow inconsistent with
the local art tradition. The bowls are
uniform in every other way as well. The
sides flare toward the top and are
slightly bowed. The corners are slanted
outward and curved. The rims of these
bowls are undulating and flanged in the
normal form.

At the upper reaches of the rivers that
lead into the high, interior plateau live
Athapaskan hunters who wear buckskin
clothing, travel on snowshoes, and form
their canoes and containers of birch
bark. Among these vessels are rectangular bowls with undulating rims. They
are folded from the bark sheet in such a

way as to leave triangular pleats lapping
the corners, in exactly the same position
as the carved grooves on square alder
bowls. The great consistency of this
design suggests that it once may have
been an important structural feature of
the bowl that has survived as a
skeuomorph, a decorative vestige of the
once functional detail. Its ancestor is
probably the folded birch-bark bowl.

118. SQUARE BOWL
Northern Northwest Coast, 19th century
Alder, opercula
H: 3 1/8 in. (8 cm.); L: 7 7/8 in. (20 cm.);
W: 6 3/4 in. (17.4 cm.)
Collection of John and Grace Putnam

119. SQUARE BOWL
Kaigani Haida, 19th century
Alder
H: 5 in. (12.7 cm.); L: 15 1/2 in. (39.4 cm.); W: 12 in. (30.5 cm.)
Collection of John and Grace Putnam

120. TRAY
Kaigani Haida, mid-19th century
Wood
H: 5 1/2 in. (14 cm.); L: 58 1/4 in. (148 cm.); W: 15 in. (38 cm.)
Collection of John H. Hauberg

Like the previous square bowl (cat. no. 117), this one has decorated ends that depict an animal's face in the formline system of design. Although they resemble one another closely, they are very different in detail. Each uses the simple face form without nostrils or pointed eyelids. Each elaborates the space above the eyes with U forms and ovoids and each fills the mouth with a pair of U forms. Even the color scheme is the same despite the pigment loss because of the saturation of the wood with oil. Following the normal arrangement, the primary formlines are black and the secondary formlines are red. Unusual, except on these square bowls, is the use of red for the inner ovoids. For some reason, perhaps related to color balance, northern artists habitually painted these bowls in this uncommon way.

Since the candlefish or seal oil that these bowls once held soaks into the wood along the fibers, it concentrates on the ends rather than on the sides. The center of the log from which the bowls are carved always runs through the bowl from end to end. The wood shrinks tangentially more than radially and stresses are set up which frequently result in splits—which can be seen here—running from the rim to the center of the ends.

This bowl was collected at Hydaburg, Alaska, and may very well be of Haida manufacture, but bowls of this sort were made by the Tlingit and Tsimshian as well. They were also made in many sizes, from miniatures less than four inches square to giant feast bowls nearly a yard long. This one is of medium size. The faces on the ends are classic in every way. The trace of staining from the infused oil suggests that it has seen less use than many bowls. Much of the color remains, and its placement is usual for these bowls. Some have lost all trace of pigment and have taken on a deep brown, or even black, color.

Long, elegant feast dishes were made by the northern people. They are related to the square bowls in their rectangular configuration and in the arrangement of the designs on the flat, raised ends. As is often the case with sculptural objects, any one perspective leaves much unknown about the piece, a fact certainly true of northern feast trays. Seen directly from the top it is a simple, rectangular shape, slightly rounded at the ends. In profile it sweeps upward at the ends and is cut away under them in a concave curve that parallels the convexity of the upper surface. A shallow recess runs under the inner edge of the rim to produce the flange characteristic of northern bowls. Even this tray of exaggerated length conforms to the bowl configuration of raised ends and lowered sides. A mid-, or even early, nineteenth century date is suggested by the somewhat angular and heavy junctures in the faces on the tray ends. The bowl was collected at Kasaan, Alaska, and was once the property of the famous Kaigani chief Son-i-hat.

121. HIGH-END BOWL
Northern Northwest Coast, mid-19th century
Alder
H: 8 in. (20.3 cm.); L: 15 in. (38 cm.); D: 12 1/2 in. (31.7 cm.)
Collection of Dr. and Mrs. Allan Lobb

Oval bowls carved of alder, with sides sweeping up to high ends, incorporate features that tie them to both birch-bark and horn bowls. Like square bowls, they are decorated on the raised ends with faces, while the sides are often very simply decorated. The sheer of the rim is exaggerated, and the tops of the high ends are squared off. Inside the bowl there is a uniform pattern of carved ridges, one paralleling the rim and joined to the upper corners by four connecting ridges. This pattern resembles an arrangement of pleats and reinforcing rods seen in certain Athapaskan bark bowls, which also have unusually high ends. To emphasize the similarities, wooden high-end bowls often show a pleatlike extension of the end design continuing onto the sides and, even more suggestive, a pattern of parallel dashes carved all over the sides that resembles the texture of birch bark.

The designs on the ends of this high-end bowl are early in style. The formlines are massive and compact, leaving very little space in the tertiary, relieved areas and confining the background to narrow slits. The composition is typical, with a large, simple formline face elaborated with U and ovoid complexes across the top. The mouth is divided by a beaklike extension that suggests the representation of a bird.

122. HIGH-END BOWL
Haida, mid-19th century
Alder
H: 4 1/2 in. (11.5 cm.); L: 9 in. (22.9 cm.); D: 9 in. (22.9 cm.)
Collection of Eugene and Martha Nester

High-end bowls were made in a wide range of sizes. This one is much smaller than the previous bowl (cat. no. 121), but still larger than many. It has lost all its paint, and the oil that permeated the wood has turned it a glossy black. The bowl shows all the characteristic features of the high-end type, but with a somewhat lower and less exaggerated curve to the rim. The design is complex, especially for a small bowl, and the formlines are beautifully shaped and

organized. They extend well onto the sides, but a panel in the center, outlined with fine grooves, carries the typical birch-barklike texture.

The bowl was collected from the Auk Tlingit in the nineteenth century, but was said to have been made by the Haida. Interpretation of highly conventionalized designs like this one is almost impossible, and even knowledgeable natives differed in their explanations, often attributing personal crest significance to the designs. This one was described as a young raven.

123. HORN BOWL
Haida, 19th century
Mountain-sheep horn
H: 4 1/2 in. (11.5 cm.); L: 8 5/8 in. (22 cm.); D: 7 1/2 in. (19 cm.)
Private collection

A most unlikely material, the heavy, furrowed spiral horn of the mountain sheep becomes, in the hands of master Northwest Coast craftsmen, the epitome of elegant bowls. Hard, tough, and resilient, horn can be softened and made somewhat flexible by soaking and heating; then the corrugated surface can be carved smooth, the walls made thin and regular, and the narrow, straight-sided vessel spread wide. In the end, the battering weapon of mountain rams is transformed into a richly ornamented, flaring bowl with a graceful sheer sweeping upward to high, broad ends.

The similarity of northern sheep-horn bowls to the wooden high-ended bowls is striking. The only difference of consequence is the slope of the sides, which in horn bowls tapers down to a narrow bottom. Both share the high, square end and the pattern of broad, shallow grooves inside the rim. Northern canoes feature a gunwale groove apparently related to the groove of the rim, and they are widened by steaming in much the same way as horn bowls. The abruptly raised ends of the sheep-horn bowls is partly the result of spreading

the sides, and this may be a source of the raised-end concept in bowls generally.

Haida bowl and spoon makers traded with the Tsimshian of the mainland for the horns of mountain sheep, which were not found on their islands. They became expert horn workers, and this fine bowl illustrates the pinnacle of that art. Perfectly regular in form, with straight, flaring sides and smoothly curved rim, the bowl form itself is a sculptural achievement. The outer surface has been carved in low relief, using the system of formline design common to every sort of decorated object on the northern coast. This artist was an expert at controlling these formline relationships. A bear's face ornaments each end, with little men grasping the lips and emerging from the bears' mouths. Similar men peer out from between the ears, their contorted bodies occupying the ears themselves. Three-dimensional bears' snouts push out from the otherwise flat rendering of the features, increasing the sculptural quality of the bowl. The designs on the sides, representing the animal's body in ovoid, U, and claw forms, are asymmetrical.

The unknown Haida carver of this bowl made a number of others of similar quality and style. It is possible that he was also the maker of the masterful sheep-horn ladle (cat. no. 140).

124. HORN BOWL
Tlingit, mid-19th century
Mountain-sheep horn
H: 5 1/2 in. (14 cm.); L: 11 1/2 in. (29 cm.); D: 6 3/4 in. (17 cm.)
Collection of John H. Hauberg

Although of the same material and the same basic configuration as the previous bowl (cat. no. 123), the effect of this mountain sheep horn bowl is very different. The gracefully outswept ends and rim are characteristic of horn bowls of the Tlingit and their interior neighbors the Athapaskans. It is thinner than the Haida bowl, and the carved ridges and grooves of the inner wall are omitted in favor of geometric patterns on the flaring surface of the rim. These patterns—nucleated circles and parallel lines—are common to Athapaskan bowls and spoons, and may even be skeuomorphic, related to the spruce root lashing of the rims of birch-bark bowls.

The formline designs on this horn bowl are massive and compact, characteristic of the early historic period of Tlingit art. They are hard to interpret, but appear to represent a thunderbird at each end of the bowl, with stylized wings occupying the sides. Thin relief slits, minimal background, and shallowly recessed tertiary spaces contrast with the deeply carved, hard-edged formlines of the later Haida horn bowl (cat. no. 123).

125. BOWL
Kwakiutl, 19th century
Alder
H: 5 1/8 in. (13 cm.); L: 12 5/8 in. (32 cm.); D: 9 in. (23 cm.)
Private collection

Although the customary Kwakiutl dish is carved to its final form from a block of alder, its bowed sides and high, inwardly curved ends give it the appearance of having been steam-spread from a narrower form—a horn bowl, for instance. The interrelationships of solid carved bowls, bent-corner bowls, and steam-spread bowls are complex but visually apparent.

The Kwakiutl made bowls of this kind in every size. A detailed record of the method of making these bowls was made by George Hunt in 1908 and published by Franz Boas (Boas 1921:57-59). A bowl of this size was described as "used for the chief's daughter and the chief's son. Two (a man and his friend) eat out of it too." Ordinarily these bowls were not decorated by carving or elaborate painting, although the rims were frequently painted, just as in this example, with simple lobes of black. They depend for their beauty on a graceful form juxtaposing acute angle and organic curve and on the varied textures of regular adzing on the outer surface and of parallel grooves in simple patterns on the inner surface and rim.

126. BOWL
Kwakiutl, 19th century
Alder
H: 7 1/2 in. (19 cm.); L: 29 in. (73.5 cm.); D: 13 in. (33 cm.)
Collection of Eugene and Martha Nester

George Hunt's description of bowl making gives the largest size of a dish as four spans in length, which is slightly longer than this one. He wrote that "This size of dish is used at a feast by six men" (Boas 1921:59). There are, of course, much larger bowls used by the Kwakiutl (cat. nos. 132 and 133) but they are of a different sort. The smallest regular size, exclusive of very tiny grease dishes, was one span (about nine inches) long, and was used by "a woman whose husband is away" (Boas 1921:59).

This alder bowl illustrates all the characteristic features of its type: flaring sides, high ends with compound-curved planes, and surface textures produced with the adze and crooked knife. Fine, regular grooving was used for decoration on much of the Northwest Coast, but the Kwakiutl, especially those tribes living on the northwestern part of Vancouver Island, made the most use of it. It is apparently a very ancient decorative technique made possible with the use of stone and shell adzes and beaver-tooth knives. A few archaeologically collected pieces and many collected by the earliest European visitors to the coast exhibit these textures.

127. CANOE BOWL
Tlingit, 19th century, collected at Sitka
Alder
H: 3 3/4 in. (9.5 cm.); L: 6 3/4 in. (17 cm.); D: 4 5/8 in. (11.7 cm.)
Collection of Jim and Marilyn Bergstrom

The very close relationship of bowls to canoes is best illustrated by bowls that are deliberately carved as stubby canoe models. This tiny vessel is complete with many of the features of giant canoes. The upswept bow and stern and the finlike extensions at each end are features of great northern canoes of the nineteenth century. More obvious canoe details are present: the flattened ends, the notch under the bow representing the angle of the cutwater, and the broad inner groove paralleling the gunwales. Even very subtle features have not escaped the bowl maker. The tiny triangular flat where the gunwale grooves converge, the broad, flat band extending from tip to tip on the outer surface, and the slight raising of the bow and stern at the ends of the gunwales are all found on large northern traveling canoes. The bowls, however, were carved to their final form, and not spread with steam as were their canoe prototypes.

Big canoes were often decorated with formline designs, and the carved figures on canoe bowls are analogous to those decorations. The design on this little canoe bowl is quite simple. The creature represented is not complete enough to allow identification.

129. SEAL BOWL
Northern Northwest Coast, 19th century
Alder
H: 5 1/2 in. (14 cm.); L: 22 3/4 in. (57.7 cm.); D: 11 in. (28 cm.)
Collection of Sylvia Duryee

An unusually large and flat seal bowl, this finely carved example is in every other way typical. The delicately carved formline designs cover the outer surface—even under the overhanging sides—delineating the anatomy of the seal. There is no sign of absorbed oil, and the flatness of the dish suggests that it was not intended to hold seal or candlefish oil but rather to serve as a feast dish. Inside the rim are rounded grooves, or flutes, which converge at the ends in elegant junctions. Multiple fluting like this is also seen on the upper surface of the rims of carved bowls and on the blades of daggers (see cat. nos. 130 and 167).

This bowl is said to have been collected by Adrian Jacobsen, a Norwegian employed by Karl Hagenbeck, a German entrepreneur, and by the Royal Ethnological Museum in Berlin to gather material on the Northwest Coast. Jacobsen collected in the Queen Charlotte Islands in 1881, but not in southeastern Alaska or the northern British Columbia Coast; if the bowl was acquired by Jacobsen it must have been from the Haida.

128. SEAL BOWL
Northern Northwest Coast, 19th century
Alder
H: 3 in. (7.7 cm.); L: 7 1/2 in. (19 cm.); D: 4 1/2 in. (11.5 cm.)
Collection of Dr. and Mrs. Allan Lobb

Fat, grey seals cluster like so many drift logs on the rocks and beaches of the coast to rest up from the business of living and to enjoy the warmth of the sun. Now and then one will stretch, arching his long hind flippers and stretching his head upward from the portly body. He is the model for the seal bowl. Perhaps by chance, he also adopts the characteristic bowl pose of high ends and lowered sides. Native hunters stalked him for his meat, his skin, and most of all for the rich blubber that makes his life in the cold northern waters possible and furnishes oil for the sustenance of the hunters—the oil for which the seal bowl was created.

Seal bowls were favorite oil containers of the northern tribes. Typically they take this form: wide, almost round bowls with the seal's head and flippers extending upward at either end. The details are flat designs spread over the rounded forms. These details extend over the bowl as stylized body parts. On the lower slope of the bowl the seal's front flippers are shown in the form of large ovoid joints and attached claws. Brown color, rich from age and infused grease, enhances the elaborate relief carving. The color varies from deep gold to near black, as the carving parallels or crosses the fibers of the wood.

130. FROG BOWL
Tlingit, early 19th century
Alder
H: 3 3/4 in. (9.5 cm.); W: 4 3/4 in. (12 cm.); L: 5 1/8 in. (13 cm.)
Collection of Jerrie and Anne Vander Houwen

A tiny, bulbous bowl, so saturated with oil that it oozes from every pore and has turned the wood completely black, is made in the image of a frog. A wide, toothless mouth, large eyes under arching brows, and lack of any tail identify him. The form is very simple—an oval bowl with the barest suggestion of sculptural elaboration in the frog's snout. The rim is typically undercut and double-grooved on its upper surface. Simply outlined legs are almost imperceptibly raised in relief by the delicate recessing of the surrounding background. The legs are in the classic formline style, but without elaborating detail. Formline ovoids represent the hip joints of the frog.

The sculpture of the creature's head is misleadingly simple. Very subtle modeling, almost invisible except for highlights from the oily surface, raises the enormous orbs from their surrounding sockets. The upper lids display a rounded fold seen on other old Tlingit pieces. And the frog's throat swells ever so slightly to evoke vibrant life in this old black relic of Tlingit culture.

131. BEAVER BOWL
Haida, mid-19th century
Alder
H: 3 in. (7.5 cm.); L: 7 in. (18 cm.); D: 4 in. (10 cm.)
Collection of John H. Hauberg

Although this little beaver bowl is undocumented, it is so nearly identical to one collected at Skidegate village in 1883 by James G. Swan (Sturtevant 1974:fig. 20) that it seems likely to be from the same place and time. With its globular body, arched back, and raised head, the beaver conforms to the rules of bowl design. Legs extend outward in high relief. He is painted black, with glossy guard hairs represented by slashes of vermilion. In contrast to the semirealistic painting of the body, the head follows the conventional arrangement of black eyebrows and eyes, vermilion lips and nostrils, and blue-green paint on the eye sockets and snout. The carving is very clean and sharp.

Beavers are identified in Northwest Coast art by a combination of features, the most important of which are the huge incisors and the flat, scaled tail—all of which this little beaver has. High, rounded nostrils and small, slanted ears are also beaver features, as are large feet, especially the webbed hind feet that act as rudders when the animal is swimming.

Although it is in every respect like grease bowls made for native use, it shows no sign of traditional use and was probably collected when new. Many were made for sale in the nineteenth century, and some of them are among the finest known.

132. SISIUTL FEAST BOWL FRAGMENT
Kwakiutl, late 19th century
Red cedar
H: 13 in. (33 cm.); L: 24 3/4 in. (63 cm.): D: 9 in. (23 cm.)
Collection of John and Grace Putnam

133. SISIUTL FEAST BOWL FRAGMENT
Kwakiutl, late 19th century
Red cedar
H: 17 3/4 in. (45 cm.); L: 41 3/8 in. (105 cm.); D: 7 7/8 in. (20 cm.)
Collection of John H. Hauberg

When privileges were transferred in a Kwakiutl noble marriage, among the most prestigious was the right to use great feast bowls carved in the shape of mythical men and beasts. The privileges were part of the dowry of the bride, and marriages among the families of chiefs were arranged with the advantages of their ownership in mind. There were often four feast dishes in a set, each representing a different creature. These fragments are among the few remaining remnants of a great three-part bowl representing the fearsome serpentlike being Sisiutl.

The bowl was the valued property of a chief of the village of Blunden Harbour, or Ba'a's, and was photographed there by Edward Curtis in 1912 (Curtis 1915:176, Holm and Quimby 1980:34-35). It was originally over fourteen feet long, including the feast ladles that formed the protruding tongues of the Sisiutl, and was made in three parts, each a dish in itself. All three bowls, a central head and two serpents' bodies with their heads and tongues, were mounted on wooden wheels so that the laden bowls could be rolled into the feast house when they were used.

Few of the monsters of Kwakiutl mythology rival the Sisiutl's power. Even looking directly at it could be fatal, but warriors who gained its power were invincible. The likeness of the Sisiutl appears on headdresses and masks, blankets, painted screens, house fronts, and, in fact, on almost every sort of decorated object in Kwakiutl art. It is a powerful and versatile image, adaptable to almost any surface. In the feast bowl it assumes one of its most effective forms.

These two fragments, one side of the central bowl (cat. no. 133) and part of one of the terminal heads (cat. no. 132), are among the few pieces that remain of the great Sisiutl bowl. The power of its sculpture and bold painting is still apparent, veiled as it is by the ravages of time and weather.

SPOONS

Hardwood, usually alder, maple, or yew, and horns of the mountain sheep and mountain goat are the materials of spoons and ladles on the Northwest Coast. In form they are remarkably uniform throughout much of the coast in spite of the variety of materials. The methods of utilizing those materials influenced the ultimate spoon shape, and both wood and horn account for at least some of the distinctive character of Northwest Coast spoons. If carved of wood, the spoon is chopped from a cylindrical section of a sapling; the tips of the bowl and handle are close to the surface on one side of the cylinder and the bottom of the bowl close to the opposite side. The heart of the tree runs through the bowl, intersecting it once near the curve of the tip and once again at the juncture with the handle. The spoon bowl's width is nearly the width of the cylindrical billet. The resulting form, with its broad and tapering bowl and S shaped profile, is the standard spoon shape from Vancouver Island to the northern limits of Tlingit country.

The simplest horn spoons are made by cutting away the inner side of the spiral horn of the mountain sheep or the tapered curve of a goat horn, softening it by steaming, spreading the basal end and forcing the tip upward, and reversing the curve of the handle. The shape achieved is almost identical with the wooden counterpart (see cat. no. 135 and cat. no. 137). Each material must have contributed to the creation of the final, traditional form.

Perfectly plain, undecorated spoons of this basic form are aesthetically rewarding, but many are also embellished with carving, painting, and inlay. Some are among the richest productions of Northwest Coast artists. There are many in collections— from miniature toys made of eagle beaks to great ladles in scale with the giant feast dishes—and they are decorated in every style and technique known to the coast.

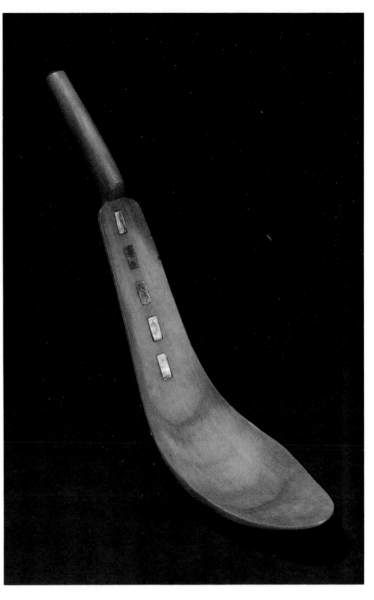

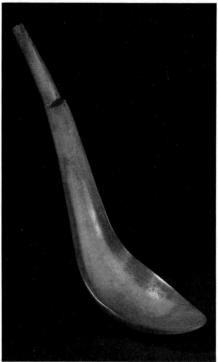

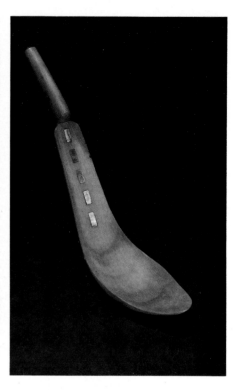

134. WOODEN SPOON
Bella Bella (?), 19th century
Hardwood
L: 13 in. (33 cm.); W: 4 in. (10 cm.)
Private collection

Judging by the angled reverse of the handle, this classic spoon is from the central coast. It is elaborated with a very abstract painting in the traditional colors of black and red which entirely fills the hollow of the bowl. The style of the painting is consistent with the spoon shape and suggests a Bella Bella origin (see cat. no. 103). Delicate formlines trace an asymmetrical grid of ovoid and U forms which no doubt delineate the parts of some fabled creature, though it remains unrecognizable. The wood is carved to a thin shell. It is a delicate object, very unlike our stereotype of a wooden ladle.

Highly decorated spoons were usually reserved for feast use. Although this one shows considerable patination, the paint itself is hardly worn, suggesting that the spoon had not seen everyday use. Many were made for sale, as long ago as the middle of the nineteenth century, and it may be that this is one.

135. HORN SPOON
Tlingit, 19th century
Mountain-sheep horn
L: 13 in. (33 cm.); W: 3 1/8 in. (8 cm.)
Collection of Bill and Marty Holm

The translucent horn of the mountain sheep carved and steam-molded to a dynamic, curved form provided spoons that transcend utility. And yet they are basically utilitarian objects, utensils that must function efficiently or be discarded. The angle of the bowl and its capacity fit the size and form of the deep bowls with which they were used. Elegant details, seemingly decorative, fulfill useful roles. On this spoon a tapered cylindrical extension of the back of the spoon is set off from the broad handle by narrow shoulders. When the spoon is held lightly with the thumb across the handle under the offset extension and with the fingers against the back of the handle, the extension rests in the crotch of the thumb and the whole spoon is balanced in position for use. It is a common detail on northern spoons and one that combines pleasurable form with function.

Sheep horn, when newly carved, is pale buff in color. With use it acquires deeper and deeper hues of amber and brown. This spoon, although probably of nineteenth century origin, has been used very little and retains the pale, translucent color of the fresh horn.

136. HORN SPOON
Tlingit, 19th century
Mountain-sheep horn, abalone shell
L: 13 in. (33 cm.); W: 3 in. (7.6 cm.)
Collection of John and Grace Putnam

Almost a perfect mate to the previous spoon (cat. no. 135) in form and dimensions, this horn ladle differs slightly in the proportions of the cylindrical tip and the shape of the transitional shoulders. Abalone-shell rectangles, expertly inlaid in the horn, provide a striking decorative touch. Although at first glance the spare geometry of the shell plaques seems at odds with northern Northwest Coast art concepts, abalone-shell embellishment like this is, in fact, fairly common. Headdress frontlets are often set with rows of rectangular shell inlays, and similar pieces are sewn to blankets and other ceremonial garments. Abalone shell was highly prized for its iridescent color, and deeply blue- and green-tinted shells were imported from the south, apparently even in prehistoric times. When Spanish explorers in the eighteenth century brought California abalone shells, by chance, to the northern coast, they quickly found that the shells were coveted by the native noblemen. Soon the shells became a staple of trade. They are still highly prized—especially those of deep color—by Northwest Coast Indians.

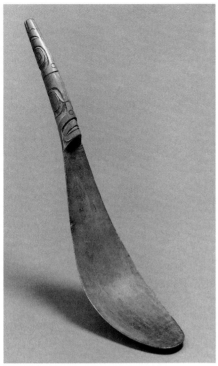

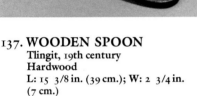

design as a two-dimensional arrangement wrapped around the handle. Fine line engraving on the inner surface of the bowl outlines formline figures of ovoids and U forms. The arrangement is too abstract to be safely interpreted.

137. WOODEN SPOON
Tlingit, 19th century
Hardwood
L: 15 3/8 in. (39 cm.); W: 2 3/4 in. (7 cm.)
Collection of John and Grace Putnam

This long, slim spoon of hardwood is from the same design tradition as the previous two horn spoons (cat. nos. 135, 136), but it was carved into its final shape from a cylinder of wood, while the other spoons were steamed and formed from pieces cut from the spiral horns of mountain rams. The round extension fairs smoothly into the flat handle, rather than flaring into angular shoulders, but otherwise the form is the same. Deeply carved formlines representing a figure of mythology wrap around the handle. Feast spoons like this were made in large sets that had similar carved decoration. Small spoons made of black mountain-goat horn, their handles carved with formline figures, often have the same configuration. Wrapped around the cylinder, the relief-carved design takes on a sculptural form; but if it could be spread out, its similarity to flat designs—on bowls, for example—would be immediately apparent.

138. HORN SPOON
Tlingit, 19th century
Mountain-sheep horn
L: 11 3/8 in. (29 cm.); W: 3 1/8 in. (8 cm.)
Collection of Bill and Marty Holm

Another spoon of the same general type is carved of mountain-sheep horn, which has taken on a golden brown color with age and use and superficially resembles wood. Mountain sheep horn objects are often misidentified as made of wood because of the similar appearance of the two materials. The growth layers of sheep horn are visible as meandering bands, or even grooves, crossing the horn perpendicular to the grain; and the material is translucent, showing colors ranging from pale yellow to deep reddish brown when seen against strong light.

The handle is carved with the head of a hook-beaked creature, perhaps a thunderbird. The eye sockets are deeply recessed, making the eyes prominent and bold like the beak and flaring nostrils. Above the head are ovoids that can be read as the shoulder joints, and above them are shallowly engraved U forms, perhaps the wing feathers. Since he engraved a single vertical line down the back that separates the eye sockets that come within a centimeter of each other, the artist obviously perceived the

139. HORN SPOON
Tlingit, early 19th century
Mountain-sheep horn
L: 13 5/8 in. (34.5 cm.); W: 3 1/2 in.
(9 cm.)
Collection of Bill and Marty Holm

Aged to a deep red-brown and showing
the signs of long use, an ancient mountain sheep horn ladle displays both delicate formline engraving and powerful
sculpture. Judging by the archaic style
of the designs and the appearance of
age, it is quite possible that this spoon
dates to the eighteenth century. Its texture and color resemble mellow wood,
and the transverse bands of deeper color
on the neck of the handle, characteristic
of sheep horn, could be mistaken for a
fiddleback figure in old maple. Hold the
thin bowl to the light, however, and it
glows a deep red.

Two creatures spread over the back of
the spoon. On the bowl, its rounded
snout filling the tip, is a sea creature,
perhaps a sea lion. The head is in classic
northern style, with massive formlines
defining the features. A long, rectangular panel connects the head to the pelvis
and flippers. In the panel are squared U
forms suggesting fins, or perhaps a dorsal fin which would imply a supernatural, composite creature. Another
formline face fills the pelvis area, and a
pair of clawed flippers and a rounded
tail rise from it. At the base of the tail is
carved a tiny human face. The end of the

handle is carved as the head of the second figure, which resembles a whale.
Long pectoral fins, or perhaps wings,
extend along the sides of the handle,
stopping just short of the feathered tail
joint of the strange part-bird and part-
whale creature. Framed in the rim of the
whale's blowhole is a powerful, sculptured face, and tucked under the whale's
jaw is another.

140. HORN LADLE
Haida, 19th century
Mountain-sheep horn
L: 14 1/2 in. (37 cm.); W: 6 3/4 in.
(17 cm.)
Collection of John H. Hauberg

Among the artists of the Northwest
Coast there were some who had complete mastery of the materials, techniques, and design system with which
they worked. The maker of this horn
ladle was one of those artists. He has
chosen a raven as the subject of his
sculpture. At least two other raven
ladles appear to be by this artist, one in
the Portland Art Museum (64.19.3) and
the other in the American Museum of
Natural History (16.1/1073). Both are
larger and more elaborate than this one,
but all three share the same masterful
workmanship and perfection of form.
The raven is the most frequently represented creature in large mountain sheep
horn ladles.

The bird's head forms the finial of the
handle, and his body, represented in
beautifully integrated formline structure, covers the bowl. On the raven's
breast is a simple, round-eyed face, perhaps analogous to the faces on the
breasts of raven rattles. His wings sweep
around the rim, flanking claws and legs
that are drawn tightly against the body.

At the tip of the ladle's bowl is the
raven's tail, a human face surrounded by
a broad formline ovoid and surmounted
by two broad feathers. The feathers are
earlike and give the face the appearance
of a humanoid bear. The formlines com-
prising the design are broad and simple,
without extraneous elaboration. Their
execution is flawless.

The narrow sheep horn from which
the ladle was made has been spread until
the bowl is nearly as wide as it is long.
The inner rim is recessed in a broad
groove on each side, like those on a
bowl or a canoe. The grooves converge
at the ends, running up into a deep
groove in the handle. Rich, red-brown
color complements the form.

141. HORN SPOON
Haida, 19th century
Mountain-goat horn, mountain-sheep horn
L: 11 1/4 in. (28.6 cm.); W: 3 in. (7.5 cm.)
Collection of John H. Hauberg

The mountain goat, source of wool for Northwest Coast weavers, also furnished curved, black horns that were made into spoons and handles. Fine feast spoons, the "family silver" of northern Northwest Coast nobility, were made with bowls of mountain-sheep horn riveted to the black, elaborately carved handles. The figures were crests and illustrations of myths, and were arranged and rendered just as they were on the monumental totem poles that proclaimed the privileges of the noble families—except that it would take fifty spoon handles to equal the width of a typical Haida totem pole. The surprising thing is that the complexity of the figures and the degree of detail are essentially the same in these two distinct but closely related products of the carvers' art.

The raven bites the tongue of a whale-tailed frog. The raven's wings, with ovoid shoulders and U form feathers, flank the tiny creature. A human figure, inverted between the raven's ears, holds the wing-tips of a thunderbird in his mouth. Between the thunderbird's ears sits a humanoid figure with a dorsal fin protruding from his head. As the horn tapers, the figures become smaller, yet each is rendered in perfect detail. The finest Haida spoons, like this one, are true masterpieces.

142. HORN SPOON
Haida, 19th century
Mountain-goat horn
L: 10 1/4 in. (26 cm.); W: 2 5/8 in. (6.7 cm.)
Collection of John H. Hauberg

Both the handle and the bowl of this Haida spoon are made of mountain-goat horn. On two-piece spoons the natural curve of the goat horn is retained in the handle, while the horn for the bowl is spread open. When the two parts are riveted together the usual S curve results.

The figure at the base of the handle is a sea creature, perhaps a sculpin. A raven stands above him with his long bill pointed downward touching the lips of an inverted human between his wings. Above the raven squats a figure with cloven hooves and an animal's head from which rises a hornlike projection. It probably represents the one-horned mountain goat, a figure in Tsimshian and Haida mythology. The goat's front feet rest on the head of a man who squats between his hind legs, grasping them with his hands.

Many Haida spoon makers were also carvers of argillite. The conventions of representing the details of figures, the intertwined compositions, and the complex piercing of the goat horn is mirrored in argillite pipes of the same period. The pipes and spoons are almost identical in style and workmanship, although the spoons were made for native use and were almost never for sale, and the pipes were almost all made to sell to non-Indians.

143. HORN SPOON
Tlingit, 19th century
Mountain-goat horn, mountain-sheep horn, abalone shell
L: 10 3/4 in. (27.5 cm.); W: 2 3/4 in. (7 cm.)
Collection of John and Grace Putnam

This spoon is attributed to the Tlingit on the basis of the style of carving, which is less compact and not so rigidly governed by formline principles as that on documented Haida spoon handles. The figures are elongated and separated by piercing. Abalone inlays sparkle in the eyes and joints of the figures. Both the handle and bowl are of mountain-goat horn. A plug of a reddish horn, perhaps of the mountain sheep, has been inserted to form the tongue of the lower figure, an inverted man. A frog, head down and held by a bear, bites the man's tongue. Between the bear's abalone-inlaid ears stands an eagle. Carving of the tip of the horn, above the eagle's head, is unfinished. No doubt the artist planned another figure, but the carving didn't progress far enough to make it recognizable.

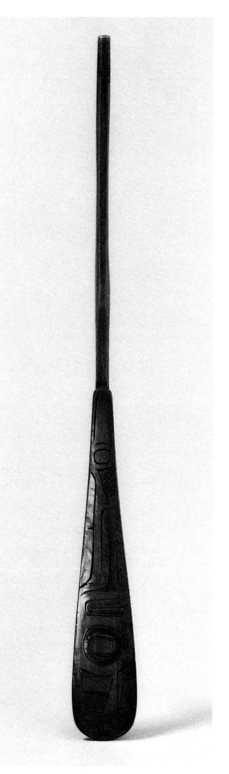

144. SOAPBERRY SPOON
Tlingit, mid-19th century
Hardwood
L: 14 5/8 in. (37.1 cm.); W: 1 1/2 in. (3.9 cm.)
Collection of Eugene and Martha Nester

A favorite dessert everywhere on the Northwest Coast was a stiff foam beaten from water and soapberries, the fruit of the shrub *Shepherdia canadensis*. Soapberries grow in dryer climates and are not universally available on the humid coast. Those people who lived where the berries grew harvested a surplus and traded them to less fortunate tribes. They are still highly prized today, and are still bartered and sold from tribe to tribe. They can be preserved by drying, as they were in times past, or by canning or freezing. A few berries make a lot of foam, and great quantities were eaten at feasts. They will not whip if any oil or grease is present in the utensils, so special care was needed to prepare them.

Special paddle-shaped spoons were used to eat the foam. Some of them are perfectly plain but elegantly formed. Many, however, are decorated by carving, painting, or both. Judging by the style of carving and painting, this spoon is a very old Tlingit example. A black and red ovoid and U complex with an attached clawed foot is painted in an early style. A bear's head on the handle bites the butt of the blade. Once he was painted black, with red ears, lips, and nostrils, but much of the paint has worn away.

145. SOAPBERRY SPOON
Tlingit, mid-19th century
Yew wood
L: 18 1/2 in. (47 cm.); W: 1 3/4 in. (4.5 cm.)
Collection of Dr. and Mrs. Allan Lobb

A very long, slender and elegant soapberry spoon is carved in shallow relief with the figure of a crouching animal. The spatulate blade is gently spooned, and the flattened handle merges with the blade's ridged back. The handle itself is subtly modeled, swelling upward near the juncture of the handle and blade. Soapberry spoons were made in sets that were similar in form but represented different figures. This one is not readily identifiable.

Soapberry foam has a fruity, but slightly bitter, taste; it was sometimes sweetened with berries and, in later times, sugar. Experienced eaters swish the foam in and out between their lips to break the bubbles in order to avoid swallowing too much air. Eating soapberry foam is a lighthearted activity, often accompanied by joking and horseplay.

146. SOAPBERRY SPOON
Tlingit, mid-19th century
Hardwood
L: 17 7/8 in. (45.5 cm.); W: 2 in. (5 cm.)
Collection of John and Grace Putnam

Occasionally the blades of soapberry spoons are carved in a form other than the usual paddle shape. This fine old Tlingit spoon takes the outline of a salmon. The details are in the massive, angular formlines. Compressed faces that are Tlingit in style fill the bases of the dorsal fin and the tail. The spoons were made to be used in a festive, social gathering, which explains the elaborate decoration of such essentially functional utensils.

147. SOAPBERRY SPOON
Tlingit, mid-19th century
Hardwood
L: 17 7/8 in. (45.5 cm.); W: 1 3/4 in.
(4.5 cm.)
Collection of John and Grace Putnam

This spoon is elaborated with a little formline man, wearing a hat with potlatch rings, crouching at the end of the handle. The blade is the usual spatulate form, with a highly conventionalized animal engraved over its surface. It could be interpreted as an eagle, the head occupying the proximal two-thirds of the blade and the hook of the beak pointing toward the handle. The bird's foot fills the tip of the blade, with a stubby wing compressed between it and the eagle's head.

148. SOAPBERRY SPOON
Tlingit, mid-19th century
Hardwood
L: 16 3/4 in. (42.5 cm.); W: 1 3/4 in.
(4.6 cm.)
Collection of John and Grace Putnam

Probably part of the same set as the previous two spoons (cat. nos. 146, 147), this one carries the elaboration of the handle a step further. The blade is held in the beak of a bird, probably a raven. A little man, similar to the one on the handle of the eagle spoon, crouches above the raven. On the spoon blade, a long-snouted animal with narrow ears and claws, perhaps a wolf, stretches toward the end. The formlines are angular and compact, with thin relieving slits and very little background.

HUNTING AND FISHING

The Northwest Coast tribes have been classified as hunting and gathering societies since agriculture, with the exception of the tobacco growing done by the Tlingit and Haida, wasn't practiced by them in precontact times. They depended on the resources of nature for food and materials. Yet they developed cultural complexities such as their permanent villages of large houses—which were unusual for hunter-gatherers. Special conditions on the Northwest Coast probably account for much of this. The seasonal round of harvesting the bounty of the sea—especially the anadromous fish like salmon and eulachon, and shellfish—was not unlike agriculture in that the "crop" became available at predictable times and locations and was harvested in quantities capable of sustaining the people during the off-seasons. The same can be said for the natural fruit and root grounds, which were considered real property among some coastal tribes and were tended much like gardens.

The technologies of fishing and hunting were highly developed. Fishermen perfected ingenious devices adapted to the living and feeding habits of each of their quarries (Stewart 1977). The harpoons and arrows of sea hunters were sophisticated and uniquely suited to the taking of game ranging from whales to sea otters. Land hunters and trappers developed traps, snares, and deadfalls, and even the creatures hidden in the tide flats were brought to the gathering baskets with digging sticks of specialized design. Many of these utilitarian implements are the art objects of today's collections.

149. HALIBUT HOOK
Tlingit, early 19th century
Wood, spruce root, iron
L: 11 in. (28 cm.); W: 2 in. (5 cm.)
Collection of John and Grace Putnam

Early European and Euro-American visitors to the coast were amazed and chagrined at the efficiency of native fishing equipment, which was crude in appearance by their standards. They frequently recorded their frustration at being unable to catch fish, while the Indians seemed to have an endless supply. The two-piece wooden halibut hook of the northern coast was a particularly awkward-looking contrivance. Yet it was actually a marvel of practical design, perfectly suited to the taking of the great flatfish (Stewart 1977:46-55). Although the two pieces of wood and a bone barb, lashed together with split spruce root, seem haphazard in form, every angle, curve, and measurement was standardized through generations of experience to the most efficient arrangement.

Sir George Simpson, a governor of the Hudson's Bay Company for nearly forty years until his death in 1860, was the collector of this halibut hook. Simpson, one of the most important figures in the history of the fur trade, visited the Northwest Coast several times during that period, and probably acquired the hook on one of those trips. It is a fine example. The decorated arm is carved to represent a bird, probably either a cormorant or a merganser. The long neck, attenuated beak sharply hooked at the tip, and crest of feathers on the head are features that fit either bird. Carving of the wings and tail follow northern formline conventions, with ovoid joints in the shoulders and a human face at the base of the tail. The barb, lashed in place with split spruce root, is apparently a square iron nail.

150. HALIBUT HOOK
Tlingit, 19th century
Wood, spruce root, iron, cotton cord
L: 8 in. (20.5 cm.); W: 1 3/4 in. (4.5 cm.)
Collection of Mr. and Mrs. Alan Backstrom

Two-piece halibut hooks are designed to be loosely attached to, and to float upward from, a sinker. The barbed arm is above, and the carved arm below. Bait is tied to the barb, and the halibut takes the entire arm into his mouth; in its ragged and torn surface, the arm usually shows the marks of the fish's stuggles.

The carving on this hook is of a composite figure of a raven and a halibut, a combination seen on a number of hooks. The raven's head, flanked by his feet, protrudes from the halibut's body, which is bordered by a continuous fin on each side. The carving is fairly rough but typical of halibut hooks, which range in workmanship from extremely crude to finely finished, beautifully designed carvings. Fishing equipment was probably made by the fishermen themselves, rather than by the professional artists who produced the rattles and masks for which Northwest Coast art is known. Expertly carved examples are few. The importance of the figures lies in the magic they bring to luring the halibut, not in impressive display.

151. HALIBUT HOOK
Tlingit, 19th century
Yew wood, yellow cedar, spruce root, iron
L: 11 in. (28 cm.); W: 1 3/4 in. (4.5 cm.)
Collection of John H. Hauberg

This fine halibut hook was made by an expert carver, a trained artist. The carved figure is a humanoid animal, probably a bear to judge by this long claws. He holds a small creature of uncertain identity, possibly a grub or woodworm, in each hand.

That halibut hooks were made by the fishermen who used them is corroborated by the fact that each hook was made to the measure of the individual user. The spread of the two arms is measured according to the width of the clenched fist, and the barb is set so that the fisherman's thumb can just pass between its point and the opposite arm. These proportions are important to successful halibut fishing. Since halibut are tremendously powerful fish ranging up to several hundred pounds in weight, it was vital that any fish caught be small enough to be killed and boated by the fisherman. The width of his fist and the thickness of his thumb limit the size of the halibut that can take the hook to one he can safely bring into the canoe by himself. Native fishermen who have used these hooks claim that the halibut will not fight it as they would a conven-

tional steel hook, perhaps because the hook tends to turn the halibut on his back when being hauled in.

152. SEAL CLUB
Northern Northwest Coast
Yew wood
L: 23 1/2 in. (59.7 cm.); W: 2 1/2 in.
(6.4 cm.)
Collection of John H. Hauberg

Clubs for killing the seals and sea otters
that were taken with harpoons or har-
poon-type arrows, as well as for halibut
and salmon, were often elaborately decorated with carving. Usually they were
made of a hardwood, such as yew,
although some were made of whale
bone.

A favorite subject for the design was
the sea lion, a rival and very efficient sea
hunter. This typical northern seal club
probably represents that animal, with
his large, clawed flippers and formida-
bly toothed mouth. He is rendered in
traditional northern style. The ovoid eye
socket is bordered by a broad, raised
formline, repeated in the flipper joints.
Its use in sealing is suggested by near
black patination, perhaps derived from
the oily and bloody hands of the hunter.

Many fish and seal clubs are relatively
simple, handled knobs that are more or
less well finished. They are often seen in
ethnographic collections; but elaborately decorated clubs like this one are
better known, having been frequently
illustrated and exhibited.

153. TRAP-STICK
Tlingit, 19th century
Whalebone
L: 11 in. (28 cm.); W: 1 in. (2.7 cm.)
Collection of John and Grace Putnam

There are many mysterious objects in
collections of Northwest Coast material,
but none is less understood than the
bone trap-stick. Many have found their
way into museums, sometimes misidentified as shamans' charms or tool handles. George Emmons collected
numbers of them from the Tlingit, and
his typically detailed collection notes

refer to them as "trap sticks." In some of
his descriptions Emmons referred to
them as the stakes to which snares were
attached, and at other times he called
them triggers for deadfalls. That they
were in some way part of a trap mechanism seems certain, but that they were
simply snare stakes seems highly
improbable. Their very specific and uniform shape implies a much more complex function than a tethering pin. Some
trap-sticks are complete with two other
unusually shaped wooden pieces, which
are clearly part of the mechanism. No
amount of experimentation, or digging
through old accounts and the ethnogra-
phies of the Northwestern tribes, has
produced a credible explanation of how
the trap-stick functioned. At one time
there were probably hundreds of native
trappers who used the sticks as a matter
of course. The steel trap sealed the fate
of the bone trap-stick and left us with a
mysterious relic.

Almost all trap-sticks are elaborated
with complex carvings at the broad end,
which are perhaps analogous to the
magical carvings on halibut hooks.
Many, like this one, represent animals,
or animals associated with humans. The
figures always protrude from the convex
side of the stick, and this projection is
probably linked to the object's function.
The swelling curve of the stick itself and
the sometimes chisel-shaped point are
probably also functional. Regardless of
our ignorance of these functions, the
whole object is a visually satisfying piece
of Northwest Coast art.

CANOES

Wherever Northwest Coast people traveled or gathered, there were canoes. The canoe made the coast livable. It gave the people the means to harvest the produce of the sea, the ability to transport cargoes of food and goods and to visit far-off villages. Whole tribes moved by canoe to their seasonal camps to fish and to gather berries and roots. Canoe-borne emissaries traveled to distant tribes to woo the daughters of chiefs. Inviters called the tribes by canoe, and the invited guests arrived in great fleets drawn up in a line, dancers in the bows and all the paddlers singing. By canoe, warriors brought destruction to their enemies, and in later days families traveled the length of the coast to sell their baskets or find work in the hop fields of Puget Sound.

The prodigious western red cedar was the canoe tree. In the northern Tlingit area, where cedar did not grow, large traveling canoes were imported, and small hunting canoes were made of cottonwood or yellow cedar. With stands of giant, clear-grained cedar at their disposal, the Haida of the Queen Charlotte Islands and the people of the west coast of Vancouver Island, became professional canoe builders, trading their vessels to tribes with surpluses of goods that were scarce or not available to them, such as candlefish oil and goat wool. But every tribe made some canoes in a variety of types and sizes. The canoes all shared basic features: they were carved of red cedar, double-ended with fine lines, and each almost always had its thin-walled hull spread by steaming to its final vital, elegant form.

154. CANOE MODEL
Makah, late 19th century
Alder
H: 5 1/2 in. (14 cm.); L: 33 1/2 in. (85 cm.); D: 6 1/2 in. (16.5 cm.)
Collection of Dr. and Mrs. Allan Lobb

The tribes of the southwest coast of Vancouver Island and the northwestern shore of the Olympic Peninsula in Washington State were daring and skilled canoemen who hunted the mammals of the open sea in light, graceful canoes with narrow, upswept bows and vertical, flaring sterns. Their most prestigious prey were great whales, which they pursued in eight-man canoes, using heavy yew harpoons tipped with points of sharpened mussel shell barbed with elk antler. Fur and hair seals, sea otters, sea lions, and porpoises were hunted in the sleak dugouts.

A hunting canoe with three crewmen and a seal aboard is represented in this model. All the figures are carved in one piece with the canoe. It accurately depicts the salient features of the boat, the elegant prow with its earlike gunwale extensions and snout looking like an alert animal head. Jutting from the smoothly arched cutwater is a narrow projection, always present on Westcoast canoes and apparently purely aesthetic in function. The flare of the gunwales, extending from the "ears" to the after end of the raised stern, is carefully calculated in width and form to turn the seas away from the canoe. When plunging into a wave, or in a following sea, the flare buoys the boat, which rides up the wave like a ski.

155. MODEL CANOE
Westcoast, late century
Alder
H: 4 1/2 in. (11.5 cm.); L: 33 in. (83.7 cm.); D: 4 3/4 in. (12 cm.)
Collection of Dr. and Mrs. Allan Lobb

The maker of this model was a master carver and painter. Several of his models are known, and all are of the same high standard of workmanship and design as this one. The low bow, thrusting forward rather than sweeping up like the bow of the previous model (cat. no. 154), is an early characteristic, seen on models recovered from the precontact Ozette site and in drawings from the earliest European expeditions to the coast until those of the middle of the nineteenth century. Meticulous attention to detail marks this model. Delicate grooving on the gunwales at the bow and stern duplicates a feature of well-made nineteenth century canoes. The painting is particularly fine, illustrating an abstract geometric aspect of Westcoast art seen in the details of masks and the paintings of ceremonial screens.

Wilson Duff has presented striking skeuomorphic evidence for a relationship between the Westcoast canoe and the framed, skin-covered Eskimo umiak (Duff 1964). Both peoples were whalers and sea hunters, but differ radically in culture, language, and physical characteristics. The nature of any contact that might have led to umiak skeuomorphs in Westcoast dugout canoes is unknown. A remarkable skeuomorph, not mentioned by Duff but perfectly illustrated in this model, is the wavy line painted under the gunwales. This wavy line exactly duplicates the appearance and placement of walrus-hide thong lacing that secures the skin cover to the first frame-stringer below the umiak's gunwale. The design appears on all the known models by this artist.

156. MODEL CANOE
Northern Northwest Coast, mid-19th century
Yellow cedar
H: 6 3/4 in. (17 cm.); L: 33 7/8 in. (86 cm.); D: 6 1/4 in. (15.8 cm.)
Private collection

When the first Europeans reached the northern coast some of the canoes that met their ships had broad, vertical fins at bow and stern, many of them elaborately painted with enigmatic designs in black and red. This canoe form lost favor sometime in the early nineteenth century, and by the time Paul Kane painted one in the early 1840s he used a model like this one as his source. Proof that he did not see the actual canoe in use is the fact that he mistook the slanting stern for the bow, representing the canoe being paddled stern first. "Head canoes," as they are called, exist only in the form of models today.

The painting on the canoe is typical: an animal's head is depicted in formline style on the bow and the hindquarters shown on the lower, slanting stern. No clear identifying features are present and so the animal cannot be identified with confidence. The painting uses red as the primary color, with black secondary elements and inner ovoids. A characteristic of many Northwest Coast canoe models, including this one, is a disproportionate shortness in relation to width and height. An actual canoe would be nearly twice as long in beam to length ratio. The shallow groove under the gunwales, analogous to the grooves under the rims of bowls, is seen in this old model.

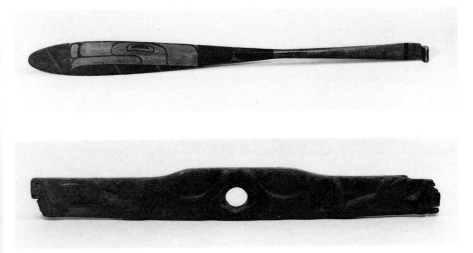

157. CANOE PADDLE
Northern Northwest Coast, mid-19th century
Yellow cedar
L: 48 in. (122 cm.); W: 6 in. (15 cm.)
Collection of John and Grace Putnam

Just as canoe types differed from one part of the coast to another, so did the paddles that were used to propel them. This beautifully formed and painted paddle is from the northern coast, probably Haida or Tlingit. The painting includes an unusual variant on ultraprimary design (see cat. nos. 111 and 158) in which large formlinelike areas are painted within the decorated space prior to painting the true formline design in the remaining spaces. In this example the ultraprimary painting is not solid, but is covered with a red, hatched pattern in one section and red lines paralleling the ultraprimary shape in another.

The true formline painting is masterfully done all in black, as is often the case in designs incorporating red ultraprimary. Secondary areas that would ordinarily be painted red are crosshatched. The figure is abstract and appears to represent a bird. Paddles were made in sets, the number varying according to the size of the canoe. The paintings on such paddles were similar to one another in style and composition, but usually differed in detail. Even the designs on the two sides of the same paddle were rarely exactly alike.

158. CANOE PADDLE
Bella Bella, 19th century
Yellow cedar
L: 52 3/4 in. (134 cm.); W: 6 in. (15.2 cm.)
Collection of John and Grace Putnam

Another example of ultraprimary painting is seen in this Bella Bella paddle. Here both the ultraprimary and the primary designs are black, which is somewhat uncommon. Secondary patterns in the main figure are red. The paddle, with its long, elliptical blade, lack of shoulders at the base of the blade, and convex-sided shaft is typically Bella Bella. The formline style is consistent with that identification (see cat. no. 103).

Northwest Coast canoe paddles typically have very long blades and short shafts, with a transverse grip or "crutch" handle. The paddlers generally took rather short, quick strokes, often to the beat of a paddling song. On large canoes the steersman, seated in the stern, used a large and broad paddle as a rudder. In the late nineteenth century, when many canoes were sailed, real rudders were sometimes attached to the stern. At the same time, oars came into use on canoes, and most late nineteenth century canoes of any size were fitted with oarlocks. Paddles continued to be used, however, as long as canoes were made. Many were also made for sale, and those were frequently decorated with carved designs. Paddles made for actual canoe use were never carved; the blades thinned by carving would almost surely break if used.

159. CANOE MAST THWART
Tlingit, early 19th century
Red cedar
L: 72 1/4 in. (183.5 cm.); H: 8 5/8 in. (22 cm.)
Collection of John and Grace Putnam

Judging by the length of this thwart it probably came from a canoe of about forty-five feet in length, a large canoe for its period. Some later canoes approached seventy feet. The thwart is pierced to act as a mast partner. Most canoes of any size during the historic period were equipped to be sailed, and large canoes were usually fitted with two masts. They were unstayed, held upright by the mast thwarts. The usual rig was a square spritsail, which was derived from the form of sail used by ships' boats in the early historic period. Before Europeans came to the Northwest Coast, canoes were only sailed before the wind, using very simple sails of cedar bark matting or wooden slats. Journals of early explorers often mention making sails for the Indian canoemen and teaching them to sail in the European manner.

Mast thwarts on large canoes were often carved with figures, and a favorite theme was a creature with mouth open to receive the mast. This one is a human figure with legs and arms stretched to the sides. It is very reminiscent of the figures between the ears of the bears on carved horn bowls (see cat. no. 123). The carving is much worn and must be of considerable age. It is said to have belonged to Shartrich, a chief at Klukwan.

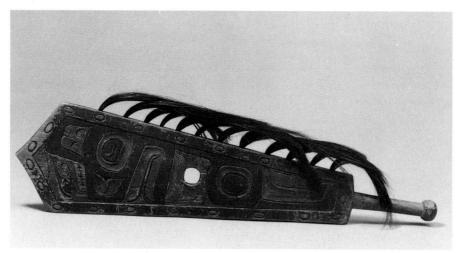

STAFFS AND WANDS

Carved staffs and wands of many varieties were used in ceremonial contexts by the people of the Northwest Coast. Some of them were "speakers' staffs," totem-polelike carvings held by chiefs or their speakers in formal oratory. Among the northern tribes, especially the Tlingit, dance leaders carried staffs that they waved and thrust to mark time and to signal the movements of the dance. These were often in the form of fins, sometimes several meters long, with shaftlike handles called "dance paddles" because of their resemblance to canoe paddles. Some of them were, in fact, in the form of paddles, elaborately decorated with painting, inlay, and fringes of human hair.

160. DANCE WAND
Tlingit, 19th century
Yellow cedar, human hair
L: 19 5/8 in. (50 cm.); W: 3 in. (7.7 cm.)
Collection of Jim and Marilyn Bergstrom

Tlingit dancers often carried carved wooden wands or small paddles, usually in pairs. Shamans also used wands or batons in their practice, some of which represented magical weapons with which they battled the malevolent powers opposing them. This wand was probably for dancing. The animal figure represented in the painted and carved formline design is not identifiable, nor is the significance of the hole through the center known. Fins of supernatural killer whales were often shown perforated like this, but the shape of this wand is unlike the usual representatons of the whale's fin.

The border of the wand is decorated with carved ovals that represent opercula inlay. Probably when the piece was new the light yellow of the wood contrasting with the black border gave a satisfactory imitation of the inlaid shell. A typical fringe of hair falls from the edge.

Dancers carrying wands like this one gestured with them in time to the dance song, responding to the words with appropriate movements. In certain dances, especially those imitating the Athapaskan Indians of the interior, the dancers held white bald eagle tails. Old photographs also show dancers carrying daggers.

161. CEREMONIAL STAFF
Tlingit, 19th century
Yellow cedar, abalone shell, human hair
L: 53 1/8 in. (135 cm.); W: 3 3/4 in. (9.5 cm.)
Collection of Bill and Marty Holm

The shaft of this dance staff is carved into nineteen spoollike segments painted red and black and resembling vertebrae, which they may represent. At the lower end, the cylinder of the staff is elaborated with an abstract pattern of carved formlines resembling an animal's head with attached fins and claws. The upper end flares into a flat, asymmetrical blade that probably represents the tail of the creature depicted on the whole staff. Massive, angular formlines in black and red, with traces of pale blue in the tertiary areas, resemble early nineteenth century Tlingit work (see cat. no. 47). Inner ovoids and secondary U forms are inlaid with abalone-shell plaques; some of these have been drilled, which indicates a previous use where the shell pieces had been sewn in place.

A fringe of human hair, dark reddish brown in color, sways from the edge of the fin. Hair fringes were often used by the Tlingit artists on crest objects (see cat. nos. 47, 48, 49) and on the equipment of shamans (see cat. nos. 199, 200) The hair was usually set into drilled holes and wedged in place with hardwood pegs.

COPPERS

The copper is a unique and enigmatic emblem of the Northwest Coast. The object gets its English name from the metal from which it is made. When Europeans first came to the Northwest Coast they found copper to be prized above almost all other materials. This scarce material, acquired only through trade from sources in the interior, was workable with techniques available to Northwest Coast people. It was beautiful in its warm, metallic brilliance. Sheet copper became an important material of barter in the early days of the fur trade.

All the tribes from northern Vancouver Island northward use coppers and have traditions accounting for their origin. Interestingly, all coppers that have been subjected to metallurgical testing have proven to have been made of commercial sheet copper. Yet there seems no reason to doubt that there were coppers made of the native material before European contact. Several early accounts mention that when commercial copper became available, coppers made of it were of less value than those made of the native metal, and yet historically coppers of the commercial material have been considered by their native owners to be of immense value.

The peculiar shape of the copper, with its flaring top and ridged lower half, has intrigued scholars, and many have suggested possible origins for it. To date, none can be considered to be more than conjectural. Even the uses of the copper are imperfectly understood. They certainly vary from one area of the coast to another, but everywhere the copper is a symbol of wealth and prestige and has an important place in the ceremonial life of the people.

162. COPPER

Tsimshian (Gitksan), Kitwanga, 19th century
Copper
H: 41 1/8 in. (104.5 cm.); W: 29 7/8 in. (76 cm.)
Private collection

This very large and beautifully engraved copper was collected at the Gitksan village of Kitwanga, on the upper Skeena River. It has the typical shape of a northern copper, with broad proportions and flared, curving top. The T shaped ridge, usually referred to as the backbone of the copper, has been hammered to a sharp V form and the face has been raised into an even bulge. The head and forepaws of a bear have been engraved on the face, outlining broad, classic formline elements that have been painted black. The natural color of the copper shows as a background.

The copper was damaged in a house fire, which melted away its lower corner. Coppers were sometimes intentionally destroyed by burning or by sinking in deep water, especially by the Kwakiutl chiefs to the south. Here, however, the damage was accidental.

163. COPPER
Haida, Skidegate, 19th century
Copper
H: 30 in. (76.2 cm.); W: 21 in. (53.3 cm.)
Collection of Sylvia Duryee

Large, heavy coppers were used by northern chiefs to proclaim the importance of their lineages. They were displayed at potlatches and were particularly important at the memorial for a deceased chief. Since they were so valuable, they were used in the transfer of property, and there are many stories about the use of coppers to pay for the rights to village sites, fishing stations, and so forth.

Not all northern coppers have designs, although apparently all valuable coppers were named. The face, feathers, and feet of a bird appear on this copper. The eyes have been domed to stand out from the surface, and the outlines of the figure have been engraved. Although the shapes are traditional, the formlines are only minimally suggested by the engraved lines. The bird's feet, claws touching at the center, appear under his hooked beak. Ovoid and U patterns at the sides apparently represent his wing feathers. A stylized human face is engraved between the upright ears.

This copper is very broad for its height and has an unusually flat top. It is said to have been collected from the Haida village of Skidegate, on the Queen Charlotte Islands.

164. COPPER
Kwakiutl, 19th century
Copper
H: 34 1/4 in. (87 cm.); W: 13 in. (33 cm.)
Collection of John and Grace Putnam

Kwakiutl coppers have a number of characteristics that differ from those of their northern counterparts. Often they are much slimmer than northern coppers and of thinner copper, although this one is quite thick. They also are typically strongly arched, or even angled, at the top. Frequently the painting continues down the sides of the lower half. The usual design for this area is a series of bars extending outward from the central, vertical ridge. They may be horizontal, as in this copper, or angled downward. They represent ribs; the T shaped ridge is called the "rib place" by the Kwakiutl. The upper part of the copper is called the face, and, as in northern coppers, is painted with a design representing the face of the creature for which the copper is named. Kwakiutl coppers are rarely engraved; the design is merely painted on. But since it is customary to brighten the unpainted areas by scraping from time

to time, they eventually become recessed so that the black designs stand out in relief.

The most distinctive characteristic of Kwakiutl coppers is probably their cut and patched condition. Any copper that has seen traditional Kwakiutl use will have, at the least, a piece cut from it, and old coppers of great value will have been cut up, pieced together, and cut again. A chief uses his copper to retaliate against anyone who has insulted or injured him or his family by cutting a piece from the copper and presenting it to the offending person. That person is obligated to reciprocate in order to avoid shame. The copper can be renewed by assembling pieces of broken coppers or even remaking the copper on the old T ridge, which is the last part left of it after many cuttings, and which contains the life and name of the copper. This copper has been cut in a characteristic way, one half of the upper part having been removed.

WEAPONS

Warfare on the Northwest Coast was a mixture of raiding for booty, retaliation, or revenge and a kind of stylized combat similar to that known to us from the age of chivalry. On the northern coast especially war seemed to demand certain rules of behavior in which the honor of the combatants' clans was to be upheld above all, and the loss of high-ranking warriors had to be compensated before peace was established. Formal hostages, who were honored and given special status, were exchanged during the negotiations.

In keeping with the ceremonial character of war customs, weapons were frequently elaborate and beautifully crafted. All the materials available to the artist found their way into the manufacture of weapons. Some of them became family heirlooms and even achieved the status of emblems or crests. For a few of these noble weapons the native traditions have been recorded. However, we can only guess at the history of most of them.

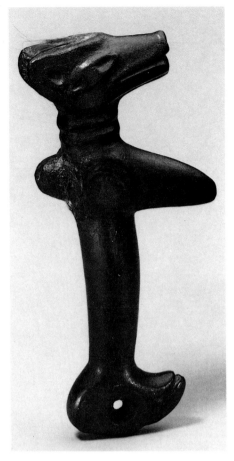

165. WAR CLUB
Westcoast, Nootka Sound, 18th century
Stone, hair
H: 14 in. (35.5 cm.); W: 6 in. (15 cm.);
D: 2 in. (5 cm.)
Collection of John H. Hauberg

The earliest piece with historic documentation in the exhibition is this sculptured stone war club from Nootka Sound. It was collected in April 1778 by some member of Captain James Cook's expedition to the Pacific. Although it has been through a number of hands since, its Cook association is firmly established by a sketch made by Sarah Stone in 1783, recording it as part of the Leverian Museum collection in London (Force and Force 1968: 149). Since the only British ships to return to England from the Northwest Coast by that time were Cook's, the club certainly was brought by them. A 1790 guide to the Leverian Museum also describes it. It is one of only two known and documented Northwest Coast pieces from Cook's expedition in the United States.

Cook and other early visitors to the west coast of Vancouver Island collected war clubs of yew wood with transverse striking blades of stone. This war club imitates the form of those composite clubs in a single piece of hard stone, probably shaped by pecking with a hard pebble and grinding the forms to their final finish with abrasive stone. Both the wolf's head at the striking end and the bird at the pommel are in traditional Westcoast style, and closely resemble sculpture in wood from that area. At one time there was a considerable amount of human hair and, according to the Leverian catalogue, "beautiful green feathers" attached to the club. Traces of some adhesive substance and hair remain.

The hole through the eye of the bird probably held a thong that circled the wrist of the warrior and prevented the loss of the club. It has been called a "slave killer," as many different kinds of Northwest Coast weapons have been, but there is little reason to believe that it was not a warrior's weapon.

166. DAGGER

Tlingit, Klukwan, late 18th century (?)
Iron, copper, buckskin
H: 21 1/2 in. (54.5 cm.); W: 4 1/8 in.
(10.5 cm.)
Collection of John H. Hauberg

Some of the first Europeans to meet Northwest Coast natives found them in possession of iron daggers skillfully made and decorated, which left them impressed with the Indians' ability to produce such elegant weapons. We still wonder at it today, knowing how difficult it is to do comparable work with all the tools and techniques we have at our disposal. Some Northwest Coast people, however, have traditions of native smiths working iron before the Euro-Americans came to their country, and families have kept examples of their work as valued heirlooms. This dagger is such an heirloom.

According to the tradition of the family from which the dagger was collected, it was made by a woman, Saw-Ye-Na-Aught, from a meteor that fell at the head of the Chilkat River above Klukwan. This story of a precontact female smith was widely known in the nineteenth century and was recorded by Holmberg in 1854 (Holmberg 1856: 28). The dagger was a treasure of the Tluqwaxadi clan at Klukwan and has the name "Witch Doctor's Thrust." It was said to have been used to kill slaves, whose heads were thrown into the Chilkat River in order to bring shrimp into the area.

The dagger is made in a single piece. The details of the face have been added on both sides by riveting separate pieces of shaped iron for the eyebrows, lips, nose, and cheeks, and copper for the ears. The eyes and teeth are drilled. Apparently the head once had a symmetrical corona of U shaped projections, each pierced with a single hole. Much of this has been worn away. The skill needed to shape and apply the features was considerable, but nothing compared to that required to forge the blade with its broad fluting on both faces. It was probably forged to nearly its finished form, and then the surface was ground with abrasive stone to its final shape. The grip of smoked moose hide is a recent addition. It's very possible that it was originally wrapped

tightly with a winding of braided hide or human hair.

167. DAGGER

Tlingit, Angoon, late 18th century (?)
Iron, copper, leather
H: 26 3/8 in. (67 cm.); W: 4 3/4 in.
(12 cm.)
Collection of John H. Hauberg

This magnificent dagger, or, perhaps more properly, sword, is one of the finest examples of Northwest Coast metal art known. Like the previous dagger it is an ancient heirloom, believed to date to precontact times on the coast. Tradition identifies the artist as Kuch-Kee-Ees, or Black Wolf, of Klukwan, who is said to have made it nine generations ago. The dagger has the name Keet Kwatla, Killer Whale Dagger, referring to the double whale-head and high-dorsal fin on the pommel.

The carving is deep and bold. Metal sculpture like this has not been done on the coast since the early nineteenth century, and we have no idea what techniques were used by the artists. The

fluting on the blade is expertly done, with the three grooves tapering uniformly to their convergence near the point. The back of the blade is slightly concave and without fluting—the usual form of Tlingit daggers of this type. Copper overlays at the hilt are also typical of one-piece iron daggers.

Although daggers were the principal weapons of Tlingit warriors, they also came to be chiefly emblems. They were displayed at potlatches in much the same way as crest hats and other prerogatives. An old photograph shows this dagger resting on the body of a deceased noble person lying in state.

168. DAGGER
Tlingit, Wrangell, early 19th century
Wood, iron, cloth, hide
H: 14 1/2 in. (36.7 cm.); W: 2 in. (5 cm.)
Collection of Dr. and Mrs. Allan Lobb

Although many daggers from the northern coast were made in a single piece with the pommel forged as an extension of the tang, many were also made with the blade set in a carved hilt of some other material. Wood was the most common, but bone, walrus, and sperm-whale ivory, mountain-sheep horn, and even whale baleen were used. A popular material was walnut, salvaged from the stocks of worn-out or damaged muskets. This dagger hilt appears to be of gunstock walnut.

Daggers with separate, carved hilts never have fluted blades. The blade of this small dagger, double-edged with the surface beveled from a ridge at the center line, is of typical form. The grip is made of two flat strips of wood, one of which is part of the carved pommel. The long tang fits in a recess in this piece, and the other strip is bound tightly over it with a wrapping of skin thong. A hook at the end of the tang fits into a corresponding slot, anchoring it tightly in the hilt.

A bear carved of walnut, heavily patinated with age and holding a human in its mouth, forms the pommel. The animal's head is highly stylized, with the features rendered as formlines over the sculptured surface. The tiny man is boldly modeled in early Tlingit style.

169. DAGGER HANDLE
Tlingit, early 19th century
Mountain-sheep horn, abalone shell, hide
H: 7 in. (17.7 cm.); W: 2 in. (5 cm.); D: 1 3/4 in. (4.5 cm.)
Collection of Sylvia Duryee

The head of a fiercely scowling warrior, or perhaps warrior spirit, serves as an appropriate finial for the hilt of a dagger. The form of the head, very deep from front to back, is influenced by the shape of the mountain-sheep horn from which it is made. Large, round eyes with open lids, short rounded nose, and broad lips are all Tlingit sculptural characteristics. Deep, curved wrinkles framing the nostrils and mouth and at the corners of the eyes emphasize the angry grimace; they appear on war helmets and shamans' masks as well.

Iridescent abalone shell, expertly inlaid, complements the deep, orange-brown translucence of the sheep horn. Reflections from the lustrous surface sharpen the bold planes of the face and the wrinkles' smooth curves. A row of spirals whirling over the head and on the cheeks is unusual, and whether they represent hair, headdress, or some other concept is unknown.

The horn dagger hilt is a little masterpiece, dramatic and expressive as a warrior's implement should be. It probably comes from the early historic period, although it was collected in the late years of the nineteenth century by Lieutenant David Lyle. He was the inventor of the Lyle gun, which was used to throw the lines that carry the breeches buoy in lifesaving operations.

PIPES

Although the custom of smoking tobacco came to Europe from North America, it was Europeans who introduced it to the northern Northwest Coast. Haida and Tlingit planted and grew tobacco—the only example of true agriculture on the coast in precontact times—but they did not smoke it. Instead, the dried leaves were ground and mixed with lime, made into pellets, and sucked. When European seamen arrived on the coast with their commercial tobacco and pipes, the custom of growing and sucking the native plant quickly gave way to trading for and smoking imported tobacco. Since the use of tobacco had been not only a pleasurable habit but also an integral part of house-building potlatches and memorial feasts for the dead, the new custom of smoking quickly became a feature of those ceremonial activities. Pipes are among the most interesting examples of northern Northwest Coast sculpture.

170. **PIPE**
 Tlingit, early 19th century
 Walnut, metal
 H: 3 1/8 in. (8 cm.); W: 3 1/2 in. (9 cm.);
 D: 2 in. (5 cm.)
 Collection of Eugene and Martha Nester

At about the same time that trade tobacco and the custom of smoking it were introduced to the people of the northern coast, the musket came on the scene. Although some traders were initially reluctant to arm the aggressive northerners, the demand for firearms soon induced traders to supply them in great numbers, and by the beginning of the nineteenth century muskets were plentiful. They changed patterns of hunting and warfare, and they also influenced art. Broken and worn out muskets supplied two prized materials, iron and walnut, which came to be used in pipes. Sections of musket barrels made fine pipe bowls and the walnut stocks supplied a superb carving wood.

In this pipe an eagle crouches over the inverted head of a man, probably a corpse to judge by the expression of closed eyes and half-protruding tongue between the drawn lips of the bony face.

The eagle seems to be holding the head in his hooked beak. His wings wrap around the body, a naturalistic rendering of the stance of an eagle over his prey. The shoulder joint is carved as a massive formline ovoid with the feathers attached. The spread tailfeathers continue the design around the back.

The bowl of the pipe protruding from the eagle's neck was probably once capped with a copper flange, and the corroded remnant of a metal lining remains. The pipe utilizes the full thickness of the trade gun-butt from which it was carved.

171. PIPE
　　Tlingit, early 19th century
　　Hardwood, copper
　　H: 4 3/8 in. (11 cm.); W: 2 1/4 in.
　　(5.7 cm.); D: 2 1/2 in. (6.3 cm.)
　　Collection of John H. Hauberg

A manlike figure with a dorsal fin protruding from his back crouches on a pedestal, perhaps representing a box, carved on this old Tlingit pipe. In the Raven House in Klukwan are four house posts with similar figures crouching on carved chests. They are said to represent Raven in human form. Although the house posts are very similar in arrangement to the pipe design, they probably do not represent the same story. The crouching men-Ravens are surmounted by coppers and formline designs of some quadruped, while the figure on the pipe has a whale's fin on his back. In this he very closely resembles a series of carved figures collected by George Emmons, and eventually dispersed to various museums. The figures are crouching men, heads upright, with tall dorsal fins standing up from their backs. Emmons described them as figures attached to a shaman's blanket and representing the Gonakadet, a supernatural undersea being who brings wealth and good luck to anyone who makes contact with him. The Gonakadet is sometimes described as looking like a

carved and painted box; the boxlike pedestal upon which the figure crouches may reinforce that identification.

The compact figure is carved in true Tlingit style. Massive formlines with minimal background and narrow tertiary spaces are characteristic of early northern work. This pipe is too thick to have been made from a gunstock. A copper flange rims the pipe bowl. A short stem made of a shoot with the pith removed was inserted in a hole in the back of the pipe, but, as usual, the stem is missing from this pipe. Very few of these pipestems have survived.

172. PIPE
　　Tlingit, 19th century
　　Antler, copper
　　H: 4 1/2 in. (11.5 cm.); W: 4 in. (10.3 cm.); D: 1 3/8 in. (3.5 cm.)
　　Private collection

Most smoking pipes of the Tlingit were made of wood, but there are examples made of stone, ivory, and antler. This is an example of the latter, probably made from the antler of a caribou. Antler was widely used on the Northwest Coast for wedges and tool handles, harpoon points and barbs, war clubs, and shamans' paraphernalia such as bracelets, necklace pendants, and amulets. It is a tough material, fairly easily carved, and capable of being softened for slight

bending by soaking and heating.

The artist used a prong of the antler for the stem of the pipe, and represented the dorsal fin of a whale on it. A small bird crouches between the halves of the split fin, which is turned back at the tip to join at the back of the pipe stem. The whale's tail is represented by two large ovoid joints with appended flukes next to the copper rim of the pipe bowl. When smoked, the pipe would have been held with the whale's head down. The carving is a good example of the way in which Northwest Coast artists used the available space, in this case the natural form of the antler, in representing the creatures of their art. Antler prongs gave them an extension of the main form from which the artists often carved fins or beaks.

173. PIPE

Tlingit, early 19th century
Walnut, iron gun barrel
H: 3 1/2 in. (9 cm.); W: 5 3/4 in.
(14.5 cm.); D: 1 5/8 in. (4 cm.)
Collection of John H. Hauberg

This handsome little sculpin pipe makes use not only of the stock wood of the trade gun, but also of a piece of the barrel. The spiny fish is graphically portrayed with an outsized head, bulging eyes, and wide mouth. Without sacrificing any of the formal stylization of Tlingit art, the carver has shown the long, spiny dorsal and anal fins, the pectoral and ventral fins, the broad gill covers, and the spines on the nose and the back of the head. Elegant formlines cover the entire carving, defining the anatomical detail. A bird's face decorates the downturned tail, which is more like a whale's flukes than like a sculpin's caudal fin.

Segments of gun barrels were favorite material for pipe bowls. Most of them are made from the 24-gauge barrels of Hudson's Bay Company trade muskets, but this one is larger and possibly from a musket of military calibre. Usually, as in this pipe, the gun-barrel bowl is inserted in a likely spot without any thought of symbolism; sometimes it is used as part of the design—often as the segmented top of a crest hat. If it is used as a crest hat, grooves are filed around it to represent the separation of the stacked potlatch cylinders (see cat. no. 57).

174. PIPE

Haida (?), mid-19th century
Walnut, brass
H: 2 1/2 in. (6.5 cm.); L: 5 1/2 in.
(14 cm.); D: 1 1/2 in. (4 cm.)
Private collection

Around the middle of the nineteenth century clay pipe-bowls ornamented with portraitlike heads were manufactured in the eastern states, and some of these made their way to the Northwest Coast. They were the inspiration for the many argillite pipes with Euro-American faces on the bowls, some of which are virtual copies of the clay pipes (Wright 1980:44-47). A very few similar pipes carved of wood are known; this is one of the finest. The fillet of leaves and berries, curly hair, and shoulder knobs are features shared with many argillite pipes. The features of this face are so distinctive and portraitlike that it seems possible that the pipe was made to represent an actual person. If it weren't for the characteristics it shares with Haida argillite pipes, and some very Northwest Coast stylistic conventions such as the form of the nostrils, we might fail to recognize it as an Indian piece. The brass cap and funnel of the pipe bowl are also like well-documented Northwest Coast pipes.

Traces of vermilion remaining in the recessed areas alongside the nose and under the fillet suggest that the pipe was

once painted. What appears to be black paint remains as a slight stain on the shoulders. A few traditional style pipes retain their paint, and perhaps most were painted at one time.

175. PIPE
Haida, mid-19th century
Walnut, bone, baleen, brass, glass, paper
H: 4 1/8 in. (10.3 cm.); L: 15 in. (38 cm.);
D: 7/8 in. (2.3 cm.)
Private collection

Haida artists of the early nineteenth century who carved pipes of argillite intended for sale to the Euro-American visitors to their islands took their inspiration from exotic sources as well as from their own well-stocked repertoire of mythology. The ships of the European and American traders were of great interest to island-dwelling seafarers, and very early they and their crews became the subject of Haida sculpture (Wright 1979:40-47). "Ship pipes" were sometimes rather naturalistic representations of the vessels, but more often they were highly stylized designs. Certain features that identified them as ships were a long, flat keel with upturned stem often ending in a spiral derived from the ship's billet head, cabinlike structures along the deck, and often a smokestack and paddle wheels. Some were carved of wood rather than argillite, and these resembled the black stone pipes in most of their salient features.

The most fully documented group of wooden ship pipes are those that were given by officers of the Hudson's Bay Company to Lieutenant Charles Wilkes, part of the United States Exploring Expedition, in October 1841. But even for these pipes the only information we have is the date and place of the gift. Most have no accompanying information or existing information is frequently erroneous. This pipe was regarded as Hawaiian, probably because the little captain, seated in the cabin at the bow, is reading a book printed in the Hawaiian language! Since there were many native Hawaiians working for the Hudson's Bay Company on the Northwest Coast it is not at all unlikely that a page of Hawaiian printing could come into the possession of a Haida pipe carver, who glued a scrap of it to the captain's book, which is visible through the bone-framed glass window.

ARGILLITE

One of the best known and least understood of the materials of Northwest Coast Indian art is argillite, the black shale that Haida artists have carved into complex curios for sale to seamen, traders, missionaries, anthropologists, and tourists from the early years of the nineteenth century to the present day. There is some evidence that at least a few argillite objects were made for native use, but the overwhelming majority of that production was for sale to non-Indians. In the days before the works of Northwest Coast Indian carvers were recognized and accepted as art, argillite carvings were highly regarded as the cleverest of curios and brought higher prices than almost any other kind of object from the coast. Later, when collectors began to respect the aesthetic and emotional qualities of masks, rattles, and other carvings, especially those made for ceremonial use, work in argillite lost favor and was often thought of as an acculturative craft without any artistic merit. In fact, some of the great masterpieces of Haida art as well as some of the most trite souvenirs have been carved of this rare, black shale.

The material itself has been greatly misunderstood. It is very rare, and although there may be other sources, the only known quarry with fine-grain argillite in any quantity is on a rugged mountainside in the Queen Charlotte Islands. It is soft enough to carve with woodworking tools, and it remains soft, although the common conception is that it hardens with exposure to air. This old tale, which is also used to describe catlinite, or red pipe stone, a closely related material, has been refuted again and again but it continues to crop up. The material takes a fine luster from

the blades of the tools used to carve it and does not need polishing or rubbing with graphite to bring out its sheen. It is very brittle but remarkably resistant to changes in temperature; although most pipes made from it were not smoked, argillite pipes can be (and were) smoked without damage. Haida argillite is one of the most interesting and beautiful materials in Northwest Coast Indian art, and the best argillite carvings rank as masterpieces.

176. ARGILLITE PIPE
Haida, early 19th century
Argillite
H: 2 3/8 in. (6 cm.); L: 8 5/8 in.
(22 cm.); D: 1 1/8 in. (3 cm.)
Collection of Eugene and Martha Nester

The exact year when argillite carvings first appeared among objects collected on the Northwest Coast has not been determined to our satisfaction, but it appears to have been around 1820. The earliest known carvings were pipes carved either as clusters of figures from Haida mythology or as stylized models of European ships. The earliest of these Haida motif pipes had bowls large enough to be practical for smoking and were rather compactly designed, in a style quite like that of the wooden figural pipes that were smoked by the northern tribes. As the artists experimented with the material and the techniques of working it, they began to elongate the format, clustering more figures in more and more complex relationships. Freedom from the restrictions of material limitations, such as the shape of

the mountain-goat horn used for spoon handles, or of grain direction of wood, facilitated the development of convoluted, pierced compositions.

This fine little pipe was probably made in the 1820s, or 1830s at the latest. It illustrates the beginning of the elongated, pierced style, but is still within the period of solid, compact form. The formline detail on the wings and fins is skillfully carved in the early, classic northern style. There are seven figures represented. The principal figure is a raven; the pipe bowl is in his head. He bites the throat of a man whose body appears to penetrate the barrel of the pipe, which he grasps with his hands. The man's head rests on the snout of a whale, whose pectoral fins lay against the pipe barrel. Another human face with open mouth behind the whale's head may represent his blowhole. Under the pipe, and grasping the stem end with his hind feet, is a frog. He holds the tongue of a large, humanoid face, whose arms and hands stretch along the pipe and grasp the end of the whale's flippers. At the bowl end of the pipe a tiny killer whale hangs head down, his flippers clasping the raven's wings and his dorsal fin in the shape of a small raven's head. He is probably the mythical killer whale, Raven-Fin.

177. ARGILLITE PIPE
Haida, early 19th century
Argillite
H: 3 in. (7.7 cm.); L: 14 1/2 in. (36.5 cm.); D: 1 in. (2.4 cm.)
Collection of Donn Charnley

During the 1830s, the second decade of the argillite carving tradition, pipes began to be carved that were longer and flatter than those of the early years. This pipe probably represents an early departure from that compact style. The bowl, which is nearly in the center of the pipe, is still large enough to be functional, and the figures are fully carved on the bottom of the pipe, a characteristic of the early period.

The largest figure represented is one found more often on argillite pipes than on any other object of Northwest Coast art. It is the dragonfly, and can be recognized by its large, round eyes, paired, cross-hatched wings, and segmented body. Often the dragonfly has a small human face between his large eyes (see cat. nos. 192 and 216); here the face has become a complete figure seated on the insect's nose, with his feet in the creature's mouth. A frog crouches under the dragonfly's tail and extends its tongue, which is bitten by the humanoid raven occupying the stem end of the pipe. A small figure sits between the raven's ears, grasping them with his hands. Under the pipe, at the center, the joint of the raven's tail has the form of a human face with arms and hands stretched forward toward the wings of the dragonfly.

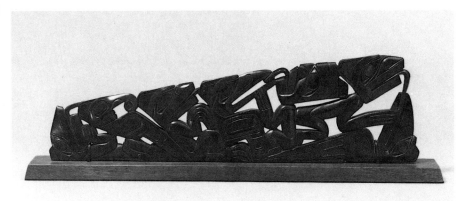

178. ARGILLITE PIPE
Haida, mid-19th century
Argillite
H: 4 3/4 in. (12 cm.); L: 17 in. (43 cm.); D: 5/8 in. (1.5 cm.)
Collection of Bill and Marty Holm

We are particularly fortunate to have in this exhibition three of the eight identified pipes by the "Master of the Long Fingers" (see Wright's essay, p. 139). This unknown Haida artist developed, sometime in the first half of the last century, a very distinctive style of carving argillite. His style was characterized by many interconnected figures in one plane, multiple piercing, and easily recognized handling of sculptural forms and two-dimensional detail. Pipes by this artist are among the thinnest of all panel pipes; this one is only one and a half centimeters thick and forty-three centimeters long. Although the figures have the appearance of being sculptured in the round, they can perhaps be more accurately described as double-faced relief carvings. This thinness and the extensive piercing between figures has made them very fragile, and, since they were carved a century and a half ago, it is remarkable that they have survived so well.

The figures here are fairly straightforward. At the stem end is a reclining bear whose tongue touches the top of the head of a coiled-nosed creature, perhaps a butterfly. Another bear reclines against the insect, his tongue extended to touch the ears of a raven with formline wings and large, clawed feet. The raven faces a man whose tongue he bites. The man's head rests on the back of yet a third bear, who shares a tongue with the second, reclining raven.

179. ARGILLITE PIPE
Haida, mid-19th century
Argillite
H: 4 1/8 in. (10.4 cm.); L: 15 in. (38 cm.);
D: 5/8 in. (1.5 cm.)
Private collection

The second of the "Long Fingers" pipes is similarly thin and pierced, and sometime in its long life the head of the terminal bird, probably another raven, has been lost. Each of these compositions begins with a reclining figure at the stem end, the ensuing figures becoming more and more erect as they proceed along the pipe until the pattern reverses and the last figure is again reclining. This pipe is more freely sculptural than the preceding one (cat. no. 178). The silhouettes of the various figures' heads are clearly distinguishable along the top of the pipe, whereas on the first example (cat. no. 178) they fall on an almost perfectly straight line.

There is also a greater variety of figures on this pipe. At the narrow end a bird, perhaps an eagle, reclines, his beak holding the head of a frog. The frog extends his tongue to the ears of a raven, which he also touches with his claws. The raven's wings and beak frame the double-dorsal fin of a supernatural killer whale. Tongue, pectoral flippers, and tail of the killer whale join a man with bearlike ears, whose tongue reaches the head of a round-eyed creature with a missing nose. This is probably an insect whose proboscis touched the now missing beak of the raven.

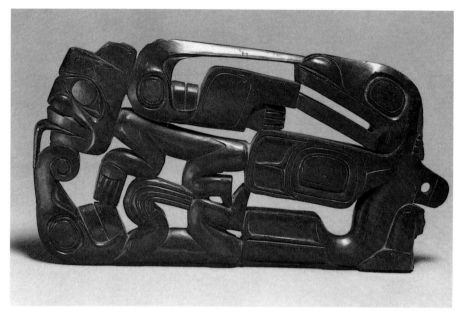

180. ARGILLITE PIPE
Haida, mid-19th century
Argillite
H: 4 in. (10.3 cm.); L: 8 in. (20.4 cm.);
D: 5/8 in. (1.5 cm.)
Collection of John and Grace Putnam

Only the larger end of this handsome "Long Fingers" pipe remains, but it is enough to indicate its fine quality. All the characteristics of the artist's style are apparent. Each of the four surviving figures is a different creature, two of which are probably insects. Although the figure with the coiled proboscis has no wings, the head is so much like that on the first of the three pipes that it may represent the butterfly in human form. The other bird has a long, straight, or uncoiled, nose. His wings appear to be unfinished, with only a single line marking the edge of the wing ovoid and no detail at all in the extension. However, the artist also habitually left the ears of his creatures undetailed, and perhaps this simplicity was deliberate.

The pipe bowl is in the top of the whale's head, as it is in the previous pipe. This placement was a favorite and appropriate choice of argillite pipe carvers. In all three of the Long Fingers pipes the hole drilled for the pipe bowl is only four millimeters in diameter, about the same width as the stem hole. There is no practical reason for drilling such a small hole. Probably Haida pipe carvers, reluctant to make a decorated object without function, chose to drill the hole even if it was too small for any practical use.

181. ARGILLITE FIGURE
Haida, mid-19th century
Argillite, white stone
H: 12 1/8 in. (31 cm.); W: 4 1/8 in. (10.5 cm.); D: 2 in. (5 cm.)
Collection of John H. Hauberg

The strange men with their exotic dress who manned the ships from Boston and England were favorite subjects for Haida argillite carvers of the early and mid-nineteenth century. Officers and crews struck busy poses aboard fanciful argillite ship pipes, often in the company of horses, monkeys, or creatures of Haida mythology (Wright 1979:40-47). Proud captains, feet apart and hands thrust into coat or trouser pockets, were recorded in polished, black stone. Fascination with the curious activity and alien dress of the foreigners probably accounted for much of the interest that the Haida carvers had in them, but no doubt there was a commercial motivation to these carvings as well. The customers were the subjects themselves, and a fanciful impression of one's self or one's shipmates by a savage of the Northwest Coast of America probably made a better conversation piece back

home in Boston than an incomprehensible monster of mythology would.

In 1869 Frederick Whymper collected this proud captain when he visited Sitka during his travels in connection with the survey of a route for the proposed America-trans-Siberia telegraph line. Assuming it had originated in Sitka, he identified it as "representing a Russian soldier"; but it is a Haida carving and probably represents one of the English or New England sea captains who called at the Queen Charlottes (Whymper 1869:105). The officer strikes the usual pose. The stripes on his waistcoat, the buttons and seams of his trousers and coat, his heavy boots, and peaked cap are all faithfully recorded. His face is made of some kind of soft, white stone which contrasts with argillite muttonchop whiskers. Other sea captain figures have faces of red argillite, bone, or ivory (Vaughan and Holm 1982: 132-142).

182. ARGILLITE FIGURE
Haida, late 19th century
Argillite, abalone shell, sea lion whiskers, ivory, eagle down
H: 10 5/8 in. (27 cm.); W: 3 3/8 in. (8.5 cm.); D: 2 5/8 in. (6.5 cm.)
Collection of Bill and Marty Holm

Much later in the century the Haida figure carvers began to produce sculptural groups illustrating incidents in myths, figures of shamans at their work, and dancing chiefs. It has been suggested that the Haida artists turned to these subjects after traditional native values had been eroded by the forces of acculturation (Gunther 1956 and Kaufmann 1969:135), and certainly most of them were carved around the turn of the century when almost all art production was slated for the market. Nevertheless, many of these figures are remarkably powerful sculptural expressions.

A chief in his dancing regalia—frontlet headdress with ermine trailer and sea lion whisker crown, Chilkat blanket, fringed apron, and raven rattle—was a dramatic figure without peer. His haughty expression and animated stance—shoulders tilted, head cocked, and raven rattle thrust forward—have been caught by the artist. This sort of animation was rare in earlier Haida sculpture. The formline designs of the blanket and apron are in the style of the turn of the century when considerable freedom had crept into the formerly rigid rules of the art.

Abalone-shell inlay in the frontlet border and the tips of actual sea lion whiskers set into the top of the headdress intensify the naturalism of the figure. Even whisps of eagle down have been tucked into the crown. The chief's ivory dancing rattle is a replacement, but the missing original must have been much like it.

183. ARGILLITE CHEST
Haida, late 19th century
Argillite
H: 6 1/8 in. (15.6 cm.); L: 12 in. (30.2 cm.); D: 7 5/8 in. (19.4 cm.)
Collection of John H. Hauberg

Another product of the argillite carvers' repertoire was the miniature chest, inspired by the great wooden containers that held chiefs' ceremonial materials and served as their coffins after death. Although basically like bent-corner chests in proportions, argillite chests are much more fanciful in their decorations, frequently incorporating high relief detail and full sculptural figures. The compositions of the formline designs, which follow only a few standardized arrangements in the larger, functional chests, are much more individualistic in argillite. They were all made for sale and the artists certainly catered to the foreign market.

John Robson, a chief at Skidegate and a renowned carver, was the maker of this argillite chest (Holm 1981:190-192). He was a contemporary of the famous artist Charles Edenshaw, and became his stepfather after marrying his uncle's widow, Edenshaw's mother. Robson's and Edenshaw's carving and painting styles were sufficiently similar that their works have often been confused, but on the basis of present understanding this chest must be attributed to John Robson.

The chest has a number of figures represented on it. On one of the long sides a bear is shown as a formline design (illustrated), but with his snout carved in full three-dimensional form. The bear's shoulders are represented by ovoids in the upper corners of the chest and his forefeet and claws stretch under his jaw. On the opposite side a bird, probably a raven with beak turned

down, is flanked by his wings, their long feathers turned under his beak. Sculptural beaver heads protrude from the ends of the chest, and the beavers' bodies are represented by abstract formline patterns. On the lid Robson carved an illustration of a mythical incident which shows Raven caught by a naturalistically represented crab. Raven in his travels went to play with a crab, which pinched his wings and dragged him into the sea, releasing him only after the water flowed over them.

184. ARGILLITE CHEST
Haida, late 19th century
Argillite, abalone shell, wood
H: 10 5/8 in. (27 cm.); L: 20 7/8 in. (53 cm.); D: 12 1/4 in. (31 cm.)
Collection of Bill and Marty Holm

Grizzly bears loom from all four sides of this large argillite chest, the work of a prolific carver of argillite who has been tentatively identified as Tom Price (Gessler 1981: 13, Holm 1981:193-7). Price's style is bold and angular and the bears, with their narrow eye sockets, bared teeth, and snarling lips, are properly ferocious. Deeply carved formline patterns use many of the standard features of wooden chest designs rearranged in a multi-angled composition. These bears suggest by their finlike shapes that they might be the mythical undersea grizzly. The protruding heads and claws are all separately carved pieces of argillite glued in place. On the lid, crouching in a network of indecipherable formlines, are two frogs. All the eyes of the six sculptured creatures and the paw joints of the two large bears are of abalone shell.

Argillite, when quarried, can be split into somewhat irregular, flat slabs, and chests were made of those slabs carved to the proper thickness and glued together. Some of them were reinforced, like this one, by fastening the side slabs to a wooden box. To join the pieces of argillite the Haida carvers used a glue said to have been made by boiling fish skin. The glue often failed with age, consequently many composite argillite objects have come apart. Both of these chests (cat. nos. 183, 184) are among the many that have been reassembled with modern adhesive.

185. ARGILLITE PLATTER
Haida, mid-19th century
Argillite, bone
Diam: 14 in. (35.5 cm.)
Private collection

The Haida became acquainted with round, decorated tableware in the earliest days of European contact, and early in the argillite-carving period they began to make circular platters to sell to Euro-American buyers. Many of these are so perfectly shaped that they look like they have been turned on a lathe, but there is no evidence to show that this was done. They were probably carved by hand with the assistance of a compass.

The early examples are elaborately engraved with combinations of compass-drawn circles and arcs, flowers, leaves, berries, and cross-hatching. The circles were often elaborated with radiating grooves that give them a resemblance to a compass rose. A similar motif is used to represent the paddle wheels on argillite ship pipes. There is some reason to believe that American pressed glassware, which was becoming popular when the maritime fur trade

was still active on the Northwest Coast, may have been the most direct prototype for the argillite platters. Certainly the resemblance is remarkable.

This platter is especially light and elegant in its design. The arrangement of decorated border, central circle, four rosettes, curved tendrils, and clusters of leaves is typical. The bone inlay contrasts nicely with the lustrous black of the argillite. Ropelike molding is common on later, figural platters, but it is seldom seen on circular, floral-patterned platters such as this one.

186. ARGILLITE PLATTER
Haida, mid-19th century
Argillite
Diam: 12 1/4 in. (31.2 cm.)
Collection of Sylvia Duryee

Several argillite platters are known that are copies of American coins. Although the maker of this platter represented the letters UNITED STATES OF AMERICA HALF DOL. accurately enough, his irregular spacing shows that he was copying them as a design rather than as meaningful words. Some other examples have letters omitted, reversed, or even invented. Much of the platter's detail is faithfully copied from the coin: the eagle's stance, his cluster of arrows and olive branch, the shield with its proliferation of stripes, and even the S mark of the San Francisco mint. The mint began producing in 1854, which dates this platter to sometime after that. The feathers of the eagle are unlike those in traditional Haida art, and represent an attempt by the artist to copy those on the coin. American eagles on ships' carvings, official documents, and bank notes also furnished inspiration to Haida artists (see cat. no. 208).

The opposite side of this platter is decorated with circular rosettes, tendrils, leaves, and berries in the traditional manner of mid-nineteenth century circular platters. The platters, very brittle and subject to scratching and abrasion, are not functional. One fine one did serve as a birdbath in Brooklyn for many years before being rescued by a knowledgeable collector!

187. ARGILLITE PLATTER
Haida, early 20th century
Argillite
L: 16 1/2 in. (42 cm.); W: 9 3/4 in. (25 cm.)
Collection of John H. Hauberg

Toward the end of the nineteenth century the argillite carvers began to produce great numbers of platters, many of which incorporated sculptural figures in their designs. These turn-of-the-century platters were frequently oval rather than round, and almost none of them were carved on both top and bottom, as the earlier platters had been. Platter making continued on into the early decades of this century before giving way almost entirely to model totem poles. A few platters are again being made, but they are usually small.

The story illustrated by the carving on this platter is of a young prince who was chastised unfairly and went away from his home. He was taken by the salmon people to their village where he was well treated. When the salmon tribe went upriver to spawn he was caught, as a salmon, by his own people. The salmon was cut open, and he appeared as a tiny person who grew magically. He brought the knowledge of how to treat the bones of salmon respectfully in order to ensure their return. The two-dimensional designs surrounding the salmon-prince are difficult to interpret. They may represent the Wasgo, or sea wolf. What appears to be a wolf's head with a long ear and many teeth occupies one side of the design while a whalelike tail is engraved on the other side. The space between is filled with fins and flippers.

The multi-angled composition, with tapered, constricted U forms often overlapping one another, is characteristic of the work of some early twentieth century Skidegate argillite carvers (Holm 1981:192-3).

188. ARGILLITE PLATTER
Haida, late 19th century
Argillite
Diam: 12 7/8 in. (32.7 cm.)
Collection of John H. Hauberg

The renowned Haida artist, Charles Edenshaw, was one of the most prolific argillite carvers of all time, and he carried the art to a point of perfection seldom matched. Examples of almost every sort of object produced in argillite were made by Edenshaw—except for pipes. His model totem poles cover the full range of sizes, and he carved single figures of men and mythical beasts, chests, model houses, at least one ashtray, miniature cockleshells—and, of course, platters.

A favorite theme of Charles Edenshaw's was the story of Raven's creation of mankind (Hoover 1983: 62-67). The unpredictable culture-hero, trickster Yehl, the same one who opened the Box of Daylight to the world, created humans from a cockle. He then discovered that they were all male, and he set out to find the means of changing some to female. This incident in the Raven story was chosen by the artist for illustration in a series of at least three argillite platters, of which this is one. Each platter shows the same moment in the myth, in nearly the same composition, but they differ in detail and style, and so provide interesting comparisons bearing on the development of Edenshaw's art.

Here is Raven, part bird and part man, wearing a painted hat with prestige rings on top. His arms are human, but he has the bird's wings and legs. Behind him is his steersman, made by Raven out of a bracket fungus and rendered powerless by the supernatural power of the female genitalia that Raven is hunting. The canoe is magnificently decorated with formline figures and is divided into bow and stern designs and a central panel just as in a real canoe. In design and workmanship the platter is a model of perfection.

TOTEM POLES AND CARVED FIGURES

Totem poles are the universally recognized symbol of the Northwest Coast. Until the last half of the nineteenth century, though, the range of tall, fully carved exterior poles was limited to the country of the northern tribes. Their functions varied from one area to another and with each particular type of pole. Most were illustrations of myths or incidents in myths; they were raised as memorials to deceased noble persons or to commemorate the building of a house where they displayed the crests of the owner. Some carved posts, functional in a more practical sense, held up the massive roof beams of the great plank houses.

In the latter part of the nineteenth century Northwest Coast carvers took advantage of the fascination that totem poles had for visitors to the coast and began turning out models for sale. Some of these carvers were from tribes that had no tradition of carved poles; they invented new types or produced fanciful copies of familiar poles, often based on book and postcard illustrations. The technical and artistic quality of model poles made for sale ranges from abysmal to inspired. The model totem-pole industry continues to this day.

Carved figures other than totem poles were made in profusion and for various purposes. Some were made for native use in ceremonial drama or in shamans' work, while others represented Indians in traditional dress and were designed to appeal to the curiosity of non-Indian buyers.

189. ARGILLITE TOTEM POLE
Haida, late 19th century
Argillite
H: 18 7/8 in. (48 cm.); W: 3 in. (7.5 cm.);
D: 2 3/4 in. (7 cm.)
Collection of John H. Hauberg

Although Charles Edenshaw was born at Skidegate he spent much of his life at Massett where his uncle and predecessor Albert Edward Edenshaw lived. This fine argillite pole is very much like, in the upper figures at least, the frontal pole of Fort House at Massett. Although the same myths and legendary figures fill them, argillite poles were ordinarily not accurate models of the large wooden totem poles; seldom do they match in all respects.

At the top of the argillite pole a small bear climbs on the potlatch cylinders. Flanking them are two hatted faces, which are called the watchmen. At the base of the cylinder between the ears of a large bear that has an enormously extended tongue is an eagle's face. The bear may be a sea bear, as flippers appear along his sides, apparently pendant from his forelegs. Dr. Charles Newcombe, who collected the Fort House pole, identified its almost identical figure as the Bear Hunter (MacDonald 1983:152). The long tongue lays along the back of a small and exquisitely carved figure that seems to be a small bear. Newcombe identified the comparable figure as a sea dog. A seal is held transversely under the tongue.

The lower figures are very different from those on the Fort House frontal pole. On the argillite pole a large bear holds the tail of a fish with large head and round eyes, perhaps, judging by the spines over the eyes and nostrils, a sculpin. His flat tail and broad pectoral fins are scored with rays. As is characteristic of Edenshaw's model poles, each figure interrelates with those adjacent to it by means of grasping claws and overlapping limbs (Holm 1981:188-190). The hand of a master is evident in the perfect execution and control of form.

190. ARGILLITE TOTEM POLE
Haida, late 19th century
Argillite
H: 20 7/8 in. (53 cm.); W: 3 1/8 in. (8 cm.); D: 2 3/8 in. (6 cm.)
Collection of Bill and Marty Holm

Parts of two stories are illustrated in this large argillite pole by Charles Edenshaw. At the bottom a sea bear grasps and bites a smaller bear, a theme similar to that shown on the previous pole. On the large bear's head a beaver squats and holds, head down, a small beaver, who bites the tip of his tail, the joint of which is an eagle's face. These figures probably refer to the tale in which Raven, having heard that the beaver owned a lake full of salmon, played on the beaver's sympathies to take him, a poor orphan boy, into his home. When the beaver was away, Raven went to the lake, rolled it up with the fish in it and flew away, dribbling drops of water that became the rivers and lakes of the Haida country. Above the beaver's head, clutching his eyebrows with clawed feet, sits a strange figure. He has a human form, but wings droop from his arms and his powerful

beak with rounded, flaring nostrils bites the head of a salmon. His eyes peer out under heavy eyebrows. Perhaps this is man-Raven, enjoying the fruits of his deception. At the top of the pole perches Raven in bird form; in his beak he holds the stolen lake and its load of salmon.

Like many of Charles Edenshaw's model poles, this one is deeply carved, pierced and open between the legs and bodies of the intertwined figures. Innovative details, like the asymmetrical crossed hands of the man-Raven and the sinuous salmon he holds, characterize Edenshaw's carving. Compact, rounded formlines in the two-dimensional detail of wings, fins, and ears match similar sculptured forms in the faces and limbs of the figures (Holm 1982: 181-190).

191. ARGILLITE TOTEM POLE
Haida, late 19th century
Argillite, bone
H: 29 in. (73.7 cm.); W: 4 1/8 in. (10.5 cm.)
Private collection

Raven with his beak turned down tops this extremely large argillite pole by an unknown Haida master. There is a good possibility that it is the work of the artist who carved the spectacular interior house post of Easy to Enter House at Tanu (MacDonald 1983: pl. 112), since both the sculptural forms and the formline detail of the two poles are remarkably similar. Whoever the artist was, he was completely in control of the Haida sculptural tradition.

The figure below Raven is difficult to identify because of the strange combination of mammalian head and feathered wings. It may be Raven again in one of his manifestations; a small bird's head emerging from his abdomen might be a clue to his identity. Below him a fierce bear grabs a human, head down, with his long claws. A split killer whale wraps around the base of the pole. The whale's head, with a blowhole on the forehead, protrudes from the front of the pole and each side of the body—with flipper, dorsal fin, and tail—is carved on the sides.

This unknown master artist and Charles Edenshaw were Haida contemporaries who illustrated the same crests and stories in the same media and artistic tradition, but in very different, individual styles.

192. MODEL TOTEM POLE

Haida, late 19th century
Yew wood
**H: 35 in. (89 cm.); W: 4 1/2 in. (11.5
cm.); D: 4 1/2 in. (11.5 cm.)**
**Collection of Mr. and Mrs. Alan
Backstrom**

Haida model-makers were given a boost
by the World Columbian Exposition in
Chicago in 1893 when James Deans, a
collector and student of Northwest
Coast culture, commissioned a number
of them to make the complete village of
Skidegate in miniature. Most of these
model houses and totem poles were of
high quality. Anthropologists at the turn
of the century were also interested in
totem poles for more scholarly reasons,
and some of the best carvers, John Robson and Charles Edenshaw among
them, were commissioned to carve models of poles that had stood in their villages or that illustrated particular myths
or types of totem poles that intrigued
the anthropologists.

Edenshaw made many wooden mod-
els. This large model, carved of yew, is a
fine example. It appears to be slightly
earlier in style than his poles commissioned about 1900 by John Swanton for
the American Museum of Natural History (Swanton 1905). As in other
Edenshaw models, the figures are
carved deeply, in the round, with many
undercuts and some piercing, unlike the
monumental, full-sized poles of the
Haida. Full-sized poles typically
retained the essential cylindrical form of
the cedar log from which they were
carved.

At the top a little bear climbs out over
the head of an eagle who bites the tail of
a dragonfly, which is very reminiscent of
the insect on a bracelet by the same carver (cat. no. 216). The dragonfly holds
the eyelids of a large sea bear, from
whose mouth emerges a small whale, his
traditional food. Intertwined with the
sea bear's hind legs is a small bear with a
dorsal fin, probably its cub. At the base
of the pole a great humanoid thunderbird bites the tail of a small killer whale
that in turn holds the unfinished tail of
the thunderbird in his teeth. Each figure
in this complex composition of interlocking creatures is masterfully sculptured, and the formline details of wings,
flippers, and tails are arranged and
executed with great sensitivity and skill.
Edenshaw finished his carving with the
knife, rather than smoothing the surfaces with abrasives such as shark skin,
and the tiny facet of each final cut is visible and produces a vibrant, crisp
surface.

193. MODEL TOTEM POLE
Kwakiutl, late 19th century
Red cedar
**H: 31 3/4 in. (80.7 cm.); W: 4 1/2 in.
(11.5 cm.)**
Collection of Sylvia Duryee

Sculptural styles varied widely on the coast; this model pole from the northern Vancouver Island region illustrates very well a nineteenth century Kwakiutl approach in which figures were carved fully in the round and extended limbs were separated from bodies and even from the column itself by piercing. Kwakiutl artists were quite willing to cut deeply into the log and to add pieces—arms, wings, and beaks, for example—to increase the reach of the sculpture. Most large poles were more compact than this, but many included at least some figures attached to the column in the open style of this model.

The figure at the top, a woman nursing her child, resembles similar carvings made on several parts of the coast (see cat. no. 198) and is unusual on a model pole. The head on which she sits probably represents a sea monster like the Tseygis, a malevolent undersea creature resembling a giant bullhead. Under this monster's head is a wolf, carved in the round so that only his feet touch the planklike pole. His long tail is turned up along his back. At the base of the pole a grimacing man grips two of the tentacles of an octopus over his head. Each of these figures is rendered in a naturalistic, figurative manner that is characteristic of Kwakiutl sculpture of the nineteenth century. The colors are black, red, and blue—the red and blue, at least, acquired in trade. The red is vermilion, which was brought to the coast by fur traders in the earliest years of European contact. The blue paint is also an introduced pigment. It may be powdered ultramarine, which was supplied by trading companies all over North America in the mid-nineteenth century, or it may be a solid, ultramarine laundry bluing that has been a popular source of pigment for Northwest Coast artists for many years. An ink inscription on the back of the pole appears to read "Collected in North America July 4, 1811 by myself Jos(?) Thompson(?)," but the style is consistent with late nineteenth century Kwakiutl sculpture, and no other model poles are known from such an early date.

194. HOUSE POST
Kwakiutl, early 19th century
Red cedar
**H: 72 in. (183 cm.); W: 26 in. (66 cm.);
D: 9 7/8 in. (25 cm.)**
Collection of John H. Hauberg

The great plank houses of the Northwest Coast were constructed on frames of massive posts and beams. Kwakiutl houses generally were built with a roof frame consisting of relatively small, post-supported beams along the eaves and either one or two long, heavy beams spanning the length of the central part of the roof. Stout rafters were laid on these and, across them, poles on which long, split cedar boards were placed in overlapping rows. The posts that held up the central beams were often carved in the form of ancestral figures or mythical creatures with which the ancestor had had an adventure. These giant, looming figures, shadow-contoured in the firelight, enlivened the memory of lineage heroes. Only those who could recount such family tales and afford the heavy expense of the carving and the potlatch that validated them could display carved posts in their houses.

Captain D. F. Tozier, an officer of the Revenue Cutter Service (predecessor of the Coast Guard), collected the post in the Quatsino Sound area of northwestern Vancouver Island in 1910. Judging by its style, it was very old then; the weathered condition is deceptive since it can develop very quickly in that mold-rich environment. An unknown giant squats on the shoulders of a man's torso. Deep eye sockets with round, bulging orbs, a northwestern Vancouver Island stylistic feature, give the monster a fearsome stare. His tongue protrudes, touching a band crossing his chest that resembles a burden strap. The monster clutches the head of the man, whose trachea appears as a row of round spots carved in his neck. The post was, no doubt, once painted. The blackened surface may be the remains of a preservative coating that was applied to all the large carvings collected by Tozier.

195. RETAINING PLANK
Tlingit, Klukwan, early 19th century
Spruce
H: 26 in. (66 cm.); L: 50 in. (127 cm.);
D: 2 3/4 in. (7 cm.)
Collection of John and Grace Putnam

One of the many prerogatives that certain chiefs claimed was the right to excavate the center of the house and face the walls of the central pit with massive planks. In a very few houses of this kind the retaining planks were carved with figures. One of these was the famous Whale House at Klukwan. The Whale House was a treasury of artistic masterpieces, including a magnificent painted and carved screen and four house posts that are recognized as great achievements of Northwest Coast art. These clan treasures are still in the modern successor to the old Whale House in Klukwan.

When the old house still stood, it had a two-step excavation. Each of the retaining planks of the lower level was carved with the likeness of a humanoid figure—head in the center, legs and arms stretched to the sides. George Emmons, who visited the Whale House in 1885 and later wrote an illustrated report on it, was told that the figures represented "'Kee-war-kow' the highest heaven where those who were killed in war and died violent deaths went, and are seen at play in the Aurora Borealis" (Emmons 1916:22). Another explanation was that they were men warming themselves at the fire.

When the house was dismantled, the central faces were preserved and this is one of them. The face is surrounded by a formline ovoid of broad, angular form.

Carving on the face itself is typical of early nineteenth century Tlingit work, with convex forms, large eyes on smooth orbs, widely spaced, rounded nostrils, and a broad-lipped, toothed mouth. The surface of the spruce plank shows the pattern of closely and evenly spaced adze marks favored as a surface finish by Northwest Coast craftsmen.

196. POTLATCH FIGURE
Kwakiutl, late 19th century
Red cedar
H: 48 1/2 in. (123.3 cm.); W: 13 1/2 in.
(34.3 cm.); D: 9 1/4 in. (23.5 cm.)
Private collection

Northwest Coast sculpture, especially from the northern part of the coast, was for the most part a formal, intellectualized art. To the south, in the Kwakiutl country, sculpture was exuberant and expressionistic. Kwakiutl artists felt few of the restraints that their more northerly counterparts worked under and utilized in the production of their tensely structured art. Most northern sculpture has a timeless quality—the bear, or the raven, is there with his salmon or moon, he relates to other figures in the composition, and we know what he is up to if we know the story. In contrast, some Kwakiutl carvings, especially the figures of chiefs and their rivals, have a quality of immediacy and action.

The figures were commissioned by chiefs to represent a rival in a compromising situation, or themselves in a prestigious act such as breaking or displaying a copper. Either representation symbolized chiefs going to war against their rivals. The rivals were shown emaciated, suggesting their lack of wealth, or represented in a ridiculing caricature. This figure was called "Hawinayus" (or Going to War) by George Hunt when it was acquired at Fort Rupert in 1933. He identified it as the figure of a chief who had led a raid on the Salish to avenge the death of relatives who were lost at sea when returning from Victoria. The description matches the war described in detail in *Ethnology of the Kwakiutl* (Boas 1921:1363-81), and the chief was probably Nukapunkyim.

Originally the figure had an attached arm, which was probably raised in a gesture. The meaning of the distended belly is unknown. It may refer to the quantities of food, signifying wealth, available to the chief.

197. CARVED FIGURE
Westcoast, late 19th century
Yellow cedar
H: 21 in. (53.3 cm.); W: 3 in. (7.7 cm.);
D: 2 in. (5 cm.)
Collection of Jim and Marilyn Bergstrom

The purpose of this small carving is unknown, but it is a fine example of Westcoast sculpture at the turn of the century. The human face is closely related to masks from the same period and area (see cat. nos. 29, 30). It is similar to the work of a famous artist, Chiletus, whose painting and sculpture have been an inspiration recently for the new generation of Westcoast artists who are re-animating their art tradition.

The carving on this wandlike object is direct and subtle. It exhibits a traditional Westcoast face, deep from front to back, with large, round eyes and tapered lids shallowly modeled under long, angular brows. The nostrils are larger and more flaring than most, but their form, long and slanting down to the rear, is perfectly typical. The little bear, clutching a plaque on which is painted a simple face, recalls Chiletus' work.

198. CARVED FIGURE
Westcoast, late 19th century
Alder, yellow cedar bark
H: 14 1/8 in. (36 cm.); W: 6 1/4 in.
(16 cm.)
Collection of Jerrie and Anne
Vander Houwen

When Captain Cook's ships left Nootka Sound in 1778 there were on board, among the masks, blankets, and weapons collected from the native inhabitants, small figures of mothers and children—at least one of them represented in its cradle. A century and a quarter later Westcoast carvers were still making similar figures for sale to tourists and collectors. This little Westcoast lady, nursing her child, is the equivalent of the turn-of-the-century Haida argillite figure groups: representations of native customs and concepts of the past made for the curio trade. The Westcoast artist who carved the mother and child made many others like her, and a few of them have survived.

Although no longer in use by the women of the Westcoast tribes, the cradle, the dress of yellow cedar bark, the robe, and the kilt, and the face painting, were close enough in time that the artist was able to reproduce them. It is very possible that the cedar bark work was done by a woman. The vermilion paint in the part of the hair and delicate dots under the eyes is probably an accurate rendition of an earlier style. Tiny metal rings pierce the lobes of the mother's ears. A similar figure, probably by the same artist, has earrings made of bird quills, imitating dentalium shells. That figure wears a robe of fur rather than of shredded and twined cedar bark like this one.

SHAMANS' OBJECTS

The supernatural powers available to Tlingit shamans took the form of spirits of animals and humans, often those of dead Tlingits. They were represented in masks, carved amulets, paintings on robes, aprons, and drums, and as figures ranging in size from four or five inches high to larger than life. These figures were used in various ways. Small ones may have been handled in much the same way as the bone and ivory amulets brought in contact with a patient to vanquish the malevolent power responsible for illness. Larger figures were used as a shaman's grave guards, protecting his body in death from the negative forces he opposed in life.

199. SHAMAN'S FIGURE
Tlingit, Sitka, mid-19th century
Yellow cedar, human hair
H: 14 1/2 in. (37 cm.); W: 4 in. (10 cm.);
D: 3 in. (7.5 cm.)
Collection of John H. Hauberg

Collected in Sitka at the time of the transfer of Alaska from Russian administration in 1869, this little shaman's figure probably represents a spirit of a Tlingit carrying a club to fight the shaman's supernatural enemies. The peculiar form of the mouth is like that identified by George Emmons as representing an angry spirit or a spirit singing. The carving and painting are rough, as are many shaman's articles. There is good reason to believe that many of these objects were made by the shamans themselves, rather than by professional artists. The power of the figure, mask, or amulet was not dependent on the perfection of the object. On the other hand, there are many exquisitely carved shaman's figures and other paraphernalia. Aldona Jonaitis' essay (p. 129) offers another view on the possible significance of the quality of craftsmanship in Tlingit shamans' art.

200. SHAMAN'S FIGURE
Tlingit, early 19th century
Red cedar, human hair
H: 7 1/4 in. (18.5 cm.); W: 2 in. (5 cm.);
D: 1 1/2 in. (3.7 cm.)
Private collection

A tiny shaman's figure, expertly and sensitively carved, stands with a hand raised as if holding some object. There are a number of similar little figures in collections, some of them equipped with complete outfits of apron, robe, headdresses, masks, rattles, and weapons. George Emmons collected several of them and believed them to be dolls made for boys' play, meant to teach them something of a shaman's work. They are so finely made and complete, with accurately carved miniature masks, that it seems unlikely that they were simply playthings.

The face of this figure is very well carved. Naturalistically modeled features are only slightly stylized in form. Traces of dark blue paint in the eye sockets and in abstract patterns on the forehead and cheeks remain. Following the typical form, the body and limbs are red, the hands and feet natural.

201. AMULETS
Tlingit, 19th century
Bone, stone, leather
Diam: (largest) (irreg.) 2 1/2 in. (6.3 cm.)
Collection of Dr. and Mrs. Allan Lobb

Shamans of the northern tribes used amulets attached to their robes and aprons, or hung around their necks, to concentrate power on their patients. Many materials were used, but bone, antler, and ivory were the favorites. Two of these amulets appear to be of whale bone, and the third is of stone, perhaps argillite. It is possible, although by no means certain, that the black stone beast's head is a fragment of a Haida pipe, drilled for suspension and well worn from its use as an amulet and perhaps a scratcher. On many parts of the Northwest Coast, people in critical life phases or in certain occupations that required spiritual cleanliness for success avoided scratching their heads or their bodies with their fingernails, and instead used rubbing or scratching stones similar to this one. That use would account for the very rounded, worn surface.

The other two amulets of bone are interesting because of their rough, expressive carving. Although they clearly relate to classic Northwest Coast art in their use of eyes with pointed lids, U and ovoid forms, and lipped, toothed mouths, the ordinary rules of flat design are ignored. Again, the explanation could be in the relative unimportance of fine workmanship on objects associated with supernatural power—in deliberate opposition to secular standards of art— or in the artistic naiveté of the shaman-carver.

202. SOUL CATCHER
Tsimshian (?), 19th century
Bone, abalone shell, leather
H: 1 3/4 in. (4.5 cm.); L: 7 1/2 in. (19 cm.); D: 1 1/8 in. (3 cm.)
Collection of John and Grace Putnam

In spectacular contrast to the simple whalebone amulets, the bone soul catchers of the Tsimshian shamans make full use of the conventions of the northern design system and fine craftsmanship. This specialized amulet always follows a certain form: a hollow bone tube slightly flaring toward the ends, which is cut out to silhouette the open mouth of a beast's head at each end and engraved with formlines to delineate the features of the beings represented. Many are also inlaid in the teeth, eyes, and other details with abalone shell. Bone soul catchers are hung on buckskin neck thongs.

The figure represented on the soul catcher has mistakenly been called Sisiutl because of the open-mouthed head at each end; this term refers to a specific Kwakiutl supernatural creature that is certainly not represented here. This is some other beast—whale, wolf, or bear. Interestingly the designs, although symmetrical from end to end, are almost never the same on both sides. This soul catcher is almost perfectly plain on the reverse. On the designed side, however, it shows an expert's hand, with perfectly formed ovoids and U complexes forming the features of the heads and flippers. They surround a broad human face, very similar in proportion and form to that on the retaining plank of the Klukwan Whale House (cat. no. 195).

203. SOUL CATCHER
Tsimshian, 19th century
Bone, abalone shell, buckskin
H: 1 3/4 in. (4.2 cm.); L: 7 5/8 in. (19.5 cm.); D: 1 1/8 in. (3 cm.)
Collection of John H. Hauberg

The attribution to the Tsimshian for these two soul catchers is based primarily on the fact that most very well documented examples were collected from that tribe, and information on them comes almost exclusively from the Tsimshian. Stylistically they follow the system of two-dimensional design used by artists of all the northern tribes. The similarity of form in the many soul catchers in collections is remarkable. Judging by the extreme wear of the hard, bone surface and their deep color, some of them are very old. There are also many bone amulets made of fragments of older soul catchers. This one probably dates to the 1860s, and is a beautiful example of northern art executed in bone. The full-cheeked little man pressed between the jaws and ears of the two wolflike creatures wraps around under the bone cylinder, his legs and feet appear on the other side.

Soul catchers were said to have been used by shamans in capturing and retrieving the soul of a person whose illness could be attributed to its loss or theft. The soul would be caught in the bone tube and stoppered there for its return. Descriptions are meager and contradictory, suggesting that there may be much more to their use than the term soul catcher conveys.

SEATED HUMAN FIGURE BOWLS

Up the Fraser River to the interior of British Columbia, on the mainland and islands around Georgia Strait, and in the northern Puget Sound basin, mysterious stone bowls have been found and over the years come to be recognized and referred to as "seated human figure bowls." They are mysterious because we have a very superficial and imperfect understanding of what they were and how they were used, and some of them display characteristics of form that are unexpected in work from their area and time.

The common term describes their form: a more or less defined human figure, seated with a shallow bowl between its legs. Many also have another face or animal carved on the front side of the bowl, and a long headdress, often resembling a snake, frequently hangs down the back of the figure. Most also have a hole or knob on the top of the head which could be used for a suspension cord. They vary in quality of carving from extremely crude to very refined.

204. SEATED HUMAN FIGURE BOWL
Salish, precontact
Soapstone
H: 14 3/4 in. (37.5 cm.); W: 4 3/8 in. (11 cm.); D: 7 1/4 in. (18.5 cm.)
Collection of John H. Hauberg

This example, found below the surface of the ground at North Saanich on Vancouver Island, is made of soapstone, the most common material for seated human figure bowls. It is quite large. According to Wilson Duff (1956:49), the figures range from small in the interior to large on Vancouver Island. This one is noteworthy for its boldly carved head with large, round eyes and pointed eyelids. The modeled cheeks, the orb of the eye, and the wide mouth with heavy lips and exposed teeth are all features that are uncommon, if present at all, in historic wood sculpture on southern Vancouver Island. This anomaly of sculptural characteristics that seem more

northern than Salish cannot be explained on the basis of our present knowledge.

Equally mystifying is the small bowl depression and its possible use. Ethnographic accounts (Duff 1956:55-59) are contradictory, but at least two suggest that the bowls were used in purification ceremonies connected with female puberty rites. Other native accounts suggest the bowls held water into which a shaman gazed to prophesy or to see distant places. There is no doubt that they were powerful shamans' objects.

205. SEATED HUMAN FIGURE BOWL
Salish, precontact
Stone
H: 11 in. (28 cm.); W: 5 7/8 in. (15 cm.);
D: 5 1/2 in. (14 cm.)
Collection of John and Grace Putnam

A very different version of the seated human figure bowl is made of a coarse sandstone, rather than the fine-grained soapstone that allows crisp lines and smooth surface. The bowl illustrates the basic formal characteristics but with very little detail. The arms, however, are carved in high relief, and shallow indentations define the fingers. Even this very simple carving has facial characteristics unlike later Salish sculpture from its area, which is thought to be from near the Washington-British Columbia border.

206. SEATED HUMAN FIGURE BOWL
Salish, precontact
Vesicular lava
H: 15 1/2 in. (39.3 cm.); W: 12 in. (30.5 cm.); D: 9 in. (22.7 cm.)
Collection of Dr. and Mrs. Allan Lobb

Another large seated human figure bowl was found on Shaw Island in the San Juan Islands. The material is a vesicular lava, the third most common material for the bowls. Although it does not allow the refinement possible with soapstone, bold, dramatic sculpture is possible. All three materials—soapstone, sandstone and lava—were worked in much the same manner. A suitable boulder was shaped by pecking, or striking, the boulder with a hard pebble to pulverize the surface. All of these materials are quite soft, so the pecking technique works well. Further refinements were made by sawing and scraping with stone blades, and the final finish, at least on soapstone, was achieved by grinding with abrasive stones.

Again the sculptural form of the face in this example is very different from historic Salish work. The strongly modeled features stand out from a headdress that appears to be made of reptiles' heads. The arms are wrapped around the bowl and the legs are drawn up, knees bent, along the under slope. A round face fills the space between hands and feet.

SILVER

Metal ornaments for personal adornment have a long history of use on the Northwest Coast. Copper was the precious metal of prehistory. Plaques beaten from nuggets of native copper were worn as ear and nose ornaments or rolled into tubes and used as beads. Even bracelets and anklets were made of tightly rolled copper bent into a C shape. Some of these were complex, consisting of several small, rolled rods twisted together or wrapped spirally around a rolled core. When commercial copper wire came to the coast it was used just as the rolled rods had been for bracelets. Copper and brass wire bracelets became a standard medium of potlatch payments among the nineteenth century Kwakiutl.

Ornaments of other materials figure in the ancestry of the engraved silver bracelet. Tlingit shamans wore arm rings of flat strips of antler engraved with geometric designs and bent into ring shapes. Straight lines and rows of incised triangles suggest a non-Tlingit origin for these bracelets. They are almost identical to U shaped Eskimo bucket handles bent into closed rings. Bracelets formed of strips of mountain-goat horn were worn throughout the range of that animal. Prior to the advent of engraved silver the most elaborately embellished bracelets of the Northwest Coast were those of carved goat horn made by artists of the Georgia Strait Salish (Feder 1983: 54,55; Vaughan & Holm 1982:156). Although they came from a region far to the south of the silver bracelet's place of origin, they exhibit features that later appear as characteristics in silver: elaborate, all-over engraved patterns, end-tapered configuration, crowned surface, and integral clasp. It is quite possible that they influenced the silver bracelet even though none are documented as having been collected on the northern coast.

Tlingit and Haida artists demonstrated virtuoso engraving technique on copper and iron, especially on dagger pommels, in the early nineteenth century (Vaughan & Holm 1982:64-72). The transfer of these perfected techniques to silver required only the introduction of that metal in the handy form of coins, as described by Nancy Harris (see essay, p. 132). From that time on, silver and gold became the engraver's media of choice, almost completely superceding iron, goat horn, and antler, and leaving copper a poor third.

Bracelets, brooches, and earrings of coin metal were fashioned primarily for wear by native women, although a substantial portion of the production went to non-Indian buyers. Great numbers of bracelets were distributed as payment in late nineteenth and early twentieth century potlatches, as confirmed by George Hunt's record of the payment of 260 silver and 20 gold bracelets in a Kwakiutl potlatch (Boas 1921:1351). Engraved silver and gold have taken a proportionally more important role in Northwest Coast artists' production since the recent florescence of the art tradition. Any large, social gathering on the northern coast will bring out a dazzling and sumptuous display of gold and silver—old heirloom treasures as well as modern masterpieces rivaling their predecessors in quality of design, craftsmanship, and in the lustre of white silver and deep yellow coin gold.

207. SILVER BRACELET
Northern coast, 19th century
Silver
Diam: 2 1/4 in. (5.7 cm.); H: 1 in.
(2.5 cm.)
Collection of Delbert L. Brink

Even though there had been an earlier tradition on the northern coast of engraving copper and iron with totemic figures, many of the earliest examples of decorated silverwork show intrusive designs derived directly from eighteenth and early nineteenth century European engraving conventions. Whether these patterns of stylized scrolls and leaflike sprays were merely copied from examples seen by native engravers or actually taught by European tradesmen is not clear. The technical details of European, Euro-American, or native Northwest Coast foliate scroll engraving are so similar it seems possible, if not plausible that these patterns were learned from European tradesmen.

This expertly fashioned silver bracelet is a fine example of early floral engraving. Beveling, lining, and shading exactly reproduce the details of scroll engraving on early nineteenth century silver and related decoration, such as that on firearms. The "rococo scroll" engraving on the brass and silver inlays of early eastern American rifles represents another, very similar "folk" adaptation of formal European engraving style.

208. SILVER BRACELET
Haida, 19th century
Silver
Diam: 2 3/4 in. (6.8 cm.); H: 1 3/4 in.
(4.1 cm.)
Collection of Delbert L. Brink

The eagle as a motif was popular with engravers everywhere. The emblematic American eagle came to the Northwest Coast on coins, military insignia, ships' carvings, and engraved documents very early in the historic period, and native artists quickly adopted the motif (cat. no. 186). This expertly executed American eagle—with defiant thrust of beak and arrogant glance and shield, arrows, and olive branch proudly displayed—is one of the finest examples of this type. Classic foliate scrolls, with flawless curves and spirals deeply cut, flank the eagle's cartouche.

This bracelet is of heavy gauge silver, probably hammered from an ingot cast of melted coins in a wooden or stone mold. Many bracelets were hammered from whole coins, but they are usually thinner and show creases and overlaps on the inner side—the result of folding and refolding the silver to achieve the proper shape. A cross-hatched background, while not unique to the Northwest Coast, was the usual choice of Indian engravers and was very uncommon on the European prototype.

209. SILVER BRACELET
Tlingit (?), late 19th century
Diam: 2 3/8 in. (6 cm.); H: 1 1/2 in.
(3.8 cm.)
Collection of Delbert L. Brink

The eagle has become more Indian in this northern bracelet, perhaps Tlingit in origin. The native ideal of two-dimensional design, figures fitted to space, avoidance of overlaps, and flat diagramatic representation of the features prevails, but European scrolls still swirl from the bird's head and wings.

The design is a combination of stylized naturalism with formline details of wing joints and features of the heads. Implicit formlines defining the eye and shoulder are narrow and rounded. The engraving technique on this bracelet is of high quality, but is not so clean and bold as that on the previous eagle and scroll bracelet.

210. SILVER BRACELET
Tlingit, late 19th century
Silver
Diam: 2 3/4 in. (6.8 cm.); H: 1 1/2 in.
(3.9 cm.)
Collection of Delbert L. Brink

211. SILVER BRACELET
Haida, late 19th century
Silver
Diam: 2 1/4 in. (5.7 cm.); H: 1 1/2 in.
(3.8 cm.)
Collection of Delbert L. Brink

212. SILVER BRACELET
Haida, early 20th century
Silver
Diam: 2 1/4 in. (5.7 cm.); H: 1 3/8 in.
(3.5 cm.)
Collection of Jim and Marilyn Bergstrom

Tlingit artists of the late nineteenth century often rendered the creatures of crest art as silhouetted figures. Rather than constructing the animal of interconnected formline patterns, their salient features were detailed with formline elements, such as the ovoid joints of flipper and tail. This stout killer whale is an excellent example of this style. The configuration is unusual, but not unique, with the two halves of the split whale joined at the tail, and the heads coming together on each side of the double-hook clasp. Sure, bold engraving delineates the various parts: the broad pectoral fin with its clawlike divisions, the downturned dorsal fin, and the spread flukes. Ovoid joints and eyes are absolutely uniform in their rounded, arched form—an indication of an artist whose style is mature and individualized.

Asymmetrical designs are very unusual on classic northern bracelets. This Haida artist chose to depict a thunderbird in an intensely active composition of formline complexes sweeping around the bracelet from one end to the other. Most Haida flat design of the late nineteenth century is reserved and steady, with calmly symmetrical creatures whose formline structures are based on a few solid, slightly diverging curves. Here the joints and feathers shoot off at wild angles, but always eventually accommodate the formlines they join.

The U forms taper strongly and together with the broad arch of the ovoids mark an individual artist's style. He might be John Cross, as the work resembles later, signed work by that Haida artist. The background and some of the tertiary areas are hatched in single, diagonal lines. It is an integrated, energetic, and highly innovative example of Haida art.

Charles Edenshaw, the versatile Haida master, was probably the maker of this bracelet. From time to time, Edenshaw departed from his more characteristic, modeled engraving to produce silver objects of thin metal without beveling or hollowing in the tertiary areas and relieving slits. This choice probably stemmed from an economic motivation. A little silver goes a long way if the bracelet is thin and tapered, and that thinness precludes deep carving. It is also apparent that the thin, tapered bracelets attributed to Charles Edenshaw are simpler in detail and often less precise in execution than the heavier, more deeply carved examples.

The design shows a symmetrical, split raven joined at the back of the head, with the wings and body parts arranged in the tapered ends. Open rounded formlines are typical of Edenshaw's mature work. This bracelet was probably made in the late years of his career.

213. SILVER BRACELET
Haida, late 19th century
Silver
Diam: 2 1/2 in. (3 cm.); H: 1 3/16 in.
(6.4 cm.)
Collection of John H. Hauberg

This fine bracelet by Charles Edenshaw, although probably considerably earlier than the raven bracelet (cat. no. 212), shares many of its features. The bird, this one a thunderbird, tilts his head, split and joined at the back, to touch an elaborated shoulder joint with his hooked beak. Although of heavier silver, the background and tertiary area, except the eye sockets, are single-hatched like the raven bracelet. Charles Edenshaw's diagnostic formline shapes and complexes abound. The general composition is reserved, enlivened by the angled thrust of the bird's head.

Edenshaw often left the divisions between the bird's ears and jaws undefined, to balance the formline weight perhaps, and to give the viewer, and himself, the joy of recognizing the unstated form. The swelling juncture at the corner of the shoulder ovoid is another example of Edenshaw's frequent choice of the implicit relief.

214. SILVER BRACELET
Haida, late 19th century
Silver
Diam: 2 3/8 in. (6 cm.); H: 1 1/2 in.
(4 cm.)
Collection of Jerrie and Anne
Vander Houwen

The earliest of these Edenshaw bracelets, if our understanding of the characteristics and chronology of his work is correct, is an elaborate representation of a dogfish. The dogfish was one of the artist's crests and a favorite subject. Several other dogfish bracelets by him are known, as well as dogfish in works in wood, argillite, and painted on basketry.

The complexity and relative angularity of the design suggests an early date for the dogfish bracelet, perhaps sometime in the 1870s. Later works show a steadily increasing tendency toward rounder and more open formlines, more uniform scale of design complexes, and a general simplification. Even by the date of this bracelet, however, Edenshaw had settled on most of the identifying characteristics of his work. The "stacked U" complex, two of which are opposed next to the dogfish's head, is found on almost every Edenshaw piece of engraved silver or argillite. Double-line borders around cross-hatched areas are Edenshaw's signals, although other artists utilized this device as well.

215. SILVER BRACELET
Haida, late 19th century
Silver
Diam: 2 1/2 in. (6.3 cm.); H: 2 in. (5 cm.)
Collection of Mary Winters

Edenshaw utilized the format of the cartouche and flanking embellishments—as in the American eagle bracelet—in several examples of his unique narrative approach to art (see cat. no. 188). An aggressively posed monster encounters a frog in an oval field bordered by a ropelike molding used frequently by the artist in his argillite carvings. Although the creature, perhaps a bear, is constructed of traditional formline elements, he is shown configuratively, rather than as an overall pattern of ovoids, U forms and interconnecting formlines. The frog, also configurative, is even more naturalistic.

Flanking the cartouche is a pair of killer whales, very similar in form and detail to those on the painted hat (cat. no. 59).

This bracelet and the following one (cat. no. 216) were, according to family tradition, purchased directly from the artist by an officer of the Hudson's Bay Company at Massett for his daughter, the grandmother of the present owners.

216. SILVER BRACELET
Haida, late 19th century
Silver
Diam: 2 1/2 in. (6.3 cm.); H: 2 1/8 in.
(5.3 cm.)
Private collection

Edenshaw, at his most imaginative, designed this dragonfly bracelet. The double-winged, six-legged insect is a two-dimensional, split image of the sculptural dragonfly on Edenshaw's model totem pole (cat. no. 192). Wide, round eyes, with complex inner ovoids, stare out over a toothed mouth, the lower jaw of which is formed by the insect's front pair of legs. Large incisors suggest a beaver but all other attributes point to the identification as a dragonfly. Lacy wings, long, narrow body, three pairs of legs, and the round face between the eyes all match the features seen on other renditions of the insect (see cat. nos. 177, 192).

The unsurpassed technical skill of Charles Edenshaw at his best is apparent in this elegant and unique little bracelet.

217. SILVER SPOON
Haida, early 20th century
Silver
L: 4 1/2 in. (11 cm.); W: 1 in. (2.5 cm.)
Collection of Jerrie and Anne
Vander Houwen

Northwest Coast silversmiths began making silver spoons in the late years of the nineteenth century. Some of these were copies of European tableware, and it was possible in those years to order whole sets from enterprising engravers. All those attributed to Charles Edenshaw were made in the form of native wooden or horn spoons. Most of them have a bird-head finial, which was given a hollow, sculptural form. They are engraved on front and back with highly abstracted bird and animal figures. Since they are thin, the artist followed his custom and shaded the ordinarily hollowed details of the design with closely spaced parallel grooves, or single-hatching.

The inner bowl of the spoon is engraved with the head and foot of a bird—eagle or thunderbird. On the back, running down the handle from the raven's head finial, is a complex of U and ovoid formlines, representing another foot and a joint of the tail perhaps. It is uncertain whether these two designed areas are independent or related to one another.

218a,b. SILVER SPOONS
Haida, early 20th century
Silver
a: L: 4 3/4 in. (12 cm.): W: 1 in. (2.5 cm.)
b: L: 6 1/2 in. (16.5 cm.); W: 1 1/2 in. (3.7 cm.)
Collection of Jim and Marilyn
Bergstrom

Two Edenshaw spoons illustrate the long graceful form of native pattern spoons. They feature raven heads in three dimensional form and elaborate formline engraving inside and out. One represents a sea mammal, probably a sea lion (218a), while the other shows a variant of his familiar thunderbird. On the back of the thunderbird spoon (218b), an elaborate, two-finned killer whale swims, configured like his other whales (cat. nos. 59, 215) and replete with Edenshaw details. Single-hatching, double-line borders, rounded open formlines, and flowing composition are typical of the engraved designs of Edenshaw's late period.

BIBLIOGRAPHY

Boas, F. 1921 *Ethnology of the Kwakiutl*. 35th Annual Report of the Bureau of American Ethnology. Washington.

Curtis, E.S. 1915 *The North American Indian*, Vol. X. Norwood.

Duff, W. 1956 "Prehistoric Stone Sculpture of the Fraser River and Gulf of Georgia." *Anthropology in British Columbia*, No. 5. British Columbia Provincial Museum, Victoria.

1964 "Thoughts on the Nootka Canoe." *British Columbia Provincial Museum Annual Report*. Victoria.

Emmons, G.T. 1903 *The Basketry of the Tlingit*. Memoir of the American Museum of Natural History, Vol. III, Part II. Leiden.

1907 *The Chilkat Blanket*. Memoir of the American Museum of Natural History, Vol. III, Part IV. Leiden.

1916 *The Whale House of the Chilkat*. Anthropological Papers of the American Museum of Natural History, Vol. 19, Part 1. Cambridge.

Feder, N. 1977 "The Malaspina Collection." *American Indian Art* Magazine, Vol. 2, No. 3. Scottsdale.

1983 "Incised Relief Carving of the Halkomelem and Straits Salish." *American Indian Art Magazine*, Vol. 8, No. 2. Scottsdale.

Force, R. and M. Force 1968 *Art and Artifacts of the Eighteenth Century*. Bishop Museum, Honolulu.

Gessler, T. 1971 "A Stylistic Analysis of Twelve Haida Drawings." *SYESIS*, Vol. 4, 245-252. Victoria.

1981 *The Art of Nunstints*. Queen Charlotte Islands Museum Society.

Gunther, E. 1956 "The Social Disorganization of the Haida as Reflected in their Slate Carvings." *Davidson Journal of Anthropology*, Vol. II. University of Washington, Seattle.

Holm, B. 1965 *Northwest Coast Indian Art: An Analysis of Form*. University of Washington Press, Seattle.

1972 *Crooked Beak of Heaven*. University of Washington Press, Seattle.

1974 "Structure and Design. *Boxes and Bowls: Decorated Containers by Nineteenth Century Haida, Tlingit, Bella Bella, and Tsimshian Indian Artists*. Smithsonian Institution, Washington.

1975 "Some More Conumdrums in Northwest Coast Indian Art." Paper presented at the Symposium on Traditions and New Perspectives of Northwest Coast Art, Unversity of California, Los Angeles.

1981 "Will the Real Charles Edensaw Please Stand Up?" *The World is as Sharp as a Knife: An Anthology in Honour of Wilson Duff*. Victoria.

1982 "A Wooling Mantle Neatly Wrought: The Early Historic Record of Northwest Coast Pattern Twined Textiles, 1774-1850." *American Indian Art Magazine*, Vol. 8, No. 1. Scottsdale.

1983 *Smoky-Top: The Art and Times of Willie Seaweed*. University of Washington Press, Seattle.

Holm, B. and G. Quimby 1980 *Edward S. Curtis in the Land of the War Canoes: A Pioneer Cinematographer in the Pacific Northwest*. University of Washington Press, Seattle.

Holmberg, H.J. 1856 *Ethnograpische Skizzen uber die Volker des Russischen Amerika*. Helsingfors.

Hoover, A. 1983 "Charles Edensaw and the Creation of Human Beings." *American Indian Art Magazine*. Vol. 8, No. 3. Scottsdale.

Kaufmann, C. 1969 *Changes in Haida Argillite Carving, 1820-1910*. Ph.D. dissertation, University of California, Los Angeles.

MacDonald, G. 1983 *Haida Monumental Sculpture*. University of British Columbia Press, Vancouver.

Nordquist, D. and G.E. Nordquist 1983 *Twana Twined Basketry*. Acoma Books, Ramona, California.

Paul, F. 1944 *Spruce Root Basketry of the Alaskan Tlingit*. Lawrence.

Samuel, C. 1982 *The Chilkat Dancing Blanket*. Pacific Search Press, Seattle.

Stewart, H. 1977 *Indian Fishing: Early Methods on the Northwest Coast*. University of Washington Press, Seattle.

Sturtevant, W. 1974 *Boxes and Bowls: Decorated Containers by Nineteenth Century Haida, Tlingit, Bella Bella, and Tsimshian Artists*. Smithsonian Institution, Washington.

Suttles, W. 1982 "The Halkomelem Sxwayxwey." *American Indian Art Magazine*, Vol. 8, No. 1. Scottsdale.

Swanton, J. 1905 *Contributions to the Ethnology of the Haida*. Memoir of the American Museum of Natural History, Vol. 5, Part 1. Leiden.

Thompson, N. and C. Marr. 1980 "Twined Basketry of the Twana, Chehalis and Quinault." *American Indian Basketry*, Vol. 1, No. 3. Portland.

Vaughan, T. and B. Holm 1982 *Soft Gold: The Fur Trade and Cultural Exchange on the Northwest Coast of America*. Oregon Historical Society, Portland.

Whymper, F. 1869 *Travels in Alaska and on the Yukon*. Harper and Brothers, New York.

Wright, R. 1979 "Haida Argillite Ship Pipes." *American Indian Art Magazine*, Vol. 5, No. 1. Scottsdale.

1980 "Haida Argillite Pipes: The Influence of Clay Pipes." *American Indian Art Magazine*, Vol. 5, No. 4. Scottsdale.

STYLE AND MEANING IN THE SHAMANIC ART OF THE NORTHERN NORTHWEST COAST

Aldona Jonaitis

Dressed in ritual paraphernalia, the nineteenth century Haida, Tsimshian, or Tlingit shaman was quite impressive. The shaman covered his nakedness with a hide apron, carried a rattle, and wore on top of his long, unkempt hair a crown of claws, which pointed aggressively up towards the heavens like a circle of knives. Compared to the image of a nobleman, ceremonially clad in his finely wrought Chilkat blanket and abalone-inlaid headdress, the appearance of the shaman was particularly remarkable. But however wild his demeanor, the northern Northwest Coast shaman was a most significant member of his community, respected by all since only he could control the malevolent spirits that caused disease.

It is interesting to compare northern Northwest Coast shamanic art to secular art of the same area. In some cases, shamanic and secular art differ considerably. A dynamic and vital spirit figure (cat. no. 199) that looks nothing like a placid argillite carving of an aristocrat (cat. no. 182), and a strikingly crude necklace (cat. no. 201) that displays none of the elegance and precise detail of a secular silver bracelet (cat. no. 214) exemplify dramatic contrasts between shamanic and secular art. In other cases, however, shamanic art looks very much like its secular counterparts. For example, several of the stylistic conventions on the argillite figure and the silver bracelet appear also on the exquisitely refined ivory tubular shaman's charm (cat. no. 203). I propose that, in the northern Northwest Coast art, these similarities and differences operate in symbolically significant ways. To support this proposition, I will examine the formal qualities of the spirit figure, the necklace, and the hollow charm in greater depth, stressing their differences from, or similarities to, secular art.

The elegant silver bracelet, a superb example of Northwest Coast metalwork, depicts a crest animal in delicate relief with conventional design elements like ovoids and U forms that interconnect by

Cat. no. 214

Cat. no. 201

means of the swellings and narrowings of formlines. The sureness of carving, the subtle transitions between dark and light areas, the meticulous adherence to Northwest Coast design principles (Holm 1965) all testify to a masterwork of high quality and excellent craftsmanship. The difference between this bracelet and the necklace charms is striking. On the two light bone-pieces, we see a haphazardly arranged and unconnected incised patterns that only vaguely resemble proper ovoids and U forms. Although the darker charm is slightly more carefully carved, its large staring eye with narrow corners is a poor imitation of the conventional pinched-corner eye that appears on numerous zoomorphic and anthropomorphic beings, such as the squatting animal in high relief on the frontlet in cat. no. 5. It is difficult to believe that this frontlet, the silver bracelet, and the three unrefined charms were products of the same northern Northwest Coast culture.

The wooden carving of a spirit helper (cat. no. 199) displays both crudeness and emotional intensity, another quality of shamanic art. This figure's roughly incised fingers, rudely gouged-out

Cat. no. 199

mouth, and somewhat asymmetrically rendered legs all suggest that the artist worked quickly, in a slapdash fashion, seemingly heedless of the canons of form and detail. The wide-open mouth and eyes, wildly unkempt hair, crouching stance, and forcefully held club give this figure an intensely vital feeling as well as suggest the speed with which it was executed. How different is another anthropomorphic figure, an argillite carving of an elite man (cat. no. 182). The artist of this secular piece devoted much attention and time to details: the precisely rendered train of ermine pelts that hangs down the figure's back, the high-relief animal perched on his headdress, and the formline designs on his costume. The face is especially well done, with its carefully modeled mouth and nostrils, pinched-corner eyes, and high cheekbones covered by taut, glistening skin. The expressionless eyes that look straight ahead and pursed lips that barely smile convey a passivity that contrasts with the spirit figure's animation and energy.

Not all northern Northwest Coast sacred art, however, manifests the crudeness and energy of the necklace charms

Cat. no. 182

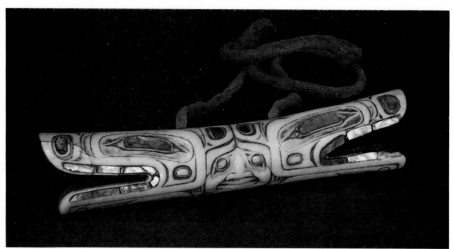

Cat. no. 203

and spirit figure. For example, the exquisitely controlled execution of the hollow ivory charm (cat. no. 203) with its conventionalized ovoids, U forms, pinched-corner eyes, formlines, and subtle transitions of plane in the central face results in an elegant carving.[1] The formal, symmetrical composition of two diverging profile faces flanking a frontal central face appears on other secular works like Chilkat blankets and creates a static image most unlike that of the dynamic spirit figure. In addition to refinement and restraint, this charm shares another element with secular art—the abalone inlay. This inlay usually appears on crest pieces, such as the rectangular frontlet, as an indication of great wealth and, by extension, social power. Unlike the necklace and spirit figure, this hollow charm displays significant similarities to secular art.

What is the explanation for the stylistic variations among these three examples of northern Northwest Coast art? Could it be simply that the artists who carved the necklace and spirit figure were unskilled whereas the one who made the hollow charm was a master? It is puzzling that in a culture that placed a

high premium on artistic excellence a man as powerful and important as a shaman would have been willing to wield articles so obviously inferior, unless that very artistic inferiority symbolized some significant aspect of his experience. The explanation I suggest for this range in style interprets what seem negative qualities—crudeness, for example—as positive, and also makes sense of the systematic and regular appearance of secular elements in a sacred context.

Northern Northwest Coast shamans performed a variety of functions, such as controlling the weather, assuring success at war, communicating with those far off. But their most important service to their community was curing the sick. The Tlingit, Tsimshian, and Haida held various theories about the causes of illness, and analysis of those theories reveals a concept unifying them. The healthy person functioned in his or her social group according to certain principles that assured order and stability. When some malevolent supernatural, like a witch, imposed his will onto that structured world, a disorder manifested itself as illness (Levi-Strauss 1963; Douglas 1975). Since these creatures were beyond the control of ordinary people, the secular leaders had no authority over them. Only the shaman could expel these malevolent beings from his community and, by so doing, re-create social order.

The specific practices of these disease-producing supernaturals varied. Sometimes they magically projected invisible objects into their victims' bodies; sometimes they stole their victims' souls and deposited them in graveyards; sometimes they cast spells over their victims' hair or nail clippings,

shreds of discarded clothing, or bits of uneaten food. Curing illnesses demanded that the shaman resort to supernatural measures. During his healing rituals, the northern Northwest Coast shaman called his spirit assistants to his side by shaking rattles, beating drums, and manipulating objects such as charms and figures. Within moments, the whole house was populated with benevolent supernatural beings who obeyed the shaman's dictates. At times, simply singing, dancing, shaking rattles, and waving charms over his patient was enough to effect a cure. However, occasionally the shaman had to suck out the disease-causing object, retrieve the lost soul, or force the sorcerer to reveal the objects over which he had cast a spell. In the course of these rituals, the shaman often fell into a trance so that he could interact more directly with his benevolent spirit helpers as well as the malevolent supernaturals who were responsible for the sickness. As he attempted to bring these disease-inducing beings under his control and thus restore the order they had destroyed, the northern Northwest Coast shaman became an active member of the spiritual world.

There is a tested art historical strategy that directs us to examine the style of the art of a group if we wish to understand its beliefs and experiences (Shapiro 1962). Following this strategy, I propose that the stylistic qualities exemplified by the necklace, spirit figure, and hollow charm analyzed here express aspects of northern Northwest Coast shamanism. The crude and energetic artworks, so different from secular pieces, symbolize the Tsimshian, Haida, and Tlingit shaman's intimate association with the world of the spirits, while the formal, conventional objects connote the shaman's re-establishment of social stability after malevolent forces created disorder.

Many cultures envision the realm of the spiritual as a kind of reversal of the secular (Mauss 1972). In northern Northwest Coast art, the several manifestations of shamanic stylistic oppositions to profane standards—crudeness when elegance is the norm, slipshod workmanship when craftsmanship is valued, disregard for conventions when those conventions constitute the basis for crest art—can be interpreted as visual representations of the supernatural. Seen in this light, those shamanic artworks that are antithetical to artistic standards are not examples of "bad art," but instead visual symbols of the shaman's participation in the realm of the spirit[2]. When the shaman wished to indicate his sacred status during his curing rituals, he displayed to the community artworks that did not adhere, perhaps intentionally, to secular conventions of artistry.

The Tsimshian, Haida, and Tlingit shaman had ultimately to correct the disturbed condition of his group. Pieces that resemble secular counterparts, like the hollow charm, embody the order that is the desired result of the shaman's rituals. The visual vocabulary that symbolized social order was well developed among the northern Northwest Coast peoples, who frequently displayed crest artworks as indications of rank and status. For example, the conventionalized and quite formal rules of design can be considered analogous to the equally conventionalized and formal rules of social behavior that governed the interactions between the leaders. The passive, restrained quality of many secular artworks is rather like the similarly self-controlled, dignified behavior thought appropriate for the elite (Douglas 1973: 49-51). And, in a society where wealth was so often an indication of social worth, it is not surprising that certain expensive materials, such as abalone, symbolized high status. When the shaman wished to express order, what better way than to possess objects that borrowed stylistic symbols of such order from the world of the secular hierarchy?

Unfortunately, we can no longer meet Tlingit, Tsimshian, and Haida shamans and observe them practicing; we can only visit museums that display their rich and varied assortments of sacred paraphernalia. During these visits, we can appreciate the exquisite delicacy of certain shamanic artworks, the vivid expressionism of others, and the uncompromising roughness of yet others. We can, by studying the style of their art, arrive at a deeper understanding of what they experienced and how they accomplished the awesome responsibilities of safeguarding the welfare of their people.

BIBLIOGRAPHY

Holm, Bill. *Northwest Coast Indian Art: An Analysis of Form.* Seattle: University of Washington Press, 1965.

Douglas, Mary. "The Healing Rite," in *Implicit Meanings*, 142-152. Boston: Routledge & Kegen Paul Ltd., 1975.

_____. *Natural Symbols.* New York: Random House, 1973.

Levi-Strauss, Claude. "The Effectiveness of Symbols," in *Structural Anthropology*, 181-201. Garden City: Doubleday, 1963.

Mauss, Marcel. *A General Theory of Magic.* New York: W. W. Norton, 1972.

Shapiro, Meyer. "Style," in *Anthropology Today*, edited by Sol Tax, 278-303. Chicago: University of Chicago Press, 1962.

NOTES

1. Although this type of charm is sometimes referred to as a "soul catcher," there is no clear indication that such an object was always used to catch lost souls. And, while the image on this charm, with its profile animal heads flanking a central anthropomorphic head has at times been identified as a *sisiutl*, that double-headed serpent of Kwakiutl mythology does not seem to be an important mythic being on the northern Northwest Coast.

2. See Esther Pasztory, "Shamanism and North American Indian Art," in *Native North American Art History: Selected Readings*, edited by Zena P. Mathews and Aldona Jonaitis, (Palo Alto, Ca: Peek Publications, 1982), 7-30, for another interpretation of the crudeness of certain shamanic artworks which suggests that "process" and "perishability" are more important to shamanism than "display" and "permanence" (p. 9). She also theorizes that the refined examples of Northwest Coast shamanic art validate status (p. 12).

Aldona Jonaitis, associate professor in art history and chairman of the Department of Art at the State University of New York at Stony Brook, has lectured and published widely on Tlingit art.

REFLECTIONS ON NORTHWEST COAST SILVER

Nancy Harris

Silver was introduced to the natives of the Northwest Coast in 1774 by the Spaniards of the Perez expedition, the first explorers to visit the area. This new, glittering metal was not immediately appreciated by the Indians for two other metals, copper and iron, were already held in high esteem.

Adequate documentation now exists to support the theory that the natives of the region that stretches from the Columbia River to Yakutat Bay, Alaska, were familiar with copper and iron long before foreign visitors ever came to their wooded shores. But in the late eighteenth century, the time of their initial contact with Europeans, there was much speculation among the explorers and fur traders as to the origin of the metal ornaments, tools, and weapons possessed by the Indians.

The logbooks from the Spanish expedition led by Juan Perez in 1774 and from the 1778 English expedition under Captain Cook reveal that a variety of metal weapons and ornaments were being used by the Northwest Coast Indians when they were first visited by Europeans. Accounts from the Perez expedition (Crespi 1891; de la Pena 1891) describe an iron-tipped harpoon and copper and iron bracelets among the Haida Indians of Dall Island in southeast Alaska. Four years later, Captain Cook observed that "neatly made" nose ornaments of brass, iron, and copper were worn by the natives on the west coast of Vancouver Island. By the time Cook reached Prince William Sound, farther north in the Gulf of Alaska, he found so much metal was available that most native weapons already were tipped with it; only the largest pieces of iron were in demand. The Indians were not interested in copper at all, indicating that they already had plenty; Cook was unaware that he was in close proximity to the major source of native copper in the region.

This part of southeastern Alaska provided much of the native copper that was widely traded on the coast; of par-

ticular importance were the areas surrounding the Copper and Chitina rivers. The supply lines to this great natural resource were controlled by the Tlingit Indians and it was through their hands that copper filtered to the other tribes. It is not surprising, then, to find that some of the earliest European records describe native metalsmithing in the Tlingit area. But it is somewhat surprising that these accounts document the Indians' ability to work iron as well as copper. Archaeological evidence suggests, however, that native copper was the metal used first; the knowledge acquired from forging it apparently was adapted to iron later. Much of this prehistoric iron is presumed to have been salvaged from driftwood wreckage; the evidence for this theory is aptly summarized by T.A. Rickard (Rickard 1939). Rickard's hypothesis is given support by a variety of coastal oral traditions that have been preserved.

One of the earliest reports of the native smithing tradition was provided by Ismailov and Bocharov, two Russian adventurers who visited Yakutat Bay, Alaska, in 1788. They described long, sharp daggers that were forged on a stone anvil and were worn by all the native men: "Their blades had projections on one surface and furrows on the reverse side...." These same words could describe daggers that Edward Fast collected eighty years later which are now in the Peabody Museum at Harvard (illustrated in Holm and Vaughan 1982). An equally ancient example of a dagger is illustrated in this catalogue (cat. no. 167). It demonstrates metalsmithing techniques similar to those exhibited in the daggers Fast collected. The Russians also noted that the Indians made iron images resembling crows' heads with copper eyes, which they carried with them as amulets.

Further proof of native metalworking skill is seen in a Tlingit wooden frontlet collected by the Malaspina expedition of 1791. This object confirms what the written records merely suggest for it

displays elaborate copper additions executed in a rather sophisticated repoussé technique. The result is a three-dimensional effect that has great visual interest. This frontlet is currently in the collection of the Museo de America in Madrid (illustrated in Weber 1976).

These artifacts indicate that the Indians already had a considerable amount of skill and experience in working metal—even at these early dates. It is important to note that although their tools (such as stone hammers and anvils) were crude, their results were not.

It is examples like these that eventually put to rest the questionable hypothesis, put forth a hundred and fifty years later by Marius Barbeau and others, that the Tlingit learned their metalworking skills from the Russians. Barbeau was a Canadian anthropologist who wrote and published extensively on the Northwest Coast Indians during the 1930s and 1940s, and was the first serious scholar to consider Northwest Coast Indian silverwork as a major art form. However, his views as to the origin of these metalsmithing skills are somewhat paternalistic, colored, perhaps, by the remnants of a nineteenth century faith in the superiority of European culture. Wilson Duff, another Canadian anthropologist, wrote about the prejudices apparent in Barbeau's writings and the pitfalls inherent in using his material indiscriminately.

It seems that it was not necessary for the Tlingit Indians to learn metalsmithing from the Russians or anyone else. Also, a careful reading of Russian accounts from this period indicate that Tlingit-Russian relations were guarded and tense during the entire tenure of the Russians in Alaska. Distrust was the rule and open violence was commonplace. The Russians preferred the more passive Aleuts, whom they uprooted from the Aleutian Islands and imported to Sitka. They employed the Aleut men as hunters and laborers; the women bore their children. The Tlingit, on the other hand, were rarely allowed inside the fortified town of Sitka, much less encouraged to apprentice in its workshops.

The Tlingit themselves have a different explanation for the origin of metalsmithing; it is part of their oral history, which is preserved in a story that was first recorded before 1840 by Ivan Veniaminov, a famous Russian priest, then based at Sitka. Veniaminov's records state that the first blacksmith was a Chilkat woman who was named Shukasaka (or "half-man") presumably because of the superiority of her skill in working metal. Her knowledge won her, apparently, an almost divine reverence. An ancient dagger that tradition suggests may have been made by her is illustrated in cat. no. 166. This dagger was handed down from generation to generation within the same Tlingit family until it passed into a private collector's hands. The story of the dagger's origin had been as carefully preserved as the dagger itself. According to the story, the dagger was made by a woman from a meteorite long, long ago; the presumption is that the woman was the first Tlingit blacksmith. (In 1979, with the generous cooperation of the collector and of Boeing Technology Services, I had the metal in the dagger analyzed. It was not determined to be of meteoric iron. This fact, however, does not diminish the quality or antiquity of the object.)

Although attempts were probably made to keep the art of forging metal a secret within certain families, the knowledge was too valuable and too available generally to remain a family privilege for long. Therefore, when Northwest Coast Indian silverware is first mentioned in written records—by John Dunn in his writings published in 1845—it is documented in several locations.

Dunn was an employee of the Hudson's Bay Company. In 1836, he noted that the Tsimshian Indians made silver nose rings from dollars purchased from American traders. These Indians lived along the east side of Hecate Strait, which separates the Queen Charlotte Islands from the mainland of British Columbia. At the same time, he described Tongass (Tlingit) and Kaigani (Haida) women wearing silver rings through their noses and on their fingers, stating also that their dress resembled the women of the Nass River (Tsimshian). In addition, he observed that maidens from the latter group also wore silver lip pins thrust through their lower lips. Dunn was the first person to record that the Northwest Coast Indians were actually creating decorative objects from silver coins, although silver had arrived on the coast, in the form of coins and tableware along with the first Spanish expedition, some sixty years earlier.

When these new and curious silver objects first came to the Northwest Coast, they usually passed into Indian hands as random gifts rather than as formal trade goods. There was little demand among the natives to trade for curiosities that had no obvious function, but they were acceptable enough as presents and were used unmodified for decorations. These objets trouvés were documented as early as 1778 when Captain James Cook collected from Indians at Nootka Sound two silver spoons that were apparently of Spanish make. One had been drilled and was being worn around the neck as a pendant. A similar affectation was recorded in a watercolor by Sigismund Backstrom, which was probably painted in 1793 (illustrated in Vaughan & Holm 1982).

Coin jewelry was also in fashion about this time. In 1790, Manuel Quimper was near Esquimault Harbor (just off the Strait of San Juan de Fuca) when he encountered natives wearing earrings made from English, Portuguese, and Chinese coins. More than fifty years later, coins had become the primary source on the Northwest Coast for this new, precious metal, but, before then, demand was so slight that silver never was part of the ordinary cargo of fur-trading vessels. It was not until the fur trade became land-based and the Hudson's Bay Company was established in the Northwest that silver began to have an influence on the creative imagination of the Indian artist.

Historic accounts indicate that coins were the primary source for silver on all parts of the Northwest Coast in the nineteenth century, and linguistic evidence confirms that fact. The words for silver in the Tlingit, Haida, and Kwakiutl languages are all variations of the English word dollar. This helps to explain the lack of reference to Indian silverwork before the 1860s; before then a barter-style economy existed on the coast and coins of any kind were very scarce. Following the Fraser River gold rush in 1858, immigrants flooded north across the U.S.-Canadian border and in 1861 the Victoria Council responded to the acute need for currency by passing a law that made foreign coinage legal tender there. After that, Dr. Helmcken, an early resident of Victoria, reported, "Money was plentiful and payments were made in American coin" (Helmcken 1975). Coins were equally scarce in Alaska until 1867 when Alaska became part of the United States. Before that time, the Russian-American Company paid its employees in leather or paper scrip and in provisions.

It is also in this period of the 1860s that we find consistent references to Indian-made silver jewelry. They begin to appear in the reminiscences of the early pioneers. Two come from what is now southern British Columbia. One describes Indians near Hope making armlets and rings from large Mexican dollar pieces (Alison 1976). The other, written in Victoria in 1861, praises Indian artistry and states that a five dollar gold piece makes a chased ring and a half dollar provides enough silver for a chased and ornamented bracelet (Cracroft 1974).

The interest in this new art form spread rapidly and it was equally popular with both Indians and non-natives. This growth was fueled by a burgeoning tourist industry and the Indian artist was quick to see the economic benefits it offered. By 1890, every village of any size seemed to have its own resident smith and the best of these made regular pilgrimages to the main trade centers of Victoria, Sitka, and Port Simpson to sell their wares.

Although the Tlingit received most of the early accolades for their smithing abilities in copper and iron, it was the Haida who received most of the praise for their work in silver. Each group, however, produced outstanding individual artisans and together they were jointly responsible for most of the truly innovative work that was created in this new medium. Other tribal groups farther south also participated, but much of the work attributed to them seems to be later in date, of poorer quality, and derivative in style.

Various types of ornaments were produced by Indian smiths including rings, earrings, and bracelets. These were most in demand, but spoons and napkin rings were also popular. Elaborate oddities such as ceremonial feathers, hatbands, and Victorian hairpieces also exist, probably the result of private commissions. Most of these objects were enhanced with elaborate, engraved designs that were applied with a tool as simple as a sharpened file.

The most popular item was the silver bracelet, and it retains that popularity to this day. Although a few, general statements can be made about bracelet shapes and designs, no single characteristic can be considered ultimately diagnostic when making tribal attributions. The collecting location is often the only evidence considered by many museums today when they make attributions and, unfortunately, it is very untrustworthy for both the artist and the art were highly mobile. The most important factors for attribution are the thickness of the silver, the width and shape of the bracelet, and, of course, the engraved design on the surface. Generally speaking, Haida bracelets are heavy silver, deeply and crisply carved, and bear the purest examples of northern

Cat. no. 211

Cat. no. 212

formline design. Tlingit bracelets tend to have bands of even width, are lighter in weight, and often combine formline designs with naturalistic elements and Euro-American motifs. Southern-style bracelets from Vancouver Island typically have strongly tapered bands and bulging surfaces. The silver is thin and the engraving is, by necessity, shallow.

Prior to 1900, many early designs used to decorate bracelet surfaces reflected the acculturation process; Euro-American motifs were as freely used as the more traditional northern formline designs. The American eagle and elaborate floral forms were two of the more popular borrowed motifs. The eagle is a major crest of both the Tlingit and the Haida, and so its popularity is understandable. Floral patterns were equally appealing during the Victorian era, but it was sheer artistic inspiration that combined both into a new and harmonious design (cat. no. 208). The eagle's breast shield testifies to its American heritage as clearly as the crisp, deep carving suggests Haida workmanship.

Entirely floral bracelets were also common and the wider examples—¾″ or more—were usually consistent in composition. The best of the northern examples are distinguished by an even width and a symmetrical arrangement of foliate forms that flank a central, stylized motif (cat. no. 207).

Eagles were also portrayed in more traditional ways. Haida artists preferred the classic, northern formline system (cat. no. 211). Somewhat unusual in this particular example is the asymetrical nature of the design, for most early bracelets display a split image that is bilaterally symmetrical. ("Early" in this context implies anything produced before the modern revival of sil-

versmithing began in the 1950s.) This bracelet is probably the work of Haida artist John Cross since it follows the design principles credited to him by Bill Holm (Holm 1981).

Tlingit-style eagles are generally more realistic in concept than those of the Haida in spite of the rigid, rather heraldic pose they assume (cat. no. 209). There is an attempt to retain the bird's natural contour and this realism is enhanced by the attention given to the textural detail in the feathers. Yet, artistic shorthand is also employed as some features are emphasized and others eliminated altogether. The head, wings, and tail are usually the dominant elements and it is here that the formlines, often limited to the eye and the joint marks in the wings, are evident.

Tlingit whale designs are also very distinctive and easily recognizable (cat. no. 210). Their most obvious characteristic is the segmented, fingerlike flipper that reflects the actual skeletal structure beneath the skin. Another clue present is the broad, asymmetrical slash on the nose that is explained by the Tlingit origin myth of the "First Blackfish" (Garfield and Forrest 1961).[1]

During the nineteenth century, both native and non-native artists shared the conviction that the Haida displayed superior talent in silversmithing. One Haida artist, Charles Edenshaw, continues to receive considerable attention today and is generally acknowledged to be one of the great masters of this medium.

Edenshaw's style evolved over the fifty productive years of his career. A very fine example of his early style is the split-representation of a dogfish that unites to form one large common head in the center of the band (cat. no. 214).

Cat. no. 213

Cat. no. 215

Cat. no. 216

Cat. no. 217

His appreciation for curvilinear forms is already apparent in this early design although the ovoids in the joints demonstrate a blocky quality that is only associated with his developmental years. A split-thunderbird design is featured on what appears to be another early example of his work (cat. no. 213). This design contains ovoids that are almost identical in structure to those in the previous bracelet design. Somewhat unusual, however, is the rather irregular nature of the single-hatching in the ground areas. In fact, it is unusual for Edenshaw to use single-hatching on a bracelet with a symmetrical band such as this one.

All other known examples of single-hatched bracelets attributed to Edenshaw occur on tapered bands. Together, they form a group of bracelets that seem to fill all the requirements for Edenshaw attributions, but they create a class by themselves because of significant variations from the generally accepted standards for his work. Characteristics of this group include: a lighter gauge of silver, a stronger, more pronounced tapering in the band, a double-engraved line around the eye, and the use of single-hatching rather than cross-hatching in the ground areas. A classic example of this particular style is illustrated in cat. no. 212.[2] Undoubtedly, these designs were inspired by Edenshaw, but today scholars do not agree as to whether these objects were actually created by him or are copies of his work.

What has come to be known as Edenshaw's "classic style" had already reached full development by 1880. This we can document because the National Museum of Man in Ottawa collected a bracelet in 1879 that is representative of his fully mature compositions (VII B103a). Formlines are now less angular, junctures more fluid, and negative spaces are more carefully planned. Even the bracelet shape has changed in time from the symmetrical band of his early years. Now, it is wider in the center and tapers gently toward the clasp. Two final examples from his classic period were created about the same time and provide an interesting study in contrasts. One is configurative in style and so an attempt has been made to retain the relatively realistic contours of the creatures portrayed (cat. no. 215). In this case they appear to be a frog and some sort of sea monster, perhaps, judging by the dorsal fin on the animal's neck, the sea bear from Haida mythology. These central figures are flanked by a pair of killer whales. The scene is narrative in nature and although Edenshaw is famous for his narrative scenes on argillite platters, they are rare on bracelets. This design is one of only two known silver examples, and both are by Edenshaw.[3]

The remaining bracelet design is a magnificent split-image representation of a dragonfly which expands to fill the space available (cat. no. 216). It is elaborate in its detail and features the bulging, baroque eyes and lacy wings that are so characteristic of this creature. The large mouthful of teeth is more difficult to explain without the assistance of the artist himself.

Spoons were also favorite objects of his and he shaped them like older, traditional forms, originally made from wood or horn. Bird designs were popular for this particular shape of spoon with the handles often ending in a bird's head. Illustrated here is an eagle or thunderbird design engraved on the back of one bowl (cat. no. 217) and what could be a raven is on another. These spoons are typical of Edenshaw's best work, exemplifying how even in very confined circumstances his attention to detail was meticulous. A larger spoon allowed him the space for a more elaborate design and he took full advantage of it (cat. no. 218b). Here, he has compressed a thunderbird design in order to fit it onto the top of the handle and has displayed a double-finned killer whale across the back of the bowl. This double-finned whale is a specific Haida crest.

All of these designs, from the classic to the flamboyant, graphically illustrate the consummate skill of a master artisan at his peak. It is for us to marvel that this silversmithing tradition all began just fifty years before with a simple hammer, a sharpened file, and a silver coin.

NOTES

1. Two old and well documented examples of Tlingit whales that demonstrate these characteristics are on display in the Thomas Burke Memorial Washington State Museum. One is a war helmet (WSM 2452), the other a feast dish. (WSM 1-1779).
2. Another example is in the collection of the Glenbow Foundation in Calgary, Alberta, Canada. (AA597).
3. The other example is in the Portland Art Museum collection (PAM 56.13). It also features a sea bear in a narrative scene, and again, the main figure is flanked by killer whales.

BIBLIOGRAPHY

Allison, Susan. *A Pioneer Gentlewoman in British Columbia: The Recollections of Susan Allison*. Edited by *Margaret A. Ormsby*. Vancouver: University of British Columbia Press, 1976.

Barbeau, Marius. "Indian Silversmiths on the Pacific Coast." *Royal Society of Canada, Proceedings and Transactions* 23, series 3, section 2 (1939): 23-28.

_____. "Old Canadian Silver," *Canadian Geographical Journal* 23, no. 3 (1941):15-162.

_____. *Alaska Beckons*. Caldwell, Idaho: The Caxton Printers, Ltd., 1947.

Cook, James. *A Voyage to the Pacific Ocean . . .* Vol. 2. London: Strahan, 1783-84.

Coxe, William. *Account of the Russian Discoveries Between Asia and America*. London: Cabbell and Davies, 1804.

Cracroft, Sophia. *Lady Franklin Visits the Pacific Northwest*. Edited by Dorothy B. Smith. Victoria: Provincial Archives of British Columbia Memoir, No. XI, 1974.

Crespi, Fray Juan. "The Diary of Fray Juan Crespi." Edited and translated by George B. Griffin. *Historical Society of Southern California Publications*, Los Angeles: Franklin Printing Co., 1891.

de la Pena, Fray Thomas. "The Diary of Fray Tomas de la Pena." Edited and translated by George B. Griffin. *Historical Society of Southern California Publications*, Los Angeles: Franklin Printing Co., 1891.

de Laguna, Frederica. *Under Mount St. Elias: The History and Culture of the Yakutat Tlingit*. Smithsonian Contributions to Knowledge, Vol. 7. Washington, D.C: Smithsonian Institution Press, 1972.

Duff, Wilson. "Contributions of Maris Barbeau to West Coast Ethnology." *Anthropologica* 6, new series, no. 1 (1964).

Dunn, John. *The Oregon Territory and the British North American Fur Trade*. Philadelphia: G.B. Zieber and Co., 1845.

Emerson, Ralph. "Silver in the Art of the Northwest Coast." Unpublished paper, Department of Archaeology, University of Washington, n.d.

Garfield, Viola and Linn A. Forrest. *The Wolf and the Raven: Totem Poles of Southeastern Alaska*. Seattle: University of Washington Press, 1961.

Helmcken, John. *The Reminiscences of Doctor John Sebastian Helmcken*. Edited by Dorothy B. Smith. Vancouver: University of British Columbia Press, 1975.

Holm, Bill. *Northwest Coast Indian Art: An Analysis of Form*. Seattle: University of Washington Press, 1965.

_____. "Will the Real Charles Edenshaw Please Stand Up?" In *The World Is As Sharp As A Knife: An Anthology in Honour of Wilson Duff*, edited by Donald N. Abbott. Victoria: British Columbia Provincial Museum, 1981.

Khlebnikov, Kyrill T. *Colonial Russian America: Kyrill T. Khlebnikov's Reports, 1817-1832*. Edited and translated by Basil Dmytryshyn and E.A.P. Crownhart-Vaughan. Portland: Oregon Historical Society, 1976.

Minutes of the Council of Vancouver Island, 1851-1861, Victoria, B.C.: Archives of British Columbia, Memoir No. II, 1918.

Quimper, Manuel. A journal in *Spanish Explorations in the Strait of Juan de Fuca*, edited by H.R. Wagner, 77-136. Santa Ana, California: Fine Arts Press, 1933.

Rickard, T.A. "The Use of Iron and Copper by the Indians of British Columbia," *British Columbia Historical Quarterly* 3 (1939):25-50.

Tikhmenev, P.A. *A History of the Russian-American Company*. Edited and translated by Richard A. Pierce and Alton S. Donnelly. Seattle: University of Washington Press, 1978.

Vaughan, Thomas and Bill Holm. *Soft Gold: The Fur Trade and Cultural Exchange on the Northwest Coast of America*. Portland: Oregon Historical Society, 1982.

Veniaminova, Innokentii. "Notes on the Atka Aleuts and Koloshi," *Notes on the Islands of the Unalaska District, Part III*, translated by Edward J. Vajda. Unpublished translation, The Russian American Company, Saint Petersburg, 1840.

Weber, Michael. "Artifacts from the Northwest Coast." *El Palacio* (Museum of New Mexico) 82, no. 4 (1976):11-15.

Nancy Harris has completed extensive research on the silver work of the Northwest Coast Indians.

TLINGIT SPRUCE ROOT BASKETRY SINCE 1903
Peter L. Corey

Cat. no. 68

Cat. no. 64

Lt. George T. Emmons published his monograph "Basketry of the Tlingit" in 1903, and since that time it has remained the most authoritative work on the subject. His writing gives us a fairly clear idea of the history and technology of spruce root basketry among the Tlingit of Southeast Alaska up to that time. However, his work raises many questions, and it falls short of the whole period of "market" basketry that came after the publication of "Basketry of the Tlingit."

At the time his work was presented, Emmons had spent approximately twenty-five years in Alaska as an officer in the United States Navy, mostly in the southeastern panhandle. His avocational interests focused on the arts and crafts of the native peoples, particularly the Tlingit. He was a good observer and a careful field-worker; he left us an important body of knowledge about certain of these craft-arts. Like many researchers, he has been quoted and excerpted in later works until—through no fault of his own—he has become accepted as the foremost expert and most cited author on Tlingit spruce root basketry. Unfortunately for people interested in this area, no other field-worker in Southeast Alaska at that time recorded similar information; as a result, Emmons' work on various phases or types of spruce root basketry remains unsubstantiated.

The lack of substantiation is most apparent in the lieutenant's statements as to the uses of spoon rests or mats, eating dishes, and the various telescoping double-basket forms for shot, gunpowder, shaman's equipment, and tobacco or snuff baskets (cat. nos. 68, 69). Translations of Tlingit oral history frequently refer to the uses of basketry, but no descriptions are given. The people of today have little, or no, first-hand experience with either use or manufacture; the knowledge they have has been gathered from grandparents or parents.

Museum curators, dealers in baskets, and collectors have all used Emmons' work to attribute pieces that pass through their hands. Although use or wear patterns may give some indication as to the original purpose, new, unused, or overly cleaned baskets do not offer needed clues. Non-Tlingit use may also have obliterated original evidence or may give false indications.

The fad of collecting American Indian basketry around the turn of the century added interesting bits of information to the background of Tlingit spruce root basketry, information often at variance with Emmons' writing. Today, it is not uncommon to find fairly large baskets, decorated with bands of self-weave decoration immediately below their rims, identified as cooking baskets. Discoloration on the inside bottom of the basket is given as evidence of charring from stone boiling; yet with analysis these markings might prove to be berry or other food stains. Emmons states quite clearly that these are berry baskets from the Chilkat-Tlingit area. By 1903 he had seen and collected only one cooking basket, giving us a single example on which to base comparison in order to either substantiate or refute future attributions.

According to Emmons and his successors, the universality of design factors in all areas of Tlingit spruce root basketry productions makes it difficult to identify geographic areas of manufacture. The one exception they present is the lack of false embroidery among the Chilkat-Tlingit and the heavy use of self-weave design. Traditional marriage patterns among the Tlingit meant that the woman left her own group and moved to her husband's village, which caused the spread of design units. Trade among the Tlingits themselves further universalized the use of designs. In collection data associated with the baskets he collected—which can be found in major museums throughout the United States—Emmons often makes statements as to the area of origin. It would be interesting to know whether he based these observations on direct information given by the person from whom he secured the piece or by attribution. If origin was by attribution it is important to know his guidelines since they could indicate a rethinking of his previous information or new knowledge that is unrecorded.

By 1903 Southeast Alaska was a major destination for coastal tourist cruises. Many of the tourists were of the social class in which the basketry-collection craze had developed. Their desire for good inexpensive baskets bought directly from the Indians helped to precipitate a major change in Tlingit spruce root basketry.

The economics of the basketry trade very quickly became apparent to the weavers. Always recognized as astute in the ways of commerce, the Tlingit women realized that they were dealing with a largely unsophisticated market where production had become more important than traditionally dictated forms. When looked at over a fifty-year period, the change was major; despite inherent craft conservatism and areas of geographical isolation, changes took place at a rapid rate.

Basketry became less essential in Tlingit life as new items from outside were introduced that would better serve the same purpose. Rapid changes in social traditions made certain types of basketry less important or unnecessary. Cooking baskets were soon replaced by metal kettles and large storage baskets were supplanted by tin buckets or trunks. Fine ceremonial hats, never numerous, as well as shaman-related basketry items, were no longer made.

Basketry associated with berry gathering remained for a longer time. The two smaller sizes of berrying baskets (cat. nos. 63, 64) became, along with rattle lid baskets (cat. no. 67), the mainstay of the trade for many years.

Although the slightly flaring, cylindrical berry-basket forms began to shrink in size, the shape remained or was exaggerated. The "weave-in-between" bottoms became more common; rims and sides didn't need to be as sturdy, nor were proportions as necessary. The design band fields were narrowed. After a period of intense use of aniline dyed weft replacing the false embroidery background, the design elements were floated on the natural root background in single colors, either with or without single lines of border in false embroidery or dyed weft. The three band arrangement so common in earlier forms was soon reduced to two, with the middle design band dropped entirely.

The rattle lid basket was also affected by the trade. Like the berry-basket shape, it decreased in size; its diameter decreased more rapidly than the height producing a different shape. The weave-in-between became more common for the bottoms and the area hidden by the overlapping side of the lid. The amount of false embroidery was also reduced, as was the complexity of the design band until it too evolved into elements floating on a natural background.

Sometime in the early tourist basket market Chilkat blanketlike design elements were introduced. The scantily documented baskets with these designs indicate production mainly among the Chilkat-Tlingit or the Sitka-Tlingit, between whom there were traditionally strong marriage ties. The "blanket faces," killer whales, eagles, birds, fish, and other representative design elements were never produced in great quantity, and there was always a ready market for them.

Cat. no. 66

Many novelty forms were experimented with to entice the buyers. Basketry-covered bottles, three-legged pots, teakettles and cups, ginger jar forms (cat. no. 66), doll hats, napkin rings, boots, booties, and contemporary hats, among other things, passed in and out of vogue. Bail handles of spruce root were tried, but never became popular due to their frailty.

Many of these changes allowed savings in time and material. It was quicker to do the weave-in-between while conserving the amount of split outer weft strand used. Less false embroidery meant time saved in the collection, preparation, and weaving of the grass. Other methods used included open "eye hole" twining and simple cut-off warp rims. Thinner spruce roots are reported to have been gathered and split only once after the initial division in half, thereby producing only a weft and a warp with no discernible heartwood portion.

The buying public seems to have considered the finer weave reflected in the baskets of this late period more desirable. The refinement of the warp and weft was at the expense of strength, but these baskets were no longer working utensils. Instead, they served as conversation pieces or did light work as calling-card trays, flowerpot covers, or catchalls on someone's bureau.

During this time of experimentation, some weavers developed technologically superior baskets by combining traditionally divergent forms and methods of decoration. The use of self-weave and false embroidery on the same basket (cat. no. 64) created an interesting visual and textural impression when combined with fine, even weaving elements. Tradi-

tional weaving of the past shows few examples of such a combination.

The Depression and the Second World War combined to bring an end to quantity production of spruce root baskets among the Tlingit. Compulsory education meant that the girls no longer learned traditional skills, including basketry. In a period of reduced market there was no remunerative incentive for them to learn. It was the older women who continued to weave; younger weavers did not come along to replace them.

The changes that occurred were not universal. They were most heavily felt in Sitka, Juneau, and, to some extent, Yakutat. However, age, individual choice, and conservatism in these areas allowed for the production of more traditionally oriented baskets as well.

Today, among the Tlingit women of late middle age and older are a number who remember sitting with mothers, aunts, or grandmothers who wove baskets. Each of them knows bits and pieces of the complex technology involved, but only a very few know all the processes from start to finish. The combination of low financial return for labor involved, increasing inacessibility to raw materials, and failing health have led Tlingit weavers to another threshold for spruce root basketry.

BIBLIOGRAPHY

Emmons, George T. *The Basketry of the Tlingit.* Memoirs, vol. 3. New York: American Museum of Natural History, 1903.

Paul, Frances. *Spruce Root Basketry of the Alaska Tlingit.* United States Department of the Interior, Bureau of Indian Affairs. Lawrence, Kansas: Haskell Indian Junior College, 1944. Reprint. Sitka, Alaska: Sheldon Jackson Museum, 1982.

Shotridge, Louis. "Tlingit Woman's Root Basket." The Museum Journal (University of Pennsylvania) 11-12 (September 1921).

Acknowledgments to: Jania Garcia
Claude Ostyn

Peter L. Corey, director of the Sheldon Jackson Museum in Sitka, Alaska, has had a lifelong affection for Northwest Coast Indian basketry.

ANONYMOUS ATTRIBUTIONS: A TRIBUTE TO A MID-19th CENTURY HAIDA ARGILLITE PIPE CARVER, THE MASTER OF THE LONG FINGERS

Robin K. Wright

An exciting increase in our understanding of the carving styles of some late nineteenth century Haida artists has occurred in recent years, and the attribution of many of their previously anonymous carvings has become possible. Careful scholarship has isolated a few documented pieces by known artists, and by detailed comparisons other pieces have been attributed to them, revealing bodies of work by single artists; these include Charles Edenshaw (cat. nos. 59, 60, 188-192, 207-218), John Robson (cat. no. 183), John Cross, Tom Price (cat. nos. 57, 58, 184), Gwaitehl, and others for whom we must rely on descriptive names such as the Master of the Chicago Settee (Holm 1981). But what of their uncles and granduncles, the master artists of the early and mid-nineteenth century? They too had distinctive and individual carving styles that can be identified by careful study of the works of art produced by Haida artists before 1865.

Unfortunately we lack documented names to associate with these carvers. Early fur traders recorded some of the names of village chiefs and people with whom they traded, but there is no documented association between these names and carvings from this period. This was the generation that thrived on the increased wealth brought by the fur trade, before the devastating cultural changes brought by the smallpox epidemics of the 1860s and the arrival of missionaries in the 1870s and 1880s. There is no doubt that many of the names that were used by Haida people in the late nineteenth century belonged to their relatives in the early nineteenth century; but since nearly 90 percent of the Haida population had been eliminated by disease by the late nineteenth century, we can assume that many carvers' families perished with no one to carry on their names, crests, or carving styles. Even without the advantage of known names, however, the individuality of the master carvers of the early and mid-nineteenth century is

enough to make them stand out as unique personalities. Their carving styles are their signatures.

One of the objects most frequently carved by Haida artists between 1820 and 1865 was the argillite pipe (cat. nos. 176-180), a tobacco pipe made of a black carbonaceous shale (argillite), which came from a single quarry near the village of Skidegate on the Queen Charlotte Islands. This stone was first carved in large quantities in the early nineteenth century to make tobacco pipes and other objects that were traded to the maritime fur traders who visited the Queen Charlotte Islands and later to the land-based fur traders of the Hudson's Bay Company. While the earliest argillite pipes were functional in design and some even show evidence of having been smoked, they quickly evolved into an ornamental tourist art. They were not meant to be smoked (even though they were drilled with bowl and stem holes) and were sold as souvenirs to the visiting fur traders (Wright 1982).

Many of these pipes now reside in museum and private collections around the world and form an ideal body of work for a stylistic study. I have been privileged to study about 750 of the argillite pipes from the pre-1865 period. The grouping of these pipes into stylistic categories clearly reveals the work of individual artists as well as stylistic changes during the fifty-year period when the early argillite pipes were being carved. The earliest pipes display traditional Haida motifs, but after 1830 Haida artists began to carve Euro-American motifs in the form of ship pipes in argillite and wood (cat. no. 175). These are based on the appearances of the Euro-American seamen, their ships, and trappings, and later the houses and settlements of the fur trading posts and towns such as Fort Simpson, Sitka, and Victoria (Wright 1979). They also carved portraitlike Euro-American seamen figures (cat. no. 181) and large argillite platters with floral and geometric patterns inspired by imported

commercial glass and chinaware (cat. no. 185). In the 1840s and 1850s pipes based on commercial clay pipes were made, many with Euro-American portrait heads for bowls (cat. no. 174) and a variety of Euro-American figures on the stems (Wright 1980).

Because of the appearance of these Euro-American motifs in Haida carvings during the 1830s and their increased production in the 1840s and 1850s, this period of the mid-nineteenth century has come to be almost exclusively associated with these motifs; the continued production of carvings with traditional motifs has frequently been ignored. Carole Kaufmann (1969:127) labeled the 1830-1865 period the "Western Period," saying "During the years 1840-1860 there is an almost exclusive interest in depicting scenes and objects found in the Euro-American sailors' or settlers' world." Carol Sheehan (1981:80) called this same period "White Man's Non-sense," saying "Euro-Americans, their ships, goods and animals first supplemented and then replaced the Haida motifs on argillite pipes." On the contrary, my research indicates that Haida carvers did not stop carving pipes with traditional Haida motifs during this period: they merely added the new Euro-American motifs to their repertoire, sometimes combining the two types of designs on the same pipes, but more often retaining the purely Haida-motif pipe as a separate type. According to my statistics for the period prior to 1865, Haida-motif pipes slightly outnumber those with Euro-American motifs. Of a total of 750 pipes studied, 396 are Haida-motif pipes, 204 are ship pipes, and 150 are trade-type pipes, combining to 354 pipes with Euro-American motifs.

Even though the same artists were probably carving both types, it is difficult to make stylistic comparisons between Haida and Euro-American motif pipes unless the motifs are mixed. Both Haida motif and ship pipes evolved during the 1830s and 1840s

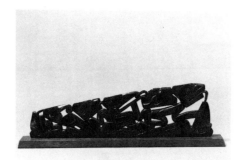

Cat. no. 178

Cat. no. 179

Cat. no. 180

from the early functional pipes with large bowls, thick cross sections, and manageable sizes into increasingly more elaborate designs with smaller bowls and thinner cross sections. Thus, at any one time, an argillite pipe carver could have roughed out a pipe blank in argillite and used it to carve either a Haida motif or a ship pipe. The early pipes were rounded and fully carved on the bottom surfaces and must be examined from all angles to see the complete designs (cat. nos. 176, 177). In later years, pipes were flattened with minimal carving on the bottom surfaces. They became highly pierced and very breakable, the longer sizes requiring two hands to hold them, making them far too unwieldy for any practical use.

In analyzing Haida-motif pipes, we have the advantage of the northern "formline" system of design that was used by the Haida carvers. This is a very formalized two-dimensional design system with rules and conventions that were carefully followed (Holm 1965). A formline is a bandlike element, always found on the plane surface of a carving, which swells and tapers, curves, and joins itself in a continuous grid that delineates the design. Formline design complexes on Haida pipes are found on the wings, flippers, tails, and ears of the figures and are made up of two major "primary" components, the "ovoid" with its floating "inner ovoid," and the "U form." Any formlines found on the plane surface within these primary components are called "secondary." The carved back or negative spaces are called "tertiary," and the thin lines on the plane surface that surround the tertiary spaces are called "tertiary lines." The facial structure also follows formline principles with ovoid eye sockets, U form nostrils, and bandlike formline lips.

Within this design system it is possible to recognize individual peculiarities in artists' styles precisely because the system is so strict. Several individual artists' styles are recognizable among the pipes I have been able to study. One of

these artists whom I have been calling the "Master of the Long Fingers," stands out as being very distinctive and perhaps the most stylistically consistent of them all. This artist's work is represented in eight Haida-motif argillite pipes, probably produced between 1840 and 1860, which are remarkably uniform in their use of the formline system. We are fortunate to have three of the eight pipes in the current exhibition, all from local private collections (cat. nos. 178, 179, 180). The other five pipes are in museum collections: the British Columbia Provincial Museum in Victoria (15686), the Lowie Museum of Anthropology, University of California, Berkeley (2-19085), the Glenbow Museum in Calgary (AA2005, illus. in Sheehan: 1981, pl. 8), the Peabody Museum of Archaeology and Ethnology (10997), and the Anthropological Museum of the University of Aberdeen, Scotland (995).

Of the eight pipes, only two have documentation that reaches back to the nineteenth century. The others were acquired through dealers or donated by people in the twentieth century and have no other documentation. The two exceptions are the Peabody Harvard pipe, which was colleted by Holmes Hinckley in 1875, and the Lowie Museum's pipe, which was part of the George Davidson Collection. Davidson was an English-born geographer and astronomer who joined the United States Coast and Geodetic Survey in 1845 and was chief of the Pacific Coast region from 1868 to 1895. He visited the northern Northwest Coast on two occasions during his lifetime, in 1867 and 1869, and probably collected the pipe during one of these trips. By association this documentation places the eight pipes before 1869. Stylistically all eight pipes fit within the period of the 1840s or 1850s, the period when Euro-American motifs were also being carved, but all eight pipes display only the traditional Haida motifs. By comparing the three pipes in the exhibition with the five other pipes attributed to the same artist, the identifying characteristics of the artist's work become clear.

The proportions of the pipes are similar to those of other argillite pipes from the same period, with long trapezoidal profiles rising in height from the stem to the bowl ends, thin depths, flat bottoms, and small bowls that are disguised in the heads of figures, often equal in diameter to the stem holes (0.4 cm.). While several of the eight pipes are fragmentary, the consistency of the artist is such that it is possible to estimate the probable total dimensions of the intact pipes. There are always either six or seven figures per pipe, and they are arranged in single file at the stem end and stacked at the bowl end so that up to three, but usually two, figures are piled one over the other. Cat. no. 178 is complete, but cat. no. 180 has been broken in half and the stem end, which probably had three figures, is missing. The

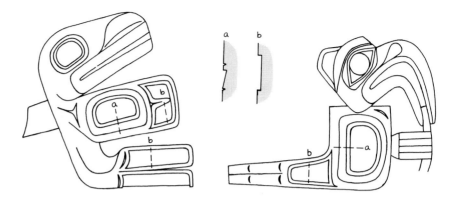

Fig. 1. Peabody Museum, Harvard, 10997

Fig. 2. Peabody Museum, Harvard, 10997

Fig. 3. British Columbia Provincial Museum, 15686

bird's head and the snout of the adjacent insect figure are missing on cat. no. 179.

The Master of the Long Fingers used a limited number of figure types in his repertoire. The identification of figures is a risky business, for only the artist himself could say for sure what he meant to represent. I will identify the figures on the pipes according to their most characteristic features, although my identifications may be questioned. Of the forty-five complete or identifiable figures on the eight pipes, fourteen are birds, five of which are ravens including one raven in human form; nine are humanoid figures, eight of which have U form or bearlike ears; eight are bearlike figures; five froglike figures appear, three of which have the addition of whalelike dorsal fins on their backs; four are whales, three with one dorsal fin, and one with two dorsal fins; and five are insectlike figures, four of which are found on the three pipes in the exhibition.

The insectlike figures are perhaps the most interesting of the figure types chosen by the Master of the Long Fingers. They all have long snouts that are either L shaped or spiral, and they may have either humanoid or winged bodies. Those with spiral noses are probably butterflies (cat. nos. 178, 180), and those with pointed L snouts may be mosquitoes (cat. no. 180). The dragonfly with a large head, segmented body, and double cross-hatched wings (a common figure on other argillite pipes—see cat. no. 177) is not found among the insect figures on this group of pipes.

The Master of the Long Fingers' style of carving formlines is unusual in that he deviated in certain ways from the conventions of formline design. These are the features that make his style stand out as the work of one artist. His formline ovoids and Us are consistently thin in width, having outer edges that are usually shaved off in favor of the square outer lines of the wings and fins, a feature that gives the formlines very

inconsistent widths (see figs. 1,2). This is an extremely distinctive feature since formline conventions dictate that the formline ovoids and Us should swell gradually and be thicker on the top and thinner on the bottom edges. The Master of the Long Fingers was very careful with the inner line of formline ovoids, but sacrificed the outer line to the overall profile of the limbs.

The formline U forms of the whales' tails and flippers, as well as U form ears, are so thin in depth that they have the appearance of tertiary lines rather than the formlines that they are. Another distinctive feature of the Master of the Long Fingers' style is that the thin formline U ears almost always have undeveloped secondary spaces (see figs. 2, 3). One exception is evident in cat. no. 178 which has a secondary double solid U complex with a tertiary line above in the middle raven's ear.

His tertiary lines are wide and are always cut completely around the outer edge separating them from adjacent

formlines. The tertiary space surrounding the inner ovoids is always beveled in toward the inner ovoid in a flat bevel, rather than being beveled out or curved (see figs. 1a, 2a). The tertiary spaces in the U forms are always cut back square and flat rather than being beveled or curved (see figs. 1b, 2b).

Each wing with feathers is handled as a formline U joining the joint ovoid (usually at a square or right angle to the ovoid) with one or two sets of stacked double solid U forms building off of the formline U with crescent reliefs at the base. These are usually quite long and thin and are squared off at the ends. The most distinctive feature of the Master of the Long Fingers' feathers is that the splitting line between the solid double U forms always cuts down into the formline U at the base, thus breaking the line of the formline U.

The Master of the Long Fingers used two basic inner ovoid shapes, one round, or nearly round, for the eye ovoids, and one more rectangular with sharp lower corners for the joint ovoids. The eye ovoids fill the eye socket area and have wide-open eyelid lines with points slightly below the center of the eye. There is always a carved line around the eye ovoid in addition to the eyelid line. The whites of the eyes slope gently back rather than being cut deeply back toward the eyelid lines. The tertiary space around the eyes is cut back toward the eyelid lines in a straight deep bevel.

The handling of the human heads in this group of pipes is also very distinctive. The heads are always bent back at either a 90° angle to the body, as we see in the three pipes in the exhibition, or bent completely back at an 180° angle, as in four of the other five pipes (see fig.

3). The eyebrows are broad and peaked in the middle, coming nearly to the top of the forehead, which is flat on top. peaked in the middle, coming nearly to the top of the forehead, which is flat on top.

All figures have wide bandlike lips, which is typical in Haida art, but the Master of the Long Fingers often curves the corners of the mouth slightly outward. On Long Fingers' eight pipes there are twenty-three extended tongues, but only five of these are held in the mouth of another figure. Fifteen of the twenty-three tongues are connected to the back of the head of the figure in front, and three touch the nose of the facing figure.

The Master of the Long Fingers didn't always carve fingers that are long, but on each pipe there is always at least one figure with extremely long fingers or claws. There are always four fingers that are either perfectly straight or bent in a long swooping curve (see fig. 3). The feet are consistently developed as simple blocklike elements with square heels, and the top of each foot slants down to the toe, which is either pointed or squared off depending on the surrounding space. It is interesting that this artist gives all figures that have feet the same type of humanoid blocklike feet, without the toes or claws one would expect to find on nonhuman feet.

Another distinctive feature of the Master of the Long Fingers' work is that there is always a carved line running from the hip to the small of the back, which makes a break in the hip line (see fig. 3). Whales' bodies always have a ridge where the planes of the belly and back come together (see fig. 1). In addition, the bottom of whales' tails as well as the bottoms of the end figures are always fully carved, while the rest of the bottom surfaces are left flat.

While no one of the stylistic features that I have described as being characteristic of this artist's work is unique to this artist or unknown on other pipes, the combination of all of them together is what defines the style of the artist and makes this group of pipes unique. I am convinced that the Master of the Long

Fingers must have carved more than eight argillite pipes, and it is probable that his other work is slightly different in style. But these eight pipes stand out as being uncommonly alike, representative of one crystalized stage in his work. There are many related pipes from the same period that are similar in many ways, but different in others. They may be by the same artist, or, more likely, by carvers who were working closely with him and knew his work. There are also many pipes from earlier periods that display many elements of the style of the Master of the Long Fingers, but have the fully carved bottom, larger bowl and thicker cross section of the 1820s and 1830s pipes. With more careful comparisons it may be possible to trace this and other pipe carvers' styles as they evolved through time, and it is expected that the styles of several artists will eventually be isolated and described. Thus, even though the master Haida artists of the early and mid-nineteenth century must remain anonymous, they need not remain unrecognized or unappreciated.

BIBLIOGRAPHY

Holm, Bill. *Northwest Coast Indian Art: An Analysis of Form.* Seattle: University of Washington Press, 1965.

_____. "Will the Real Charles Edenshaw Please Stand Up?: The Problem of Attribution in Northwest Coast Indian Art." In *The World is as Sharp as a Knife, An Anthology in Honour of Wilson Duff.* Victoria: British Columbia Provincial Museum, 1981.

Kaufmann, Carole. "Changes in Haida Indian Argillite Carvings, 1820 to 1910." Ph.D. diss., University of California, Los Angeles, 1969.

Sheehan, Carol. *Pipes That Won't Smoke; Coal That Won't Burn; Haida Sculpture in Argillite.* Calgary: Glenbow Museum, 1981.

Wright, Robin K. "Haida Argillite Ship Pipes." *American Indian Art Magazine* 5, no. 1 (1979): 40-47.

_____. "Haida Argillite Pipes—The Influence of Clay Pipes." *American Indian Art Magazine* 5, no. 4 (1980): 42-47, 88.

_____. "Haida Argillite—Made for Sale." *American Indian Art Magazine* 7, no. 4 (1982): 48-55.

Robin Wright has published and lectured on the results of her research on Haida argillite pipes.

TOWARD MORE PRECISE NORTHWEST COAST ATTRIBUTIONS: TWO SUBSTYLES OF HAISLA MASKS

Alan R. Sawyer

In recent decades Northwest Coast Indian art has received widespread recognition as one of the world's most splendid art traditions. An ever increasing number of major exhibitions and publications has fostered a better understanding and appreciation of this art and the cultural traditions of the native groups that produced it. At the same time, the scarcity of reliable collection data on a large portion of surviving artifacts limits our full understanding of the area's regional stylistic diversity and the evolution of its art traditions since precontact times.

Most well-documented Northwest Coast materials were collected more than a century after European contact at a time when native populations and their cultural traditions were in a state of serious decline. Many once thriving settlements lay abandoned and their surviving inhabitants were gathered together in a few major population centers. These circumstances tend to impose a late nineteenth century perspective on our view of Northwest Coast art. Distinct regional styles and the history of their gradual evolution have been obscured, preventing our full comprehension of the diverse creative genius of Northwest Coast peoples.

Considerable progress has been made in recent years toward the development of stylistic criteria for the establishment of more precise attributions in the field of Northwest Coast Indian art. A notable contribution to this end has been a preliminary organization by Bill Holm of stylistic traits for Northwest Coast sculpture, which first appeared as a mimeographed handout for his students (n.d.) and was later published in an exhibition catalog (1972). It lists the form characteristics of humanoid faces in the sculpture of nine major cultural groups—the Salish and Kwakiutl divided into northern and southern components. These definitions are very useful in identifying the typical mask styles of each area. What is needed now is the isolation and definition of regional

substyles within those areas and the reconstruction of their evolutionary trends.

The key to a solution of these complex problems is the recognition that the stylistic traits of a work of art constitute primary evidence of its time and place of origin. This approach has long been standard procedure in making attributions for works of art from other parts of the world. Its usefulness in the field of Northwest Coast attributions is directly proportional to the amount of well-documented material that is available from a given area. The preliminary results of my current research on Tlingit masks are highly gratifying largely because of the detailed documentation recorded by Lt. G. T. Emmons on the many examples he collected. A thorough stylistic analysis of these documented pieces has shown that each of the fourteen or more dialectic subdivisions of the Tlingit language group possessed a distinctive style of its own, and sufficient evidence has so far been found to clearly define eleven of them and reconstruct their chronological development. Space will not permit the summation of these results here. Instead, I will offer a brief discussion of Northern Wakashan masks[1] and suggest attributions of provenance and dates of manufacture for the two examples in this exhibition. The making of accurate attributions for masks from this area is far more difficult than for the Tlingit and, unfortunately, is more typical of the problems encountered in the study of Northwest Coast art.

The regions occupied by the Northern Wakashan and the Kwakiutl are closely comparable in size but cultural diversity was more pronounced in the northern area. Linguists generally divide the Northern Wakashan into four distinct dialectic subdivisions: the Heiltsuk, Haisla, Owikeno, and Haihais (see fig. 1). Drucker (1963:14) and Duff (1964: 20) show that each of these subdivisions was once composed of several independent villages, or bands, that were rapidly reduced in

⌒ Boundary of linguistic stock
- - - Dialect boundary

Fig. 1. Northern Wakashan and Adjacent Tribes (after Hawthorn).

number after 1850 by epidemic disease and the unification of survivors. Duff's population distribution map (1964:41) for 1835 indicates a wide scattering of native groups. His similar map (1964:51) for 1963 shows more than half of the region's population concentrated at the Heiltsuk town of Bella Bella, most of the remainder at Kitimat (Haisla), a small number at Rivers Inlet (Owikeno), but none in the Haihais area.

It appears evident that the wide variety of styles found in Northern Wakashan masks reflects the distinctive art traditions of the many groups that once inhabited the region. Few examples, however, are accompanied with sufficient data to support a specific attribution to one of them. Most "documented" masks were obtained at Bella Bella or Kitimat toward the end of the

1. Currently Northwest Coast scholars prefer the term Northern Wakashan for those groups formerly called "Northern Kwakiutl" and "Bella Bella," when referring to the entire area.

Northern Wakashan
Principal form—half cylinder
Subordinate forms
Planes fairly well defined
Forehead slopes back from brow
Brow medium, slight projection
Eye socket area large, defined
Underbrow, forecheek and upper cheek
    planes narrow and rather well defined
Orb large and flattened
Eyelids carved
Nostrils medium, rounded, defined
Mouth projection rather pronounced
Lips medium, continuous band
Chin may project
May have carved ears

Main identifying characteristics*
Fairly strong planes
Large flattened orb
Narrow, defined fore and upper cheek
    planes

*Many variants, some very naturalistic
    (Haida-Tsimshian-like), some very
    stylized, angular (Bella Coola-like)

Fig. 2. The Form Characteristics of
    Humanoid Bella Bella Masks
    (after Bill Holm, n.d.).

nineteenth century or later. At the time Holm offered his definitions of styles, the term "Bella Bella" was being used as a synonym for Northern Wakashan, and his list of form characteristics and illustration appear under that name (fig. 2). Holm's trait list adequately describes the shared characteristics of several interrelated Heiltsuk substyles and his illustration shows a typical example of one of them. They are, however, less applicable to the other dialectic subdivisions. His footnote indicates that he was fully aware of the wide diversity of substyles he was dealing with and the limitations of his generalized definition.

The two Northern Wakashan masks in this exhibition (fig. 3) are representative of the "many variants" noted by Holm which do not display all of the form characteristics he lists. The one from the Hauberg collection (3a) has been published as Tsimshian (Coe 1976:139) as have many other examples of the same style now generally recognized as Haisla. Most similar representatives of the Haisla style lack recorded provenance, but a few well-documented ones are identified as having been collected at Kitimat. The confusion of the Kitimat substyle with Tsimshian styles is understandable in view of that group's close proximity and obvious influence. Drucker (op. cit.) points out that both Kitimat and Kitlope are Tsimshian place-names and suggests that when the Haisla moved into the area they may have absorbed some of the local Tsimshian people.

The mask from the Backstrom collection (3b) is representative of a distinctive Northern Wakashan substyle that has not yet been attributed to a specific point of origin because of the absence of meaningful collection data on any of the known examples. In its form characteristics this substyle falls midway between the seminaturalistic Kitimat style and the more abstract Heiltsuk substyles described by Holm. This observation indicates Kitlope as a possible prove-

nance since it is located about halfway between the two centers. A study of materials collected by Rev. G. H. Raley at Kitimat and Kitlope between 1893 and 1906 has lent some credence to this hypothesis. (The items cited are now in the University of British Columbia Museum of Anthropology.) An eagle mask (Hawthorn 1976: Pl. XXV) has similar facial planes and painted decoration. It was collected at Kitimat by Raley, who recorded that it was said to have been used up to 1884. Three old masks he recovered from a burial cave near Kitlope (Hawthorn 1976: fig. 121) also show similar abstract stylistic traits though the subject matter is of a different order. Four fine old Kitimat house posts (Hawthorn 1976: fig. 492-5) display faces combining traits of both mask styles: the arched brows and broad eye sockets of Kitimat and the flattened orb, sharply defined upper cheek plane and thick square-ended lips of the other variant. This suggests that the two substyles were interrelated despite their contrasting appearance and that Kitlope reflected the original art tradition of the Northern Wakashan inhabitants. Its remote location at the southern end of Gardner Canal evidently allowed it to resist influences that transformed the art of Kitimat, located at the edge of Tsimshian territory. Figure 4 tabulates the results of a detailed stylistic analysis of my comparative samples of eleven Kitimat and eight Kitlope (?) masks; style characteristics are listed below the front and profile views of the Hauberg and Backstrom masks in figure 3 to facilitate easy comparison.

Fig. 3a. Kitimat (Haisla) mask, c. 1850 (cat. no. 45).

Fig. 3b. Kitlope (?) (Haisla) mask, c. 1860 (cat. no. 44).

	KITIMAT	: **KITLOPE (?)**
Mode	: Naturalistic	: Abstract
Form	: Oval, slightly flat sides	: Long oval, flat sides
Profile	: Hemisphere, curve at back	: Trapezoid, brow and jaw taper to flat back
Brow	: Rounded, straight slope	: Rounded, curved slope
Eyebrow	: Arched, tapers to round ends	: Arched, square ends, fur strips before 1850
Sockets	: Ovoid, soft transitions	: Constricted, filled by orb
Orbs	: Naturalistic	: Round, flattened, defined
Eyes	: Half closed, fully cut out; by 1850, open, iris pierced	: Highly arched upper lid, large pierced iris
Planes	: Curved, rounded transitions, moderate cheek pyramid	: Flattened, abrupt transitions, strong cheek pyramid
Nose	: Slightly aquiline, nostrils defined, straight base	: Straight to aquiline, nostrils defined, widely flaring
Mouth	: Half open, fur moustache to 1850— painted thereafter	: Parted, fur moustache to 1850— painted thereafter
Lips	: Smooth contour, ends join	: Blocky, ends square to cheek
Chin	: Rounded, goatee same as moustache	: Prowlike, goatee same as moustache
Ears	: Usually present, carved	: Absent
Decor	: Solid U forms, red formlines	: Solid and split U forms, no outline. Transverse bands added c. 1850

Fig. 4: Stylistic Characteristics of Two Haisla Substyle Masks.

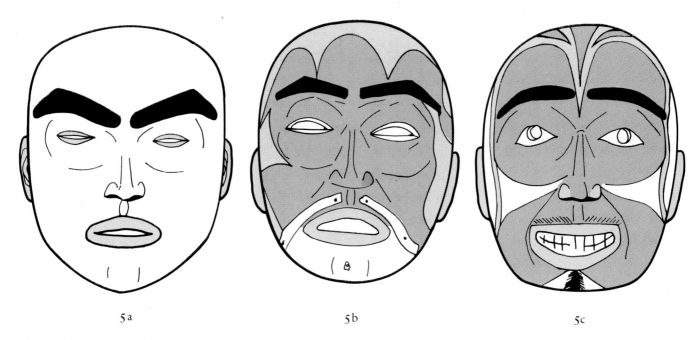

5a 5b 5c

Fig. 5. Kitimat Masks: **a.** Museum of
Ethnology, Leiden No. 122547, no data,
c. 1790. **b.** U.S. National Museum No. 688,
collected by G. Gibbs, 1862, made **c.** 1835.
c. U.S. National Museum No. 689, collected
by G. Gibbs, 1862, made c. 1860.

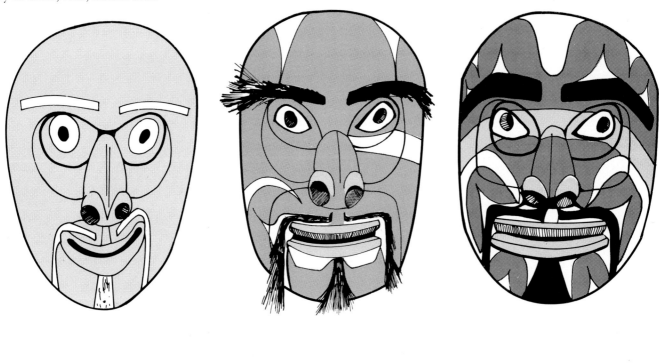

6a 6b 6c

Fig. 6. Kitlope (?) Masks: **a.** American
Museum of Natural History 16/8385, collected by G. Hunt, 1901, at Gwa'yastens,
Gilford Island, made c. 1830.
b. Rautenstrauch Joest Museum, Cologne
6601, purchased from Umlauf, 1903, made
c. 1845. c. Peabody Museum. Harvard
88.51.10/50484, collected by J.G. Swan,
1876, made c. 1860.

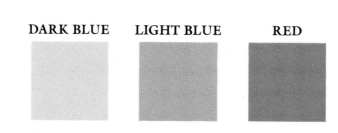

DARK BLUE   LIGHT BLUE   RED

The method used to reconstruct the stylistic chronology of Kitimat masks and estimate the date of the Hauberg example can be summarized by discussing three masks in my sample. An undocumented but very fine old mask (fig. 5a) is dated to the late eighteenth century on the basis of its subtle naturalism and physical evidence of great age, characteristics shared by masks of all Northwest Coast styles known to date from the early contact period (such as those collected by the Cook and Malaspina expeditions). The other two shown in figure 5 were collected by George Gibbs before 1862. One (5c) shows no sign of wear and is presumed to have been made for sale around 1860. The other (5b) shows considerable wear, evidence of repainting, and its forms are more softly naturalistic. Its date of manufacture is estimated at about 1835, and that of the Hauberg mask, which falls between 5b and 5c in style, is approximately 1850.

Using the same methods of deductive reasoning the Kitlope (?) sample was analyzed and dates estimated for each mask. The three shown in figure 6 were dated to 1830 (6a), 1845 (6b) and 1860 (6c). The only one with a meaningful collection date is 6c obtained by Swan in 1876, which has signs of wear indicating that it was made somewhat earlier. The very similar Backstrom mask is also estimated to date to c. 1860.

My conclusions must be regarded as tentative for much remains to be done to clarify the problems I have raised. In addition to the two substyles I have discussed there are many others from the Northern Wakashan area that need to be similarly isolated and identified.

There are, of course, other productive research techniques available that have not yet been fully exploited. These require the collaboration of specialists and the application of scientific and analytic procedures. For example, we need precise identification of materials, both native and imported, which are encountered in Northwest Coast artifacts. The interpretation of results would entail research as to the materials' origins, distribution, and time of use. What I have attempted to do in this brief essay is to demonstrate a methodology that does not require interdisciplinary collaboration, is available to all researchers in the field, and is applicable to all types of Northwest Coast art materials. I hope that it will encourage others to contribute to the formulation of what we might call "new and improved Holm remedies to faulty Northwest Coast attributions."

BIBLIOGRAPHY

Coe. Ralph T. *Sacred Circles, Two Thousand Years of North American Indian Art*. London: Arts Council of Great Britain, 1976.

Drucker, Philip. *Indians of the Northwest Coast*. Garden City: Natural History Press, 1963.

Duff, Wilson. *The Indian History of British Columbia*. Vol. 1, *The Impact of the White Man*. Memoir No. 5, Anthropology in British Columbia, 1964.

Hawthorn, Audrey. *Art of the Kwakiutl Indians and other Northwest Coast Tribes*. Vancouver: University of British Columbia; Seattle: University of Washington Press, 1967.

Holm, Bill. "Form Characteristics of Humanoid Faces in Northwest Coast Sculpture." Departments of Art and Anthropology, University of Washington, Seattle. Mimeographed copy, n.d.

_____. "Heraldic Carving Styles of the Northwest Coast." In *American Indian Art: Form and Tradition*. Minneapolis Institute of Arts, 1972.

Alan R. Sawyer, professor of art history at the University of British Columbia, is a noted authority on Peruvian and Northwest Coast Indian art.